Healing Voices

Women of Faith Who Survived Abuse Speak Out

Volume I

By J. Harris

"Healing Voices: Women of Faith Who Survived Abuse Speak Out, Volume 1" by J. Harris. ISBN: 978-0-99726-560-6 (softcover); 978-0-99726-561-3 (eBook)

Disclaimer:
Some of the women in this book have chosen to use their own names and to have their pictures presented. The names of all family members of each woman have been changed to protect their identities. Any similarities, whether in name, situation, or location to any of the family members' true identities, are purely coincidental, and not intentional.

If you note any typos or misspelled words, charge it to my head and not my heart. Please feel free to send the page number and description of the error to the comment section of www.tapestrycares.org.

Cover Art by: Rolando Diaz- www.rodiaz.com
Women's Photographs by: Hal Samples-
www.halsamples.com
Cover Design: Marcus Harris-
magikimages.mh@gmail.com

Contributing Editors:
Ann Fields, Lisa Yarbough, Antonea Bastian, Amber
Sims, and Courtney

Healing Voices Book Project is supported by:

MINISTRIES, INC.
www.tapestrycares.org

Table of Contents

Dedication

❖ To my God and my savior Jesus Christ, who has seen me through the events of this life and loved me unconditionally. Thank you God for your salvific power, mercy and grace.

❖ To my wonderful children: Johnice and her husband Jerry, Dwayne, Marcus and his wife Jessica, Veronica, and my awesome grandson Joshua (and any other grands who will someday follow). Thank you for your love and support in allowing me to be me, and loving me anyway. I love you guys so much. *2628forever!*

❖ To my family: my beautiful mother Ernestine Harris and my dad Elijah Harris, who are heaven's angels; my big sister Katherine and our angel sister Alice, who have served as sources of inspiration; my brother Eli and my nieces and nephews, who have endured much in the fire, but do not smell like smoke!

❖ To "Melony" for giving me the inspiration for this book, the women whose stories are told in this book, and to the "Melonys" everywhere all around the world whose voices have yet to be heard.

❖ To the Tapestry Ministry Board members, past and present, who have worked tirelessly to serve this

1

ministry with love and dedication: Charlane, Crystal, Johnice, Courtney, Jessica, Tikisa, Seun, Sophia, Roslyn, Monica, Lisa and Hesha.

❖ To my pastor, Rev. Richie Butler, Senior Pastor, St. Paul UMC, who recognized my call to ministry and sent me forth.

❖ To Larry James and City Square (formally Central Dallas Ministries) for allowing me the opportunity to serve in the community and to "let God out of the box."

❖ To the wonderful women of God who have assisted in the editing and writing of the powerful reflections for these stories, and who have kept this project in prayer. You all have blessed my life in so many ways.

Words of Encouragement

❖ The stories of these individual women show the strength and endurance of the human spirit. All wounds, rather emotional or physical, heal over time with or without scars." *Being strengthened with all power according to his glorious might so that you may have great endurance and patience."* Colossians 1:11 (NIV) In the telling of these testimonies, J. Harris brings an air of healing and appreciation of the wounds. Thank you, Mamma, for sharing and caring.

Mr. Dwayne Levels, B. A. Master Personal Trainer / Fitness Coach (oldest son of J. Harris)

❖ Mommy, I thank God for you hearing His voice and allowing Him to use your gift to tell the stories that will bring life and hope to those who suffer in silence. May God's word transform the lives of those who will read this book. *"And the God of all grace, who called you to His eternal glory in Christ, after you have suffered a little while, will Himself restore you and make you strong, firm and steadfast."*1 Peter 5:10 (NIV)

Mrs. Johnice Harris Woods, B. A. (daughter of J. Harris)

3

❖ I have learned the most valuable lesson in life from my mother (J. Harris): how to survive. What you do is not just for yourself, but for the next generation. I thank God for your survival that has helped to make your children strong men and women. Thank you Mom for setting the standard and exhibiting an amazing example of how a mother's love is power. Love you, Marcus.

Mr. John Marcus Harris, Barber Brothers, Master Barber (youngest son of J. Harris)

❖ God had sent you to not only be in my life, but actually be involved in it. Sometimes when I am stressed about life's decisions, I think about you saying, "Sit down somewhere and listen!" Continue to do God's work by encouraging our youth, just continue. Love you Mamma!

Ms. Veronica White, B. A. (daughter of J. Harris)

❖ Not only does J. Harris have a story to tell, but she is giving voice to the countless women who too have a message of hope, healing, and redemption that they must share with the world. She is a modern day female Moses, leading women out of the slavery of abuse to a land flowing with love, peace, promise, and possibilities.

Rev. Richie L. Butler, M. Div. , Senior Pastor, St. Paul United Methodist Church, Dallas, TX

❖ Healing Voices invites the reader to explore what is meaningful in life amidst moments of deep and personal suffering. J. Harris and friends offer themselves as what Anton T. Boisen (leading figure of CPE) refers to as "living human documents" as they affirm the redemptive power of healing and liberation.

Rev. Willacin "Precious" Gholston, Chaplain & ACPE, Inc , Supervisor

❖ J. Harris serves her community as part urban merchant of hopes and part inner city warrior! Her new book, *Healing Voices,* reflects her lifelong commitments and her deep practical faith. No doubt, her powerful stories will inspire others to live with her same courage and strength.

Rev. Larry James, M. Div,. CitySquare CEO

❖ The voices of the survivors are balm on our souls. They dared to speak up and out. They break the silence and let everyone know that there is life after trauma, and that Jesus is our healer."

Rev. Dr. Sheron C. Patterson, Pastor, Author

❖ Be free! Stay free! You are important, valuable and irreplaceable. At the end of the day, you and your life's legacy are priceless. This is the message of the stories in the Healing Voices book project. Thank you, J. Harris, for allowing God to use your gift of writing to tell your story and others as well. You poured out and allowed God to move our hearts to inspire, encourage, and uplift others. May God prosper you as you continue this work.

Minister Phyllis A. Harris, B. A. , Perkins Theological Seminary, Southern Methodist University seminarian

❖ To be the voice of the voiceless is a noble thing. To give a platform and safe place for the voiceless to tell their "own" stories is sacred. These are they—the overcomers in Christ Jesus. Thank God for the author's heart and passion to ensure the stories are told AND heard. The Divine's grace and mercy shine through as you read of the transforming love of God in Jesus Christ experienced in each life presented. I will leave you saying, "But God!"

Rev. Carol Grant Gibson, M. Div. , Senior Pastor, St. Andrew United Methodist Church, Ft. Worth, TX

❖ We all have unique and special journeys. To the women in the Healing Voices project—know that God can and will turn our tragedies, and even our own mistakes, into blessings. Your job is to keep listening to the Spirit and continue your path in faith. Learn and stay focused on the purpose that God has designed specifically for you. All of these tasks will be easier if you remember to stay surrounded by positive, loving, and encouraging people.

Mrs. Lisa R. Yarbough, Professional and Personal Development Coach; Founder of Epiphany Coaching

❖ The women in this book demonstrate that out of your pain comes your power! I applaud each woman for their bravery in sharing their stories of abuse, and how through their faith in God they were able to persevere and become victorious. My prayer is that this book will be utilized as a source of encouragement to other women, children and men who are suffering from abuse. Thank you, J. Harris, for being obedient to God's word and for providing an outlet for these women's voices to be shared with the world. You are a true inspiration and I love you dearly.

Mrs. Tikisa Jackson, M. S. , CEO and Managing Partner, CORE Institute

Preface

I ENVISION THE HEALING VOICES BOOK as the first of
many volumes to come. There are women all over the
world that have been victims of abuse, and their voices
are silent, and they and their families suffer in silence.
My prayer is that this book is a source of inspiration and
encouragement to women from all ethnic, socio-
economic, religious and racial backgrounds who have
found themselves in abusive or violent situations, and to
those that have supported and stood by them in times of
distress and despair. The book is written in an easy-to-
read style, in order that all may read and understand. I
beg the indulgence of my audience for any grammatical
errors or typos, as writing is not my profession, but my
passion is to give voice to the voiceless.

Human frailty is a condition that any of us can find
ourselves in at any given moment, but the will to survive
and press through those moments of uncertainty that
are crowded with fear is found deep in the soul, hidden
and unclaimed until it is needed. This will is God-given
and an essential part of the human condition. When our
human desires are the dominant force in our lives, we
try to fix the unfixable and mend the un-mendable. For
things to be whole and perfect, however, the perfect will
of God must be yielded to and trusted.

I encourage all of us who are human and humane,
when we encounter those who are struggling with

difficult life decisions or are in crisis situations, to be willing to provide a safe haven for those in need. A safe haven is not necessarily physical shelter, but often times a listening ear, kind or reassuring words, or a prayer on their behalf. When we are transparent and able to share our hearts with one another, the world changes, and lives are transformed. My continued prayer is that this book becomes a catalyst for change in the lives of God's people who are in need of restoration and reaffirmation.

The statistics listed below only provide a small glimpse into the urgent need to bring awareness to the reality of domestic violence, the cycle of abuse, and the effects of domestic violence on individuals, families, the community, the church, governments, nations and the world. Keep in mind that abuse can occur in many forms, and that no list can include every possible abusive situation. In addition, one does not have to suffer multiple examples of abusive behavior in order to be a victim of abuse. If a person suspects that they are the victim of abuse, it is recommended that they seek support, counseling or professional help.

Introduction

THIS WRITING HAS BEEN BOTH A CALLING AND A LABOR of love. Love of God, love of humanity, and the desire to alleviate the hurting souls of women who have been victims of abuse and injustice have been the driving forces behind these writings. I have come to the realization that there will never be a shortage of human misery and suffering brought on by the cruel acts of one human being to another. When you remove the acts of nature, accidents, and the wear and tear of living that can affect our lives as a process of aging and doing life, the only other afflictions that can account for the pain that humans suffer are those we bring one to another. I see this book as a call to action to change the attitudes of individuals, communities, institutions and the world at large toward the disrespect, violation and mistreatment of women.

I personally experienced a taste of the horrors that one human being could render on another when I was a victim of domestic violence in my marriage *(My story—J's Story—is included in this collection)*. At that time, this behavior was foreign to me, yet I knew this was not the way God wanted me to live. I witnessed the hand of God deliver me from a life of violence and fear, to one filled with love and forgiveness. As I began ministering to other women in Bible studies, I found that many of them were also suffering from the stain of violent relationships. In one of the Saturday evening women's groups I lead in the inner city of Dallas, TX, there was a moving of the Holy Spirit like I had never witnessed before. The word went forth in a mighty way as women fell to their knees, ran for joy, shouted to God, and cried tears of release.

One of the women in the group, Melony *(not her real name),* came to me the next day after Sunday service and asked to speak to me privately. She informed me that she had a spiritual revelation at the Bible class and suddenly realized why she had struggled for years with drug addiction. She went on to share how she had been raped as a child and had witnessed her mother being beaten and abused by a boyfriend. I realized that I was identifying with her pain because of what I had been through, but I had never shared my story with anyone— not my family or my closest friends. I had been ashamed for anyone to know I had allowed such a thing to happen to me.

I said to her, "Melony, you have got to tell your story to other women! I'm sure others are going through the same thing and could be helped by your message." She expressed that she did not know how to write very well, and agreed that others may be helped by what she had experienced. I said to her, "I'll write it down for you, if you tell it to me." I had no background as a formal writer and thought to myself, "What are you saying? You are not a writer!" But God spoke to me in a softer voice, saying, "Write the stories." In meeting with Melony and writing her story, the Lord helped me deal with my own scars of abuse.

At the next women's Bible class, we discussed living a life of forgiveness and dealing with past hurts. I asked the women, out of curiosity, if any of them had ever been victims of domestic violence. To my surprise about ninety percent of them raised their hands. I knew then that other stories needed to be told in order for healing to begin. That was the beginning of my journey of listening and writing down the stories of these victorious women who had survived horrific situations, and who realized that they had survived because of their faith in God and their belief in Christ. Their faith was their *"common thread."*

This has been a 12-year journey of hearing stories, and of seeing lives changed and new beginnings come forth, even in my own life. The most difficult story to write was my own, which took two years to write. The confession was more painful than I had expected, but God touched my heart with each word and affirmed that I was doing what I was called to do years ago—write the stories.

Many of the women in this book chose to be known and to reveal their faces. Their real names are used, but the characters' names in their stories have all been changed. Some of the women chose not to use their real names, and the characters in their stories are also changed. The essence of the stories and the tales of survival through their faith in God is what is important. Each woman's story is her way of ministering to other women who may be hurting.

There are stories of women survivors all over the world that need to be told to bring awareness to the devastating realities of domestic violence, rape, sex trafficking and incest in the lives of women and children, but also to give women hope that victims can live victoriously with God's help. God gave me the vision that this book would be the first of many volumes of stories to be heard and told, and I am going to keep writing them down, keep teaching and preaching the word of God and the message of Christ that will be the true healing power to women who are hurting due to violent encounters. It is only fitting that these collections of stories begin with "Melony."

"Melony"

Story by J. Harris

Reflection by Rev. Dr. Alphonetta Wines

WE TAKE FOR GRANTED the status of our lives when things are comfortable, and all are fed, clothed and safe. It is when the unexpected, the tragic occurs, that our souls are put to the test. What comes out on the other side of the disruption often times is the byproduct of human misery. What God does through us in that process is miraculous. All that He puts before us is necessary for our realization of who He is. It is when we choose not to recognize that He is speaking to us in these dark hours that we miss His blessings and can wander aimlessly through life. Thanks be to God that Melony realized God was speaking to her heart in the midst of her sorrow.

Melony was the only child of devoted black middle class parents in Memphis, Tennessee. Her father, George, worked as an elementary school teacher, and her mother, Ella, was a stay-at-home mom. They had all of the things that hard work and love could afford. Melony was a "daddy's girl," and wherever her daddy went, she was not far behind. She loved her mother dearly, but her father was her heart, and she was his. Her father insisted that they attend church each Sunday as a family, and Melony was taught at an early age that God and Christ were important in her life. Melony admired her father not only for his intelligence, but also for providing a good living for them, because they had everything they needed and more. Her father made provisions for his family's future by putting money into a savings account for Melony's college education, life insurance, and investments to ensure that they would be financially stable. They were one of just a few families on their street who did not rent, but owned their home. Ella participated in the PTA and women's organizations in the church, and enjoyed making a comfortable, loving home for her family.

Every family has its secrets that are often not spoken of, but somehow everyone knows about them. Melony's dad would often take her with him when he went to visit his friends, and there was always a little girl there named Tonya for her to play with. She and Tonya grew to be friends and looked forward to their visits. One day, Tonya and her mother came by Melony's house, and there seemed to be tension surrounding their visit. Melony ran out to greet her friend and Ella asked Melony where she knew Tonya from, and Melony told her about her dad taking her to visit Tonya's house. Heated words were exchanged between Tonya's mother, Ella, and George, and then Tonya's mother took her away quickly. Melony would not see her playmate again for years, and found out years later that she and Tonya were actually sisters. *Secrets...*

When Melony was nine years old, George began frequently complaining of a sore throat and problems with his tonsils, and had frequent throat infections. The doctor suggested he have his tonsils removed as a day surgery procedure at a local clinic, but when complications developed during surgery, the clinic transferred him to one of the larger hospitals in Memphis for more intense care. There, he was diagnosed with lung cancer. Because George worked with children, he had never been a drinker or smoker in his life, and

Melony and Ella were devastated when they got the news.

George became very ill and could not leave the hospital, so Ella and Melony stayed by his side day and night. One evening, George called Melony to his bedside to talk to her privately, because he realized that his condition was worsening, and he wanted her to take some of his wisdom with her. Melony could not stop crying in his presence, because here was the strong father she had always known, now weak and frail. He held her hand and stroked it like only he could as they discussed her future, and how he wanted her to finish school and go to college. He told her to obey her mother, and to help out at the house, and to make him proud. He then said, "Don't take any wooden nickels." This phrase would not make sense to her until much later in her life.

Melony's world came crashing down when George died the next day. Melony and Ella were at his bedside. Her daddy, her friend, her running buddy, was gone at the age of 35. The loss was unexpected and heartbreaking, causing Melony to ask hard questions of God, such as, *Why had God not healed her daddy? Why did he take her daddy away?* Her dad was supposed to be around to see her go to the prom, see her graduate from high school and college, walk her down the aisle when she married, and be a grandfather to her children. *Now what was she to do?*

Ella took the loss just as hard, but for different reasons. George had left his family well cared for financially, and with careful management, Ella and Melony should have been able to continue to live comfortably. There was insurance money that paid off the house and the two cars, in addition to a large sum of money in the bank. In addition, Ella and Melony each received $600 a month from death benefits through Social Security. But Ella had no money management skills, because George had always taken care of the finances, and this would later put the family in financial crisis.

It was at her father's funeral that Melony would first see her old playmate Tonya again, but Tonya was very cold toward her. When Melony asked her about her attitude, Tonya said that her mother had called Melony's house to speak with George, and that Melony had cursed her mother out and hung up the phone. Melony told her that she would never do that to Tonya's mother. Melony's first cousin Angela overheard the conversation and confessed to Tonya that it was she, not Melony, who had done the deed. Angela didn't want Tonya to be mad at Melony unnecessarily, because there was already enough pain going on, but it changed the relationship between Tonya and Melony forever. Angela was a few years older and understood that George had been unfaithful to Ella, and had taken matters into her own hands by wanting Tonya's mother to suffer as Ella had. Angela apologized to Melony for making trouble between her and Tonya, and because the cousins had always been close, forgiveness was easy.

As the months went on, Ella became very depressed, lonely, and filled with grief. She stopped going to church and did not encourage Melony to go either. She started to look for comfort in alcohol, and for love in other men, and Melony had never seen this behavior before in her mother. Ella was lonely and did not know how to start her life over again. Word gets around in a small community that a widow's husband has left her money, and this seemed to attract all types of shady onlookers. Because of this interest, there were many lookers looking to benefit from the dead, but Ella managed to keep her head about her—that is, until she met and started to date Jake. He was a man with a rough reputation who had been to prison for murder. Because of his charm and her loneliness, Ella fell hard for Jake. She may had even feared being alone. When he finally got his foot in the door, Ella allowed him to move in, and with him came his bedridden mother, his pregnant teenage daughter, and his brother and sister. They literally took over the house and ate up all the food Ella could bring in, ran up utility bills, and bought all of the clothes and other things they wanted, all with Ella's money. After Jake had moved into her home and heart, Ella saw another side of Jake—drug addict, alcoholic and violent abuser.

Jake's mother was always incontinent with urine and feces, and Jake demanded that Ella or Melony clean her up. The sick old woman was mean-spirited, often striking Melony if she didn't move fast enough. The house was sheer madness! Jake and his people totally defiled the home, with no respect shown to Ella. Finally, after several months of this, Melony's aunt and uncle came over and did what Ella was not strong enough to do—they made the freeloaders get out. They gave Jake and his family an ultimatum of leaving, or of having the police called on them. They left in the whirlwind they had come in, but Jake stayed.

Melony described Jake as "Satan." He had violent outbreaks toward Ella for no apparent reason. He took "reds" (speed) like candy all day, chased them with Thunderbird or Mad Dog 20/20 wine, and shot heroin in front of Melony and Ella. The combination of all these chemicals could only bring out the devil in anyone. Ella had started drinking heavily too, perhaps to deal with Jake's abuse, or to drown her loneliness, or both. Many times Jake would get high and beat Ella until she was unconscious, causing Ella to make frequent visits to the emergency room for cuts on her face, broken limbs, or head wounds, but always with the same excuse..."I fell." She was too afraid to press charges against Jake.

When Melony was 12 years old, Ella and Jake got into one of their usual violent arguments. Jake was flying high on his drug cocktails and took his violence toward Ella to another dimension. As his eyes danced wildly in his head, he seemed to almost be breathing fire. The argument moved from the living room to the kitchen, where Melony was seated at the kitchen table, reading. She had grown used to the shouting and fighting. During his ranting, Jake took a butcher's knife from the drawer, and in one wild stroke he cut Ella across the chest, almost slicing her breast completely off! Melony felt something warm hit her face and splatter on her arms and thought for a moment she had been cut, but she felt no pain. She looked at Ella clutching her chest and could see the white flesh beneath, and her breast hanging on by a small piece of tissue. Blood was everywhere! Jake stood over Ella, wild eyed, rocking back and forth and covered in blood. It looked like a scene from a horror movie.

Melony called the ambulance, and Ella was rushed to the hospital with Jake by her side, being very attentive. When they got to the hospital, Ella told the doctor that she had fallen and cut herself. Melony screamed at Ella and demanded that she tell the doctor the truth, that Jake had cut her. Melony wanted Ella to file charges against Jake, but the doctor's hands were tied if Ella did not want to file charges. All the while Jake was there, holding Ella's hand to comfort her, and threatening her under his breath about just what he would do to her if she filed on him. Ella refused to file and denied that Jake had done anything to her. The doctors worked feverishly to reattach Ella's breast, and after a few days in the hospital, she was sent home with drains and bandages. It occurred to Melony that this was the same hospital in which her father had died. *God, why didn't Jake die instead?*

After Ella recovered, Melony spent as much time as she could away from home because of Jake's constant drinking and drugging. Most of that time was spent at her friend Dana's house. It was not unusual for Melony to spend the night at Dana's house, because Dana was often left home alone at night. Dana's mother worked at a strip club as a dancer and was also bisexual, often bringing home partners from work for an "after party." Melony confided in Dana about the problems Jake was causing, but because they were both teenagers, they couldn't come up with any real solutions. But at least they were heard.

At one of those sleepovers, the girls settled in on the couches in the living room and fell asleep watching TV. Dana's 27 year old brother, Gerald, came home after working late, and had been drinking. Gerald came to Melony's couch, pulled the covers off her, and pulled her underwear down. Melony screamed for him to stop and for help from Dana, but before she could realize what he was doing, Gerald was on top of her and had penetrated her body. He was heavy and strong, and Melony's tiny body was no match for this grown man. She could smell the stale alcohol on his breath as he gave her slobbery kisses on her face and mouth between his grunting and panting. Melony continued to scream for Dana to help her as pain ripped through her young virgin body, but the more she fought, the more pleasure he seemed to get.

Melony's mind started to drift. *She needed her daddy there to protect her. This would not have happened if her daddy was alive. She wouldn't have to leave home to find peace if her daddy was alive.* Melony was hoarse from screaming for help from her friend, but Dana pretended not to hear her, and her cries fell into the night. Dana's mother wasn't home to protect her, either. No one was there to stop this maniac! *How could Dana not hear her screaming?* She was only a few feet away. Gerald was a grown man and knew he what he was doing, alcohol or not. *Was this something that he had done to Dana before? Was Dana relieved that Melony was there to be Gerald's target instead of her?*

Melony struggled, cried, and pleaded for Gerald to stop, but he acted as if he did not hear her. After he reached his climax, he gave her a sick smile, zipped his pants, and staggered to his room. Dana never turned over in recognition of what had just happened. Melony was crying, bloody, and in pain as she grabbed her underwear and clothes and ran out of the house toward her home. With blood running down her legs, she made her way to her house and woke her mother up to tell her what Gerald had done. Ella was furious and took her in her arms, and they cried together.

Ella was afraid to tell the police or Jake what had happened, because the police were always looking for him. Ella decided she would go and talk to Gerald's mother the next day, and let her know about her son. She helped Melony get cleaned up and settled into bed, and gave her some aspirin for the pain. Ella stayed by her side throughout the night as they cried softly together and lay in each other's arms. Both Ella and Melony were probably thinking of George and of how things had changed since he had been gone.

Ella could not believe what was happening to her family. She was too afraid of Jake to fight back, but she decided to file charges against Gerald, regardless of what Jake would think. A few days after the rape, Ella went to visit Gerald and Dana's mother to discuss what had happened, and to inform her that Gerald would be arrested because she was filing charges against him. Dana's mother seemed concerned and told Ella how sorry she was about what had happened, but pleaded with Ella not to file charges against Gerald because he might lose his new job. Ella told her she cared nothing about his job and that he needed to be taken off the streets before he hurt some other girl. Dana's mother continued to beg and plead for Ella to not file charges. Ella eventually agreed, but only on the condition that Melony could never come to her house again. Ella asked Dana why didn't she do something to help Melony, but Dana denied knowing anything about the attack, insisting that she was sound asleep. Ella felt guilty for the rape, because she knew Melony was at Dana's house only because she was trying to get away from Jake.

Ella was more protective of Melony after the rape by making sure Melony was comfortable and giving her extra attention. Melony missed her period the next month, and Ella suspected that she might be pregnant. Melony was afraid and had no idea what was going on with her body, so Ella called her sister because she felt she would know what to do in these matters. Melony's aunt suggested that Ella take Melony to a clinic in the neighborhood that specialized in abortions, to find out for sure if she was pregnant. The pregnancy test came back positive—Melony was pregnant, and the decision of what to do about the baby only added to her misery.

Melony was 14 and pregnant with a baby that she was not mentally mature enough to care for, and a baby fathered by a man who had raped her. She wished that she could wake up from this bad dream with her daddy holding her in his arms and that everything would be all right, but this wasn't the case. Jake forced Ella to tell him about the pregnancy and came up with his own twisted solution to the problem. He wanted Melony and Gerald to start dating each other and eventually get engaged. He felt this would help explain to the community about the pregnancy, and no one would have to know about the rape. He, of all people, had suddenly become concerned about what other people thought and about his status in the community. Ella was too afraid of

Jake not to go along with him, but she knew her 14-year-old daughter had no business marrying a 27-year-old man who had raped her. Jake's plan made Ella sick.

The idea of abortion was heatedly discussed by Ella and Jake, with time being of the essence. Ella's main concern was that Melony was not going to be able to raise a child who was the result of a rape, but with pressure from Jake, Ella informed Gerald's mother of the decision to have Gerald and Melony date, but that Melony would have an abortion, and the women agreed. The thought of dating Gerald was sickening to Melony and she was trying to trust her mother's judgment, but it did not sit well with her to be forced to date a man who had raped her.

Gerald had been told about the plan to date, but not about the abortion. He seemed pleased with himself that he would be a father, even if it was by rape. Dana and Melony's relationship changed forever, because Melony knew Dana had pretended not to hear her cries for help. She thought back on Gerald and Dana's relationship, how it was not a normal brother-sister relationship, and that there was a lot of unusual touching and feeling between them. Melony suspected that Gerald was doing the same thing to Dana that he did to her, and that Dana must have been relieved that it was not her turn that evening. Dana stuck with her story that she was sound asleep and did not hear Melony screaming. *Sure...*

The evening before the abortion was to take place, Gerald came to "call on" Melony, and she told him about the abortion plan. He was furious, and became very violent and tried to choke her. Jake had to pull Gerald off her as Gerald pleaded with Melony not to kill his baby. Melony told him she didn't have any choice, and that an abortion was probably the best thing for everyone. After all, he had raped her, and that was not her choice either. She was out of choices.

Ella took Melony to the abortion clinic the next day, and Melony's aunt came along for support. She had been there several times before for their "services" and told Melony what to expect. Melony was 1 ½ months pregnant, and the clock was ticking. The day was sad and confusing for Melony, because she was young and unsure of what was best for her. She had to trust that her mother and her aunt knew what was best.

The nurse called Melony's name, and she willingly followed the nurse's instructions and assumed the position on the procedure table. She was given medicine to relax her body enough to accept the procedure, and the doctor was emotionless and methodical. She guessed he couldn't get too emotionally involved when he extracted life from women's bodies every day. Melony was just another procedure for him. He prescribed her Valium to help with her nerves and to cope with the situation. He prescribed all of his patients Valium for coping purposes. *Melony would always wonder if the baby was a boy or girl. What would it have looked like, had it lived? What would have become of it if given a chance, in another day and time, and another set of circumstances?*

When the procedure had been completed Melony, felt empty and incomplete, a feeling she would carry through life. When a woman is either forced or chooses to separate from such an intimate part of her body, there is a piece of her soul that goes with it. After the abortion, Ella had even more sorrow added to her pile, and she became so preoccupied with Jake's madness and with her own drinking problem that there was little attention being paid to Melony. Melony became more withdrawn and angry and decided she could no longer tolerate Jake, not even while taking Valium. Melony began to go her own way by refusing to "date" Gerald any longer. Gerald had become very angry at the fact that Melony had gone through with the abortion, killing his baby, and she became afraid to be around him because he began to threaten to kill her. Melony began smoking weed, drinking alcohol and taking the Valium they had given her for her nerves, but nothing she did numbed the emptiness and the heartache.

After a year of dealing with death threats from Gerald and with Jake's madness, Melony wanted out of the house. She knew she needed her own money, so she got a job in the food service department at a big hotel in Memphis. She used her work check to support herself and let her mother keep the death benefit Social Security check. Melony knew it was time to leave home when she caught Jake peeping in on her while she undressed one evening. The sight of him made her sick, especially when he popped so many pills and drank so much that he just sat on the couch twitching and sleeping. Sometimes he would fall on the floor, twitching as if he was having a seizure, and start talking out of his head. Occasionally when Melony would catch Jake high and twitching, especially after he had beaten Ella, she would beat him with anything she could get her hands on to punish him for abusing her mother. He would later come to and not know what had happened to him.

Despite all of the drugs and alcohol in his system, Jake kept a good job unloading trucks and made a good salary, but he stole from the trucks on the side and sold the stolen goods in the community. Jake always needed a lot of money because of his heavy drug use, and he often made Ella go to the bank to withdraw large sums of money for him, even though he had money in his pocket.

When Melony started high school, she skipped class to do drugs with her friends because the drugs seemed to temporarily ease the pain that was inside of her, and because it was as close to dying as she could get. She had tried prayer to ease the pain, but with all of the things she had gone through, it seemed like God did not hear her prayers. She felt she was too damaged because of the rape, the abortion, and the drugs for God to love or care about her.

There was a lady in the neighborhood named Mama Dora who was a hard-drinking woman that liked gambling, drugs, and the company of lots of men. Melony and three of her friends began to hang out at Mama Dora's when they skipped school and did their thing. Mama Dora offered them a place to stay for a price, and Melony felt this was the answer to getting away from Jake and Gerald. She told Ella of her plan to move in with Mama Dora, and Ella begged her to stay home, but Melony told her she could no longer tolerate Jake. She hated him and refused to live in the house with him anymore. Ella knew she was too weak to fight for herself and for Melony too, so she asked Melony to keep in touch and let her know how she was doing. Melony had a job and her own money and agreed to keep in touch, and as she kissed her mother goodbye, the feelings were bittersweet. She loved her mother dearly but could feel herself dying inside each time she saw her mother battered and abused.

Melony and her friends each had to pitch in on the rent and the food, and in return, Mama Dora would let them do whatever they wanted to do. Mama Dora would take the money she got from the men she dated, and from boot-legging alcohol and selling drugs, then go to the casino to gamble and party. She had fancy clothes and shoes, and even fancier jewelry. She used the money Melony and her friends gave her to pay the bills. The girls thought Mama Dora was taking care of them, but they were really taking care of her.

Melony visited her mother often, but refused to move back. At Mama Dora's there was no adult supervision, and she could do whatever she pleased. She and her friends would do "Christmas Trees," a type of speed, and follow it with shots of scotch. When she would come down from that high, she would drink cold water and the high would start over again. Occasionally she would snort "Locker Room" (formaldehyde or "water") that would cause her to have a severe headache, become paralyzed for a few minutes, and vomit. She could not do enough drugs to erase her pain. Just when she thought her soul had seen enough tragedy, another dose came with Jake committing the ultimate abuse against Ella.

One evening after getting loaded on his banquet of drugs, Jake began beating Ella, and when she tried to defuse him he became even more violent. He was totally out of control. Ella managed to call Melony for help before he tore the phone out of the wall and began to slap her around and punch her face and her body. He then began to beat her with a chair, hitting her in the face so hard that he broke the bone around her right eye. The blow caused Ella's eyeball to come out and dangle on her face, and Jake left her for dead, unconscious on the floor. Her face looked like raw liver because she was beaten so badly, and the floor was covered in blood.

Melony suspected something was wrong when she heard Ella scream and the phone go dead, so she rushed to the house and found Ella unconscious and unrecognizable, lying in a pool of blood. Melony thought Jake had finally killed her mother. He was in the next room, high and belligerent, denying what he had done and soaked with Ella's blood. Melony cursed him with every word she knew and went next door and called an ambulance.

Jake came to his senses enough to change his clothes before the ambulance came, and he followed the ambulance to the hospital. The emergency room doctor told Melony that Ella had only a cup of blood left in her body, and that if Ella had arrived at the hospital 30 minutes later, she would have died. Of course, Jake told the doctors that Ella had been in a bad fall, but they knew that he was lying. No charges could be filed without Ella's consent, and she was in no shape to make that decision. When the doctor informed Melony that he would not be able to save Ella's right eye, Melony went into a rage and accused Jake of nearly beating her mother to death. He stood there insisting that Melony was lying and that Ella had fallen.

Ella had to be put in the ICU (Intensive Care Unit) and was given several blood transfusions to replace the blood she had lost. She stayed in the hospital for a month, and Jake visited her daily. The doctor could not convince Ella to file charges on him. Melony stayed at the hospital almost every day because she was afraid to leave her mother with Jake around, fearing that he would try to finish what he started. Melony found Jake even more sickening as time went on, and she hated him even more as he continued to do his drugs as usual and came to the hospital high and wild-eyed.

Melony finally decided that Jake had gone far enough. She got her cousin Angela to help her come up with a plan to get rid of Jake for good. After Ella returned home, Jake was very attentive toward her, probably because he was afraid that she would file charges against him. One night, Melony and Angela decided to put their plan into action with Angela's rifle and Melony's .357 Magnum. Angela hid in the trees outside the house with the rifle while Melony knocked on the door, holding her gun behind her back. Jake answered the door and Melony asked him to step outside to speak with him privately. Ella came to the door, saw the look on Melony's face and realized that something was not right. Ella placed herself between Jake and Melony and asked her what she was doing.

Melony broke down and shouted to Ella, "I'm tired of you covering for him and letting him beat on you, taking your money and destroying our family. Daddy left things in place so we would be taken care of, and you have let Jake come in and destroy all that Daddy worked so hard for!" Ella could not help but cry, because she knew it was all true. Melony told Ella that Angela was waiting outside, ready to kill Jake, and that she was planning to shoot him too. Between the two of them, they couldn't miss. Ella begged Melony to take Angela and leave, because she didn't want to see them ruin the rest of their lives on something that was her problem. Ella told her that God would take care of any punishment that Jake had coming. *Melony felt she had not seen the hand of God in action when Ella had been nearly beaten to death! God was not taking action, so she felt it was up to her to take matters into her own hands.* Melony and Angela begged Ella to move out of the way, but she stood quickly, with Jake hiding behind her. Melony and Angela eventually left with even more hatred for Jake, and feeling completely unable to help Ella.

God is sovereign and He has the last say in our destiny. A few weeks later, Ella had to go to the doctor for her follow-up appointment, and Jake went with her. Jake was doing more drugs than ever, and had been complaining of chest pain that ran down his arm. By this time, Ella had withdrawn almost all of the money that George had left her and had given it to Jake to support his drug habit. While Ella was at her doctor visit, Jake decided to check himself in to the emergency room to see about his chest pain. As he was waiting to be processed, he fell to the floor clutching his chest and had a severe seizure. He died soon after he hit the floor! The hospital staff tried to revive him, but they did not succeed.

Just like that, Ella was finally free! Ella had spoken of God having the last word, and a silent God had spoken loud and clear. Ella was broken and broke, but she was free. Melony had no tears for Jake, only feelings of relief.

Jake's relatives were notified about his death and that Jake had no insurance. Ella had to go to several of his friends to attempt to collect money to help bury him, but they had little to contribute because many of them had associated with him out of fear or were just his drug dealers, not real friends. Some of his relatives from Louisiana came to Memphis and told Ella that they didn't want her to have anything to do with burying Jake, and they would take care of everything. Ella gave the money back to those who had donated and left the matter to his family. She had tried to do the right thing, even to the end.

After a few weeks, Ella learned that the relatives had left town and not taken care of any burial arrangements, because they had no money. Perhaps they thought he had some money stashed, but he had used all of his money and Ella's money for his drug habit. When Ella found out that the family did not make any arrangements, it was too late to collect money again. The city gave Jake a pauper's burial, cremating him and disposing of the ashes. *For the first time in years, Melony felt that God had acted justly.*

Ella had continued to heal physically, but mentally and spiritually, she was a shell of herself. Pieces of her soul were gone that could never be recovered. She had lost her right eye and had to have an artificial eye implanted to replace it. Her only child's life was a confused mess, and she was about to lose the home that her husband had worked so hard to secure for her. Melony found out that during the time she was with Jake, her mother had had some siding put on the house, and the siding company had placed a lien on the house because the siding was not yet paid for. Ella thought Jake had been making the payments, but instead of sending in the payments, he had been using the money on his drug habit. The siding company acted on the lien and took possession of the house. Ella lost a house that had been paid off, and was now renting from the lien holder the house she once owned. Ella went into further depression and secluded herself from the world. Melony was still out on her own, living at Mama Dora's, trying to start her own life and felt no need to return home to live, so she just visited.

Melony later met a man who she felt was her soul mate, a 20-year-old soldier named Eddie. Even though she didn't attend school regularly, she made decent grades because she was smart and learned fast. She was a high school senior with plans to graduate when Eddie asked her to marry him. She was too young to get married on her own at 17, so she had to go to her mother to get the marriage license approved. Ella tried to discourage her from getting married so young and wanted her to finish school, but Melony was looking for some happiness in her own life, and to her, Eddie was it. Ella reluctantly signed the papers, and Melony and Eddie went to the courthouse and tied the knot. Eddie was stationed in Virginia and wanted her to come live with him there. With two months left to finish school, Melony was now someone's wife. She felt she had to do what her husband wanted, so she quit school and went to be with him.

The drugs and alcohol that Melony had been doing had to stop, because Eddie didn't play that. Melony was actually glad to give those things up, because she felt she no longer needed the effects of the drugs and the alcohol to make her happy. She had Eddie, and he was enough. Eddie took good care of her and they bought a new three-bedroom trailer home, new furniture, and a new life. Life was pretty sweet, and for a change, she was free and sober. Melony was not experienced at being married, but she worked hard at it.

After a couple of years, Melony discovered that Eddie was seeing another woman. It was like a vicious cycle: they would get into arguments about it, and Melony would leave him and go home to stay with Ella for a few weeks. But soon, Eddie would follow, begging her for forgiveness, and Melony would go back. One evening, Eddie's friends coerced him into doing some LSD that was in the form of a small star on a piece of paper. Eddie did too much of it and went crazy! Melony and one of her neighbors were at the trailer when Eddie's friends brought him home. He was a maniac! He kept running his head into the side of the trailer like a bull, and the force of the blows would knock him backwards and he would fall to the ground. Then he would shake his head, get up, and do it all over again. He was yelling and cursing and demanding Melony to come out of the house. She would not move, because she was afraid he would kill her. Eddie's friends eventually returned and took him away until he came down off the high, and Melony decided that the unfaithfulness along with the drugs was enough to make her decide to return home—this time for good. She had seen what Jake was like on drugs and did not want to go through that with Eddie.

Melony moved back to Memphis with her aunt and signed up for GED classes and a computer class, and applied for a grant to pay for her classes. She enjoyed learning again, because she had always been a good student. The idea of getting her relationship with Eddie behind her was a necessary pain. Her aunt knew the pain Melony had been through, first with her mother and now her husband, and encouraged Melony to get on with her life.

Just when Melony was getting it together, Eddie came to visit, saying he was discharged from the military and had gotten his last paycheck in the amount of $2,200. Eddie felt he had no further need for military life after his marriage had failed, so he had not reenlisted. He told Melony that he wanted her back and that they had enough money for a fresh start, but Melony told him she was going to start school, and wasn't sure if she wanted to be his wife again. He gave her an ultimatum that if she did not come with him, he was not going to share his money with her. She asked him for money to help her aunt with food until she could get her school money, but he refused. She decided that if he could not give her money for food, then it was not worth the trouble of getting back with him, so Eddie decided to get a new Cadillac with his money instead of winning his wife's affections. They decided to call it quits, but neither of them took the initiative to file for divorce.

Melony would later find out that each month while Eddie was in the military, an allotment check had been sent to Eddie's mother for Melony, since she was considered a minor, but Eddie's mother had been spending these checks for years instead of saving them for Melony. When she confronted Eddie's mother about the checks, she could only say she was sorry, and that she had spent the money because she felt she needed it more than Melony did. Melony felt used and rejected.

Soon after she called it quits with Eddie, Melony decided to join the party scene again and make some new friends. All of her plans had failed, and if she was to find any happiness, she would have to find it herself. *She still was not in agreement with God about how her life had turned out.* She met a guy named Jeff at a club. Jeff was nice, and he treated her with the respect she felt she deserved.

Jeff and his brothers all partied together with their girlfriends, and they all had nice, new cars and dressed well. They sported big money when they partied, buying drinks for all of their friends. After a few months, Jeff asked Melony out and took her to meet his parents. They all lived in a big, fancy two-story house that had a rooming house attached. Jeff offered to pay for Melony's classes so she would not have to take out a loan, but Melony told him she wanted to earn the money and not be indebted to anyone for the money.

Jeff's father was also a sporting man who had three or four new Cadillacs and wore expensive clothes. He made Melony a deal: He would pay her $50 a week to clean the rooming house, and in return, she could stay there for free. She felt it was a fair deal, and she would get to see Jeff whenever she wanted and be able to pay for her classes. Melony eventually moved in with Jeff and thought she had found love once again. Jeff's other brothers' girlfriends also stayed at the rooming house. Melony wanted to be free to marry Jeff if he asked her, so she filed for divorce from Eddie.

Melony was very observant and wanted to make sure she was making the right decision by getting involved with Jeff. She noticed that Jeff, his brothers and their father were involved in bootlegging liquor and gambling, which explained the large amounts of money they always had. Jeff's father would leave town frequently and return with suitcases of money to share with all of his sons and their girlfriends. Melony and the other girls would go shopping and buy whatever they wanted, because they were encouraged to dress well and to eat well. When they all went out to party, they would go to a certain club where they had their own tables. Jeff and his brothers would carry their shotguns with them to the club and keep them in the trunk of their cars, and they all had .38 pistols in their boots. When they partied, the drinks were endless, and they would sell drugs right there from their table. Jeff's dad had at least three prostitutes who worked the club, bringing him money each night.

One evening, Eddie came to the rooming house looking for Melony. He informed Jeff that Melony was his wife, and that he wanted her back. Eddie pulled his pistol on Jeff. Jeff smiled in disbelief and in turn pulled three pistols on Eddie, telling him to leave and forget about Melony. Jeff told Eddie if he ever came back again, he would kill him. That was the last Melony would see of Eddie for a while.

Jeff talked to Melony about how to be rid of Eddie for good and make a smooth profit as well. He suggested that Melony call Eddie up and tell him she was reconsidering his proposition, and for him to come over so they could talk. Jeff would then block his car in, have him killed, and Melony could then collect the insurance and get his car. Melony could not believe that Jeff could think up such an evil plan. *Had he done this before?* She considered it for about two seconds, and as much as she wanted to be rid of Eddie, she did not want to be a part of a murder. Her divorce would be final soon anyway. Besides, she was pretty sure that she was pregnant with Jeff's child, and she didn't want to risk being in jail and pregnant. When Jeff heard the news about the baby, he forgot about the murder plot.

There was nothing that Melony wanted that she could not ask Jeff for after he found out she was pregnant. He insisted she get prenatal care from the best doctor, and that she eat healthy foods. For the first time, with the responsibility of being a father, he felt he could share with Melony the entire inside dealings of his family. He showed her a secret room that he had built for his dad, where there were stacks and stacks of hundred- and thousand-dollar bills! Melony had never seen a thousand-dollar bill until then, and the money lined the walls on shelves. He showed her a white woman's hand wrapped in a bloody towel that had a huge diamond ring still on the hand. She couldn't believe what she was seeing!

These black men had a lot of money and power, a rare combination. *What was the risk for her knowing these secrets? What was this family really in?* She found out that Jeff's dad was a hit man for the mob, and that the suitcases of money he would come home with were from hits he had performed in other cities. The money in the secret closet came from gambling, drug deals, bootlegging, and prostitution setups all over the country, and was laundered through Jeff's family. These were some bad boys!

After exposing her to the family's business, Jeff threatened to kill her if she ever told anyone about the family's operations. *Now she knew the price of being on the inside.* Melony noticed a white man who would come over every Thursday to see Jeff's dad, and they would laugh and talk, have a few drinks, and would often play a few hands of poker. The stakes at the poker game would start at $1,000 a hand. She found out the man was moving money for Jeff's dad into legitimate avenues. One Thursday evening, the man and a friend came by as usual, and Jeff, his father, and his brothers got into the car with the men and left. The next thing Melony heard was that a white man had been found dead in a nearby park, having been beaten and killed by a shot to the back of the head. Another man was also shot, but survived and later identified Jeff's father as the trigger man. Both men had been undercover cops trying to collect information on the mob for prosecution.

Melony and the other girls were reading the newspaper and saw the man's picture, and recognized him as the man who had been coming over on Thursdays. When Melony and the girls asked about the killing, they were told not to speak to anyone about what they knew, and that if they did, they would be killed also. Jeff's dad and another man were under investigation for the murder, but the policeman doing the investigation was one of many cops on Jeff's family's payroll. One of the men working with Jeff's father was arrested for the murder instead of Jeff's father, and sentenced to 10 years in prison. Melony was sure that this man had nothing to do with the murder, but had been paid to take the fall for Jeff's dad. (*The man only served a few years, and after his release got a large sum of money and a house for his troubles.*)

When Melony had the baby, Jeff was right by her side for the birth of their beautiful baby girl, Rose. (*In Melony's heart she would always mourn the baby she was forced to abort. She felt God was giving her another chance at motherhood.*) Jeff strutted around with his chest out like a proud father and bought everything he thought the baby needed, because he did not want his child to lack anything. When they came home with the baby, Jeff showed Rose off to everyone. He loved her so because he said when he saw Rose's face, he saw his own.

Melony loved Rose with all her heart and soul. She never knew love like the love she felt for Rose. It was a sacrificial kind of love; there was nothing she would not do for her baby, she would even give her own life for her child. She took Rose to visit her mother, who was so proud of her new grandbaby. Ella was concerned about Melony's living arrangement, but she knew she could not do any better for her. Melony didn't know much about caring for babies, but Jeff's mother was a good teacher and taught her how to change diapers and how to bathe and feed Rose. Melony was determined to be a good mother and protect Rose from harm at all costs.

Just prior to Rose's birth, Jeff's dad was killed by one of Jeff's brothers over $200,000 that was in the trunk of his car. Jeff's dad had accused Jeff's brother of stealing the money, and a shoot-out had occurred. Another one of Jeff's brothers went to jail for the crime, but his share of the family business was being put aside for him upon his release. Later, Jeff's father's death caused a power struggle between the sons, and Jeff was more irritable and easily upset than usual. One evening when Rose was one month old, Jeff and Melony got into an argument, and Jeff slapped Melony. She was surprised by his behavior and knew how violent that family could be. When night came and Jeff was out with his brothers, she took Rose and their belongings and headed for her aunt's house.

Melony was determined that no man would beat her, especially after what she had witnessed her own mother go through. Her aunt was a welcome sight and she did not tell her anything about Jeff's family, because she felt the less her aunt knew, the safer she was. The next morning, Jeff appeared in front of her aunt's house, along with his mother, and he had taken a can of gasoline and poured it all around the house. With a shotgun in hand, he called for Melony to come out and to bring Rose with her, demanding that she give him the baby, or else he would burn the house down with them inside. Melony said a prayer over Rose and immediately gave the baby to him and his mother. He threatened her not to come and get her, or the child would be motherless.

Melony knew it was useless to call the police because they were all on Jeff's family's payroll, and she was afraid that if she attempted to get her daughter back, Jeff or one of his brothers would kill her. All she could do was cry and ask God to watch over Rose. *Would God hear her prayers?* Every day Melony cried and prayed for her baby, feeling so helpless. Two weeks later, Jeff and his mother brought Rose back because Jeff's mother had convinced him that Melony was worried to death about her baby, and that a baby that young needs its mother. Melony thanked him and didn't see Jeff again until three years later, when his mother died and Melony and Rose attended the funeral.

Melony and Rose thrived at her aunt's house, and Melony completed her classes and took her GED (General Educational Development) test. One day when Melony and three-year-old Rose were on the bus going downtown, a well-dressed black man got on the bus with two pretty little girls. She was admiring to herself how pretty the girls were when the man stopped by her seat. He looked down at her and asked, "Is that your daughter?" Melony said, "Yes it is, why do you ask?" He asked her, "Do you remember me?" She was afraid it was one of Jeff's connections. She said, "No, I don't." He told her his name: "I'm Gerald." Melony's heart almost stopped! Gerald looked like a totally different person, with his clean-shaven face and nice clothes. Suddenly, his face became twisted and he started yelling at her about killing his child, and that the child she killed was probably his son. Melony was frightened out of her wits! He said he had become a preacher, and that she should repent for her sin of killing his baby. People on the bus were shocked, and Melony was embarrassed about the encounter. When he and his girls sat down, she took Rose and got off the bus at the next stop without even looking to see where she was. Her entire body was trembling with fear. Gerald may have looked different on the outside, but he was still the same inside. *(She had heard that all of his sisters were strung out on drugs and working in the strip clubs, just like their mother.)*

Soon after the bus incident, Gerald's mother died, and Melony had an opportunity to see her old friends at the funeral. They acted like it was homecoming, but Melony could not get past the childhood events with their families and how Dana had ignored her cry for help when Gerald raped her. Dana was now a shell that crack cocaine had left behind. She pleaded for Melony to wait around to see Gerald after he preached his mother's funeral. *(He had gotten saved, and saved his mother from the strip club life style before she had died.)* Melony kindly told Dana she would rather not see Gerald. She decided to leave Dana to draw her own conclusions.

When Rose turned four, Melony began taking her to the library to get books to read, because she was so smart and curious to learn. At the library she met a nice guy named Alfred who frequented the reading room, and they would have long talks. She found out that he had contracted HIV (Human Immunodeficiency Virus) through drug use and was lonely like she was. He was very honest with her about his condition, but she didn't care; she liked Alfred for who he was. Because of his diagnosis of HIV, he was getting a disability check each month that helped him with his expenses. He invited Rose and Melony to move in with him, and they formed their own little family.

Melony knew she was putting herself at risk by sleeping with him, but they were more than lovers—they were sick spirits who needed each other, and they made sure to use protection. Alfred's family had disowned him when he was diagnosed with HIV because they were not sure how to deal with him. His father would come over on the first of each month when Alfred got his check to beg for money from him, and Alfred would give it to him, probably out of guilt or the need to have some contact with his family.

Melony and Al started attending a small church in a community that accepted people as they were. Melony felt the love there and slowly started to get back in touch with God. She still had her issues with God about how and why her life was the way it was, but at least she was listening. She saw how the minister came to visit Alfred and prayed for him and brought them food. As Alfred's condition progressed to full-blown AIDS (Acquired Immunodeficiency Syndrome), he became weaker and was unable to care for himself. Melony stayed with him day and night, caring for him as if he was a newborn. He often told her how much he loved her for not abandoning him, like his friends and family had.

When Alfred died, Melony contacted his father and the minister of their church to tell them of his death. The day before he died, Social Security had sent Alfred a lump sum check. Melony had acquired the ability to cash his checks when he became gravely ill, in order to take care of his finances. After his death, Melony told his father about the check, and his father took it and never offered Melony anything for caring for his son. He came the next day, packed up everything in the house that was Alfred's and left, leaving Melony and Rose with nothing and nowhere to live.

Melony was once again on her own, lonely and discarded. She felt in her heart that she had done the right thing by caring for Alfred, and that the money was not hers to keep. His father would have to deal with God on that issue. She continued to attend church, and the minister and some of the church members helped her find housing and a job. She and Rose were soon in a place where they could both grow. Melony visited her mother often, and Rose and Ella grew to be best friends. Ella had stopped drinking and found a job sitting with the elderly for support. She soon started attending church with Melony and Rose. The three of them enjoyed going to church together. Melony still liked the idea of living independently and chose not to move in with Ella, even after much insistence.

One Sunday after a riveting sermon from the minster about forgiveness, Ella began to cry uncontrollably and started screaming at the top of her voice. Melony had never seen her mother like this. Ella cried until the ushers had to take her outside. As she cried, the front of her dress became soaked with tears, and she grabbed Melony tight, begging for forgiveness for all the pain and misery she had put her through. She pleaded with Melony to forgive her before she would let her go. Melony was crying and praising God for her mother's words, and suddenly the clouds seemed to part, and for the first time in years she could breathe, really breathe! Melony told Ella how much she loved her, and that she understood she was doing what she thought was best. They both began to praise God for keeping them from being destroyed, and for allowing them to see that day.

People from the church began to surround them as they heard their outpourings of praise and pleas for forgiveness. The pastor came forth and laid hands on both of them, and the entire church began to pray for them through tears of thanksgiving. Melony and Ella rededicated their lives to Christ that day and have not looked back. Rose grew into a beautiful young woman, strong-willed and smart. Melony occasionally shares stories of her past with Rose as she tries to guide her around some situations that could harm her.

Restoration is a daily task for Melony. She often replays the tapes of the past and sometimes wants to go back to the life of drugs and alcohol. Prayer is a constant partner to get her through those dark days and nights. She remembers the depth of despair from which she had ascended, and it is an awareness of the day-to-day drawing on the word of God on which she depends, so that she does not return there.

Reflection of Melony's Story

by Rev. Dr. Alfie Wines, Ph.D.
As I traversed the twists and turns of Melony's story,

I wondered how could anyone survive all this. I considered the impact of her story on other women, because many may identify with certain parts of her story and feel led to share stories of their own. I reflected on the three days that it took for her to tell her story to her Bible study leader. I thought of the women who will be drawn to and healed by this retelling of her story, and wondered, "Does Melony know how strong she is?" Strong, you might ask? Yes, strong! The misfortunes in her life required that she use her strength for survival. The key to turning her life around was her ability to use that strength for rebuilding her life.

Like the writer of Psalm 27, Melony felt abandoned by her parents when she was just a girl with the death of her beloved father and her mother's descent into depression. She felt abandoned and alone without anyone to care for her. As with the biblical character Job, troubles came one after another. Before she could adjust to one trouble, another came on its heels. Once Jake entered Melony and Ella's lives, it took years, with many missteps along the way, for Melony to get her bearings. Angry and hurt, she turned away from God, from church, and from the Bible. Yet, somehow, she made it through. She would not have survived the horrors that she witnessed and experienced, had she not been able to draw on her inner faith and strength.

As people so often do, Melony forgot who she was. She forgot that God loves her, no matter what. She forgot that God's grace continuously reaches out to us—whether we know it or not, whether we believe it or not, whether we receive it or not.

What Melony heard and experienced during her childhood days at church was implanted deep in her soul. Though covered up by the hurt, pain, and disappointment of everyday living, God's love was still present. When Alfred invited Melony and Rose to church, the time was right. This time, the kind words and loving experiences of her childhood resonated and reconnected her to God's love. Knowing that she is loved enables Melony to redirect her strength from survival mode to the work of rebuilding a life for her daughter and herself.

Melony's story, along with the words of Psalm 27, remind us that even when the difficulties of life are so up close and personal that it feels like war, we can be confident and trust in God. We can hope and expect to see the goodness of God in the land of the living.

"Even though an army sets up camp against me, my heart will not be afraid. Even though a war breaks out against me, I will still have confidence [in the LORD]. I remain confident of this: I will see the goodness of the LORD in the land of the living." Psalm 27:3, 10

"Marsha"

Story by J. Harris

Reflection by Rev. Charlane Russell

WE HUMANS ALL HAVE GOD-GIVEN INSTINCTS that tell us that danger is near, or that we are entering an unsafe situation. Whether we are out in nature, or in a relationship, we all have that instinct. We often ignore the warnings we get in our spirit that say, "Danger!" We sometimes have such a deep-seeded need to be loved or affirmed that we willingly enter into a dangerous or harmful relationship, rather than choosing to remain alone and lonely. Loneliness can even occur when you are in a room full of people. Loneliness can be dangerous if accompanied by uncertainty, and Marsha's story is filled with loneliness and looking for love while ignoring the warning signs. Her warm and loving heart has led her to find the true love of her life, Christ. Through all of her searching for acceptance in the faces of men, she found her love for God. It is in that Godly love that she found true happiness.

Growing up in Houston, Texas, in a large African-American family can be difficult if you are the youngest of six children. The oldest child in her family was 15 years older than she, and Marsha often heard her mother saying that she felt ashamed when she was pregnant with her, because she was 38 years old when she had Marsha. This feeling that she may have been a mistake or a source of embarrassment for her parents would create a theme for Marsha's life—the need to belong and to feel wanted. She did not learn until after she had endured many trials and errors that the circumstances under which you enter this world are not what matter, but rather, what you do with your life after you arrive.

Marsha's parents, Lola and Milton, married young at the age of just 19 years old. Lola was light brown skinned with long, flowing black hair, and her beauty was undeniable. Milton was ordinary in stature and looks, and people would often wonder what Lola saw in him. He was Lola's first and only companion. They started having children after a year of marriage, and Milton did not want Lola to work. He had his own mechanic shop and worked long hours to provide for his wife and children, and he made sure he and his family attended church every Sunday. To all in their small community, they looked like a normal family. Milton made sure his family was well fed and clothed, but he did not see the need to let them know he loved them. He did what he did for them out of a sense of responsibility.

Lola did not know how to talk to her children about the things they would come against in the world, or of her life's experiences. Perhaps she did not have much experience, or was uncomfortable discussing the circumstances that drove her to want to leave home and marry young. Milton was unconcerned with the behavior issues of the children, taking the stance that as long as the bills were paid, he had done his part. He felt that being affectionate and loving was not a requirement on his part.

The children would never know Lola's side of the family, and she never pressed the issue to visit them. Perhaps she had married Milton to get away from a difficult home situation. It would remain a family secret. Together they did not know how to provide the guidance for their children to help them develop boundaries concerning what to do, and what not to do. Perhaps due to Milton and Lola's non-confrontational parenting style, Marsha's older brothers and her only sister turned to drugs and unruly lifestyles. They were a constant source of disruption in the family, always pushing the limits. Marsha's three brothers had "daredevil" spirits—one with life, one with drugs, and one with motorcycles and cars. They would try anything; no risk was too great. Marsha would also find that she had a risk-taking spirit of her own.

Because her parents never told Marsha about sex, she was curious. In high school, Marsha was an excellent student—a cheerleader, beautiful and popular, with all of the attributes for success. She did not go unnoticed by the boys at school and in the community. She was especially noticed by Randy, an 18-year-old senior star football player. He had noticed Marsha on the sideline cheering, and he approached her with his smooth and confident personality.

Marsha was an inexperienced 16year-old freshman, flattered by the handsome senior, and other freshman girls envied her because Randy chose her. Her parents were so preoccupied with trying to manage her older sister and brothers that Marsha's questions about life and love went unanswered. After years of watching her parents' relationship, there seemed to be tolerance between them, but no real affection. Marsha vowed to have more affection in her relationships and longed for someone to think that she was special and needed. Her young life was starving for affection, and Randy was there to provide it.

Their relationship moved from comforting conversation to physical passion. Marsha felt alive when she was with Randy, and all of the issues in her world seemed to disappear when they were together. He noticed her, talked to her, and saw her as a person. *What could go wrong?* Randy assured Marsha that he would not be able to get her pregnant, because he was unable to have children due to some childhood disease. This allowed Marsha to express herself sexually without the threat of becoming pregnant. Marsha was naive, and Randy knew it. After a few months of their rendezvous at Randy's house, Marsha missed her menstrual cycle and suspected that she may be pregnant. She went to her sister, Vivian, and shared that she may possibly be pregnant. Vivian was much older and had a baby, so she knew what Marsha was in for. Vivian suggested that Marsha wait one more month to make sure before telling their parents.

Marsha was worried about what the people in the community and church would say, and especially about what her mother would say. She couldn't believe that Randy had lied to her about not being able to get her pregnant in order to get her to have sex with him. She confronted him about the possibility that she may be pregnant and he confessed that he had lied, but he did not regret that Marsha was pregnant. He promised to support her and to do the best he could to help with the baby. The next month told the truth—Marsha was pregnant, and now she had to tell her parents. Vivian agreed to go with her to tell them. It took all the strength Marsha could gather to face her parents. After she broke the news to her parents, they were silent and seemed numb, and Milton looked at Lola as if to say, "You handle this." Lola expressed how disappointed she was in Marsha, and that they thought she would turn out better that her sister and brothers. Marsha really felt bad, and so did Vivian. Then, the unexpected happened.

Lola took a stand on the matter and said that Marsha had to get married. She stressed to Marsha that she did not want Randy to get off without being held responsible for the baby. Marsha liked Randy, but could not see herself being married to him. Lola and Milton were from a small country town where tradition ran strong, and when a guy got a girl pregnant out of wedlock, he "did right by her" and married her. Period.

The courthouse ceremony was simple, unromantic but official, and that was all Lola wanted—an official ceremony. The young newlyweds had no real means of support and would have to depend on their families to help them out. Randy had enrolled in college but dropped out to get a job after they got married, and Marsha got a job at an insurance company. Marsha did not want to live at home, and eventually Marsha and Randy moved in with Randy's older brother. Randy's family was close knit and had no problem taking in one more. Randy's mother had died when he was young and had left the house to his brother, and if any of the siblings fell on hard times or had no place to live, they could live there. At any given time, there were at least eight to nine people in the house.

A few months into the marriage, Marsha's family had a severe tragedy. Her older brother died from a heroin overdose, and the entire family took his death very hard. From that experience, Marsha vowed that she would never touch drugs. The family would never really know how the death occurred, just that he was found dead. This was one time that Marsha was glad Randy was around. She really needed his comfort, and being pregnant did not help with the grieving process. Randy made sure she was calm, and he was understanding of her mood swings and crying spells.

The birth of their son, Jason, seemed to soften Marsha's loss of her brother, realizing that she had a new life to take care of. Lola came to help Marsha with the baby and taught her how to care for the baby, and how to be a good mother. Marsha was so proud of Jason, and thought he was the most beautiful baby she had ever seen. Randy was a proud father but began to feel pressured and trapped, because he still wanted to go to the club and party as if he was single. Marsha wanted him to stay home and be a father and husband, and this would be the cause of many arguments. To get away from the madness, Marsha would take Jason to church on Sundays, without Randy, in search of the peace she received from the services.

Randy grew rebellious, and would make it no secret to Marsha that he had other women because he felt forced into marriage before he was ready to settle down. The arguments grew into violent attacks on Marsha by Randy. Marsha also felt trapped, and as Jason grew older she wanted to go out and have fun too, but whenever Marsha decided to go out and party, Randy confronted her and demanded she stay home. On one such occasion, when Marsha insisted that he allow her to go out with her friends, Randy pulled a gun on her and held her at home all evening. As he held the gun, he lectured her on the duties of a good wife, and how it was her duty as a mother and wife to stay home instead of going to clubs. *How could he lecture her when he went out AND had other women?*

When Marsha could finally take no more of Randy's controlling and cheating, she moved in with her sister Vivian, who lived a wild lifestyle filled with lots of men and lots of drugs. Marsha tolerated the atmosphere at Vivian's for a few weeks, but decided the environment was too unstable for Jason, and contemplated going back to Randy. He called all day every day while she was away, telling her how sorry he was and that he wanted his family back. Marsha said she would only go back to him if they moved into their own apartment to help give their marriage a fresh start. When Marsha and Jason went back to Randy in their new apartment, she warned him that if he ever tried to hurt her again, she would leave permanently. Randy promised Marsha not to harm her and to stop running around with other women.

As time went on, Randy went back to his old ways of staying out all night with the boys and with other women, so after five years of marriage, Marsha had had enough. She made and executed her plan to leave Randy, because she knew he could be violent and she had to be careful and not give him suspicions that she was leaving. She packed enough clothes for herself and for Jason, put them in her work bag, dropped Jason off at her mother's home, and went to work as usual. After a few days of her not coming home and not returning his calls, Randy realized she had moved out and was furious. He called Marsha at her mother's and left threatening phone calls vowing to get her back. Through all of the fights and moving in and out with her parents and sister, Marsha's brothers never felt the need to come to her rescue. They took the stance that whatever happened was between Marsha and her husband and was not their business, even when they saw the bruises on their sister. Marsha was alone.

One morning, when Marsha was standing on the bus stop waiting for the bus, Randy came by and hopped the curb with his car right where she was standing, almost running her over! It was 6:00 a.m., and no one was around. He had been sitting nearby waiting for her to get to the bus stop, and when he saw her, he suddenly jumped out of the car, grabbed her, and forced her into the car. As he drove off with her, they were going down the street fighting. He hit her and almost knocked her out. When he got Marsha to his house, Randy forced her at gunpoint to the bedroom, made her strip naked, and raped her repeatedly. All she could think about was that if she fought back, Randy would kill her, and Jason would be motherless.

Randy's rape rage went on from 6 a.m. to 6 p.m., with Marsha continuously crying and begging him to let her go. He continued to demand that she come back to him, and she kept insisting that it was over. She talked softly to him, trying to calm him down and make him understand that their marriage was not going to work. She told him that if he killed her, Jason would not have a mother and would never forgive him. Finally at 6 p.m., when he realized that she would never return to him, he dropped the gun, began to cry and let her go. The next day Marsha went to the police and got a restraining order against Randy, and then to the lawyer to file for divorce.

The fallout from the divorce weighed heavily on little Jason. The five-year-old had witnessed his father and mother fighting, and as a result he became quiet and withdrawn, and Marsha was afraid that the dysfunction of her marriage had scarred Jason permanently. Randy himself was a victim of what he had witnessed as a child, because his mother had married many times, and he never knew his real father. His male role models had been his uncles, who were all womanizers who would brag about the many women they'd had at one time, as if it were a badge of honor. Randy had grown up in that womanizing environment and did not know, or want to know, any other way to live. Marsha did not want that type of behavior to be Jason's reality, so she had to move on.

Temporarily, Marsha moved in with one of her single co-workers who also had a son, so they split the rent and their sons had live-in playmates. With the divorce and five years of madness behind her, Marsha wanted to live on her own terms. She enjoyed being able to come and go as she pleased, to go to parties and have fun without the threat of fights when she returned home. After a year of the carefree single life, one of her friends introduced her to Warren. He was fun to be around, made her laugh, and knew how to have a good time, and Marsha craved being around him. She and Jason eventually moved in with him.

Warren confided in Marsha things about his own troubled past that he had never shared with anyone else. He had been adopted and did not know much about his mother, and his foster mother had been very abusive toward him, beating him for no reason. The foster mother had originally not been able to have children, so they adopted Warren, and the couple eventually had two other children of their own. Warren would later find out that his adopted father was actually his birth father, which explained why his foster mother hated and abused him. Warren had been scarred from the abuse.

After six month of them living together, Marsha found out she was pregnant and she really didn't want to marry Warren, but he wanted to get married and have a normal family. He wanted his child to grow up in a home with two parents and love, so when she was nine months pregnant, they finally got married. The courthouse ceremony was unremarkable, but Warren would prove to be a loving father to their new son, Chad. Warren was determined to be a good father, but had trouble holding down a job. His emotional issues from his abusive childhood made it hard for him to deal with authority figures at work and he would eventually get fired for rebellious acts toward his bosses. The constant unemployment eventually created tension between Warren and Marsha, and the couple argued over his terminations and about their money problems.

When he would lose a job, Warren turned his anger toward Marsha and he would hit and slap her when she made comments about him losing his job. Jason told

Marsha that he could not tolerate the arguments and that he wanted to move in with his father, Randy. Marsha agreed to let him move, but she visited him every weekend and provided him with the things he needed. Marsha and Warren fought infrequently, about every three to four months, but when they did, it was violent and loud. Warren still slept with other women and expected Marsha to understand his cheating. When Marsha and Warren were getting along, they would go to church as a normal family, as if everything was fine. Even with the hidden bruises, Marsha enjoyed her time at church and prayed that God would fix her marriage. Through all she had been through, she still felt that God was with her. Marsha missed her family, but she did not want them to see her after she and Warren had been fighting.

One evening when they were fighting in the bathroom, Warren accidentally fell and hit his head on the shower door, which caused a large laceration on his scalp. Blood was everywhere! Marsha rushed him to the hospital, where he received numerous stitches in his head. The accident scared both of them so badly that they decided to separate before someone got seriously hurt. Before the accident, Warren was seldom seen in church, but the accident caused Warren to have a conversion moment. He went from rarely going to church, to being fanatical about God. He talked Marsha into moving back in with him, stating that he was a changed man for God. He convinced Jason to move back home so that they could all be a family, and promised that he would be a better father figure to him and Chad.

They started attending a small "Mom and Pop" church, where most of the members were related to each other. Warren no longer wanted Marsha to go to her family's church or to visit her family. He hung on the minister's every word, and whenever he got paid, he gave all of his money to the church. Marsha would argue with him about giving all his money away, and then they would have to go to the church to ask for money to pay their bills.

Warren's conversion did not stop him from hitting Marsha when they had arguments. Since Warren had such respect for the pastor and his wife, Marsha suggested that they go to them for counseling, and he agreed. During one of the counseling sessions, the pastor and his wife broke out into an argument between themselves. Marsha knew her marriage to Warren was really in trouble if the pastor and his wife were fighting. Soon after that counseling session, the pastor and wife separated and divorced, the church was split, and the members scattered.

Marsha and Warren also decided to call it quits, and Warren was so attached to Chad that he vowed to fight Marsha for custody of him. Warren had such a bad relationship with his own family that Chad was really his only blood relation. Jason did not like being responsible for Chad while Marsha worked at night, so he moved back with his father, Randy, and Marsha agreed to allow Chad to stay with Warren, but insisted that she be able to visit him every weekend. She was too tired to fight anymore.

Marsha felt her life was in shambles, after two failed marriages with each of her sons living with their different fathers, and her pastor and his wife's relationship had failed. *What was wrong with her that she could not find happiness?* She got her own apartment, and she found herself alone and lonely. She even felt God had left her alone, and she began to question her faith in God and to wonder if God was really real. *How could God let her go through these nightmares? She could accept her part in the tragedies, but where was God when she needed to be rescued?*

She was trying to search her mind to see where all the madness really began. *Was it because she always felt her parents did not want another child when they had her? Had she sensed the lack of love she felt growing up? Or was it that she did not have enough faith in God to direct her life?* All she knew was that she needed to do something different with her life. She regretted that she did not go to college, so she went to the local Junior College and enrolled in classes. She decided she wanted to be a social worker and try and help other young women who were in troubled relationships and marriages. Marsha enjoyed being in school and learning, because she had always been a good student in high school, and learning energized her.

After three years of living with his father, Jason moved back home with Marsha because he had seen his father for the womanizer he was, and he had seen his uncles mistreat their women, and he had decided he needed a break from that dysfunction. Marsha was glad to have him home, because she missed her baby and she missed being a full-time mother to him. Other than her dilemma with God, Marsha thought life was good. She did not go out and party like she had in the past, and felt that at 29 years old, partying did not appeal to her as it once had. She enjoyed visiting her family, having been cut off from them by Warren before. Her sister Vivian felt Marsha needed to get out more and meet new people, so she introduced her to her brother-in-law, Lance. Lance was very quiet, reserved, and generous, and worked two warehouse jobs. Marsha liked his quiet spirit immediately, and he soon introduced her to his family, where his mother welcomed her like a daughter. Marsha had found a new family.

Lance confided in Marsha that he really wanted to marry her, but that he was not officially divorced from his wife from whom he was currently separated. The fact that he did not have children attracted Marsha to him, and Lance accepted Jason and Chad as if they were his sons. Lance did not go to church, and neither did Marsha, so they had that in common. They enjoyed each other's company, and Marsha felt she had finally met her soul mate, even if he was married to someone else. They traveled frequently, and they all had family picnics and outings. Jason did not like Lance and decided to move back with his father, so Marsha did not object, but she called him often and saw him on weekends. After all, he was becoming his own man. Marsha moved in with Lance and they made plans to get married, but Lance seemed to change after Marsha moved in by becoming possessive and jealous. Lance did not want to admit that he was still attached and attracted to his wife. He would make promises of divorcing her, but never took action on it.

A job promotion caused Lance to have to travel frequently, and often when he returned home, he accused Marsha of cheating on him. No matter how hard she tried to convince him that she was faithful, he would continue to accuse her. Vivian had warned Marsha that Lance also had a steady girlfriend that he had not quite gotten over, and if she ever heard him speak of her, it may mean that they were seeing each other again. One evening when Marsha was doing laundry, she found a motel receipt in his pants pocket from where he had taken a woman to a motel. When she questioned him about it, he denied it and she began not to trust him. Later she noticed the caller ID on the phone showed the woman's name that Vivian had warned her about and she again questioned him, and he eventually admitted that he had been seeing her. Marsha gathered her things and moved in with Vivian. Even though Lance called her repeatedly, she would not respond. She was through.

Marsha heard that Lance was later diagnosed with bone cancer and died with his wife by his side.

Marsha had closed her heart off to men and God, and was in a dark place spiritually and emotionally. She was tired of the failed relationships and did not trust her own judgment. She continued to question God about why she continued to get into these unhappy relationships. She decided to concentrate again on rebuilding her life, and bought a home in the suburbs of Houston. She felt she was still young, and life was still full. Jason was in college and Chad moved with her into the new home. Chad and Jason were not close, but they loved each other in their own way. Marsha surveyed the damage and knew that she had to make some new commitments with her new life, and found a new church to attend where she could worship and be fed spiritually. With her reconnection to God, her heart was reassured that whatever she had been through, He had been there to protect her.

Marsha would need her faith to get her through the next five years as she suffered a series of losses of family members, one year after the next. Her first loss would be her mother dying from cancer. Lola had been Marsha's rock whenever she was in trouble, or just needed someone to talk to. The two of them had grown closer as Marsha cared for her during her illness, and her death would leave Marsha numb and Milton lost. He had depended on Lola to raise the children, handle the household, and keep everyone together. Now she was gone.

Milton's health began to fail after Lola's death, and Marsha had to keep watch over him also. The same year that Lola died, Marsha's brother died, and the family had to gather for yet another funeral. She saw her siblings struggling with drug and alcohol addictions and did not know how to help them. The next two years would claim her other two brothers to violent deaths and drug addictions, leaving only Vivian and Marsha of the six children as Vivian continued to struggle with her own chemically induced demons. The loss of her siblings made Marsha appreciate her relationship with God even more; it gave her strength. As Milton's health failed, Marsha was responsible for making sure he was cared for, and she thought to herself how ironic it was that the one child her parents were not sure they wanted, was the one who brought them comfort when they needed it most. Milton would not say it to Marsha, but he appreciated her kindness and her coming by daily to check on him.

Marsha felt she finally had her life on solid footing and had weathered the storms of grief and loss, but the losses had taken a lot out of her. She was tired from taking care of her parents and burying her siblings, and she needed a break. She took Chad to a Halloween party one evening and met a very exciting, somewhat younger Hispanic man named Victor. He saw Marsha, and after a brief persuasive conversation gave her his phone number. After all of the grieving and Milton being ill, Victor's electric personality was a breath of fresh air. He was fourteen years younger than Marsha but acted much older. He was handsome, charming, and confident, the perfect combination for a top car salesman at a major dealership. After a few weeks, Marsha called Victor, and he took the relationship from there.

Victor was energetic and never seemed to slow down, doing everything in fast forward. Within two weeks, he had taken Marsha and Chad to meet his mother and his very large family, and they liked them both. His mother lived in a large house that seemed to always have children, cousins, or some relative moving in or moving out.

Victor's mother liked and respected Marsha and wanted her to know the truth about her son before their relationship went any further. She made Victor tell Marsha that he had a substance abuse problem in the past, and had been released the year before from prison after serving a 12-year sentence for theft. He had gone in as a juvenile and was released as an adult. He had never been married and did not have any children. Marsha liked the fact that she would not have to deal with any ex-wives or baby-mama drama, but was not sure about Victor's mental stability. Something in her inner being sent red flags up alerting her to the fact that this relationship might be dangerous, but she could not resist her desire to be needed and wanted by this man.

The news about Victor's imprisonment unnerved Marsha, but she liked him and enjoyed his company during their whirlwind romance. He made good money selling cars, showering Marsha with whatever she wanted. They went to church together, and he knew the Bible well. *Had God finally heard her loneliness and sent someone who would care for her?* Thirty days after meeting, they were married at his mother's house. Milton was not able to attend because of his illness, but he also did not seem to care about the marriage. Victor took Marsha on a wonderful honeymoon cruise and life seemed good for a change.

After three months of marital bliss, Victor crashed! One day after going to his mother's house, he went on a drinking binge and became someone Marsha had never known him to be, but had seen in her other relationships. He was loud, verbally abusive, and mean toward her and others. Victor's cousin lived with his mother and had a boyfriend who had beaten her, and when Victor found out, he took his mother's gun, put it to the man's head and pulled the trigger. For some reason the gun jammed and did not fire. The family called 911 because Victor was in a rage, and the police came and took him to jail, where he was sentenced to six months for assault.

Jail was actually a blessing for Victor, because it was there that he was diagnosed with bipolar disorder and ADHD*(Attention Deficit Hyperactivity Disorder)*. After Marsha heard about the diagnosis, she began to put the signs together: the aggressive behavior, the constant energy, and the ability to convince people. *Had she been so lonely that she had ignored the signs?* His mother admitted to Marsha that Victor had also been sexually abused as a child but had never gotten the help he needed, because Victor would never talk about the incident. His mother noticed that his behavior changed after the abuse. Marsha felt obligated to stand by her husband and try to get him some help. Victor's gift was his ability to talk to people and get them to do what he wanted, and no matter how much trouble he got into, or how many times the dealership fired him, they would hire him back because he was such a great salesman.

Victor managed to sell Marsha and his mother on the idea that he would take his medicine and go to rehab if they bailed him out of jail, so they put their money together and bailed him out. For a while Victor went to the psychiatrist and stayed on his medications, but he would not go to his weekly therapy sessions without Marsha. She could tell when he was not taking his medications, because he would have severe mood swings, even to the point of being depressed and almost suicidal. Then he would have days where he would be up for two or three days at a time, talking and moving non-stop, wearing Marsha down with his constant talking day after day.

Eventually Victor began to make excuses for not going to the psychiatrist and for not taking his medications, and started snorting cocaine heavily and drinking constantly. Marsha was afraid of Victor's behavior when he was on drugs because she remembered her brother dying of an overdose, and the thought of finding Victor dead from an overdose was overwhelming. She would beg him to stop the drugs and to go into rehab, but he would always find an excuse not to go. The more drugs he did, the more erratic his behavior became, until he had delusions and started seeing and hearing things that were not there.

When Victor had manic days, Marsha read her Bible continuously as her safe refuge. That Christmas, Marsha and Victor went to his mother's house, and he was so hopped up on drugs and alcohol that his behavior ruined the holiday celebration and his mother asked him to leave. On the way home, Marsha and Victor got into an argument about how the drugs were ruining their lives, and that he needed to get help, so Victor agreed to go to rehab that evening. When Marsha drove him to the rehab center, he refused to get out of the car and made her take him home.

Victor could quote the Bible but never saw the need to apply it to his life. Thus, his drugging and drinking finally led to the ultimate meltdown. Marsha went to check on Milton one evening and Victor, who had been doing drugs heavily and drinking all that day, followed her. When she came out of the house, he asked her to get in the car, and while in the car he said he had seen her with another man. His eyes were red and he was driving wildly. He pulled out a large knife and told her, "I'm going to kill you!" Marsha's mind flashed back to the incident where Victor had pulled the gun on his cousin's boyfriend, and the gun had jammed.

She knew that in his condition he really meant to kill her, and she did not want to die and leave her children motherless, so for once she had to fight back. She took off her shoe and began hitting him in the head with it while they were on an access road, and in turn he stabbed her in the leg with the knife as she jumped out of the car, with the car still rolling. When she exited the moving car and landed on the pavement, she broke her ankle, and a car behind her witnessed what had happened and took her to an emergency room. Victor kept driving and never looked back, and Marsha didn't either. *(Marsha later heard that Victor had fled to Mexico, where he went on a crime spree, was arrested and sentenced to 10 years in prison).* While in the emergency room, Marsha thanked God over and over again for sparing her life. At that moment, she promised God that she would do whatever He wanted her to do in gratitude for Him saving her life. After the stabbing incident Marsha filed for divorce, because after two years of marriage to Victor, she was exhausted.

Marsha went on to complete her college studies and obtained stable employment that enabled her to send her sons to college. Marsha made good on her vow to God to dedicate the rest of her life in service to His will and way. God was calling for her to put Him first in her life. She sought out a faith community that she enjoys serving in, and has made herself available for ministry opportunities. She joined the prison ministry team to help minister to and pray with women who are incarcerated, to bring words of encouragement to them.

When you ask Marsha what lessons she learned from her life's experiences, she says:

1) When you enter a relationship, don't ignore the signs that say things might not be right. Trust your instincts and don't let your loneliness drive you to be in a relationship just for the sake of not being alone. You cannot live with anyone in peace until you learn to live with yourself in peace.

2) If you plan to get married, get to know the family history of your fiancé and how they relate to each other; it may give you a glimpse into how they will relate and respond to you.

3) When dating, pay attention to the negative signs that a person gives off, such as being controlling, being excessively jealous, throwing temper tantrums, and exhibiting manipulative and aggressive behavior. These signs are a window into who they really are.

4) Take your time and really get to know a person before committing to a serious relationship. Get pre-marital counseling if you are thinking of getting married. If you are uncomfortable with the "signs," it is all right to say NO!

5) Always pray and ask God to reveal what is best for you before entering a relationship, and listen to the answer that God gives you.

Marsha has a new partner in Christ, her savior. She wants to serve the Lord and is willing to go through the process of fulfilling her purpose in life. She no longer looks for satisfaction in the arms of natural man, but in the arms of God.

Reflection of Marsha's Story

by Rev. Charlane Russell, M.Th.

Oftentimes we spend our time and money on everything we think will fix the problem. It is not until we make our way to Jesus that the solution actually presents itself. The woman who had an issue of blood for twelve long years, found in Matt 9:20-22; Mark 5:25-34 and Luke

8:43-47, tried every doctor in town, spent all of her money, and still no one could help her. It wasn't until she made her way to the King of kings and the Lord of lords that she found her healing.

Marsha's story is much like this woman's story. She spent a great deal of time and effort trying to fix the situation herself, getting advice from others, and trying to figure out love and life. Marsha tried to assimilate into her husband's, her family's, and society's way of doing things in order to keep the peace. She thought marriage counseling would help fix the growing problem. She tried to live a life filled with fun and good times, only to be told that "a good wife" lived a certain way. She tried to leave and stay with family members, only to be manipulated back into the abuse. She even tried marriage more than once. The struggle was all too real for her.

Like the woman with the issue of blood, we too try everything before we remember that there is One who is greater than our problems. We forget that the One who holds the solution is the One we have kept on the back burner, instead of in the forefront. We tend to make Jesus the last resort instead of the first choice. Marsha's story reminds us that everything that looks good, feels good, smells good, or speaks of God, is not always good for us. It also reminds us that what we perceive as broken is not for us to fix. I once heard Dr. Lydia Waters say, and I paraphrase, "Some of us marry projects and not husbands." It is the innate ability of women to nurture and care for others that causes us to want to mother them into change, or our desire to create an environment of love and understanding that causes us to look past the faults, abuse, and utter disregard for us as the women they proclaim to love.

Marsha's story is one that is all too real for some of us, and yet the solution is closer than we think. Notice that the woman with the issue of blood is not known by her name, but by her affliction and her faith. It is her struggle that brings her to Jesus. It is her faith that made her whole. Women in abusive situations are defined by the situation until they have been delivered and set free. It is when the abused remembers her value and seeks the help needed, that she is set free from the abuser.

When Marsha remembered that she was once introduced to a man named Jesus, she too found her healing and her purpose. Her healing came from the surrender, and her purpose came from the struggle. After trying all she knew, she tried Jesus and was made whole.

"Angela"

Story by J. Harris

Reflection by Rev. Tomeca Richardson

IN THE HEAT OF LIFE, we can get caught in the inferno of our own desires—and if we allow our desires to reign, the fire can cause us to be consumed. When we allow the soothing spirit of the Lord to calm the flames, our lives will regain the order and purpose that God intended it to have. Our passion finds a new outlet: the will and way of God.

Angela was given the nickname of "Pepper" not only because of her beautiful dark hue, but also because of her fiery persona. Her life started in Dallas, Texas, with a blaze, and that blaze has shaped her path. On her journey, she has learned to let the Lord fight her battles and control the rages in her heart. She believes, as most believers do, that it is impossible to come into contact with God and not be changed for the better. That is what happened to Angela—she met God, and was forever changed.

Angela was the child of two unique individuals. Her father, Cliff, was married to another woman when Angela's mother conceived and gave birth to her. Cliff had his own fire within, as an alcoholic and a gambler, and he had a tendency toward violence. Prior to Angela's birth, Cliff was sentenced and sent to prison for 99 years for murder. He had gotten into an altercation with a man over the man's wife, and shot and killed the man, and Cliff's mother, Ada, had created a plan to dispose of the body. Cliff put the man's body in the trunk of his car, carried him to a nearby park, put him on a park bench, crossed his legs and arms, and put a hat on his head to make it appear as if he was sitting there asleep. He would have gotten away with the crime, but someone saw him place the body there and informed the police. He would be out of Angela's life for most of her younger years.

Angela's mother had five other children and battled her own demon—heroin addiction. When Angela was four years old, her mother was trying to get a fix and was unable to hit a vein, and asked another woman in the room to help her. The woman missed the vein, and the heroin went into the tissue. This caused her mother to have a violent seizure from overdosing.

Angela's final memory of her mother was of her screaming while the curtain was quickly closed by the woman who had given her the hit of heroin. In those days, other than the local funeral home's hearse, there was no ambulance service for blacks. When the funeral home hearse/ambulance arrived, there was a big commotion between the ambulance driver and the woman who had given Angela's mother the overdose. The driver wanted to know what had caused Angela's mother's condition, and the woman was unwilling to disclose the heroin use. In the rush to the hospital, the ambulance hit a telephone pole, and as a result, they did not to get to the hospital in time. Angela's mother was dead on arrival. The death was ruled an accidental overdose, and the woman who had given her the heroin did not face charges for her part in the incident. Black on black crime was not taken very seriously in those days, especially where addicts were concerned.

After the funeral, Angela, her sister Becky, and two of her brothers moved in with their grandmother, Ada.

The other children went to live with other relatives. Ada took them in out of a sense of obligation as their grandmother, and the fact that they were all receiving benefit checks helped to sweeten the deal. Ada was a woman to be reckoned with, because she was all about business. She was not the 8-to-5 type of working woman. She knew there was big money to be made if you gave the right people what they wanted.

Ada had a large two-story house with upstairs living quarters that she rented out to roomers. The first floor was a café that served food, and also served as a front for her alcohol bootlegging operation. Ada was also a loan shark, loaning people money a dollar for a dollar, and Ada always had money, nice clothes, and bought a new car every year. Angela and her siblings had nice clothes, went to the beauty shop and barbershop every two weeks, and were well fed. But, there was a price to pay if you got out of line with Ada. She could be very verbally and physically abusive. You had not been cursed out properly until Ada cursed you out. Ada's husband, Herb, helped Ada run the "business," and he had a darker side to him that would one day bring out the worst in Ada.

When Angela was five years old, Herb waited to get Angela alone one morning before the café had opened. He started with small talk, and then proceeded to pull out his penis for Angela to touch. Angela, being a child, did not know that this was inappropriate and did as she was told. Ada walked in on the incident and Herb laughed it off as being a child's curiosity. Instead of seeing the incident as Herb's fault, Ada blamed Angela for instigating the incident, and said Angela was old enough to know what she was doing. From that moment on, Ada despised Angela. She would take care of Angela, but she treated her differently from the other grandchildren. She was more abusive toward Angela, constantly pointing out her faults and then punishing her. She often told Angela that she would never amount to anything, and that she was a lost cause. Angela's exposure to Ada's abusive and violent behavior rubbed off on her own behavior in school, and she began to get into numerous fights. In the third grade, she stabbed a female classmate with a pencil during an argument. That would be the first of many stabbing incidents during her life.

A few years after the incident with Herb, Ada finally exploded, and the house became a scene of total chaos. Ada took a razor and cut Herb to ribbons when she caught him in bed with another woman. She was like a wild woman! No one was trying to stop her for fear of being cut themselves. When she got through with Herb, the ambulance came and got what was left. Ada didn't kill him; she just made him wish he was dead. Ada was taken to jail but released the same day, and Herb would not file charges against her, because Ada had friends within the police department who would protect her from being sentenced to serious jail time. Besides, it was considered another black on black crime. When Herb returned home, he was much more humble, and had lost his desire for other women. A few years after the cutting, when Angela was 10 years old, Herb died.

Shortly after Herb's death, Angela's father, Cliff, was released from prison because Ada had friends in high places, and had called in a few favors to get Cliff's case reviewed and have him released. Upon Cliff's release, Ada felt she had done all she needed to do with her grandchildren and informed Cliff that his children were now his responsibility. Angela and her brothers immediately moved into a house that Ada had purchased for Cliff.

Angela's sister Becky was Ada's favorite, and stayed with Ada. Becky had become accustomed to the plush life of nice clothes and fresh hairdos, and was willing to tolerate an occasional cursing out from Ada. During her stay with Ada, Angela had observed what seemed to be the fun and lucrative lifestyle of the prostitutes who frequented Ada's place. She would mimic their ways, and the way they acted with the men they served.

Angela decided that since she had inherited her mother's shapely figure and good looks, she would use those assets to her advantage when she got old enough. Angela's goal was to become a high-priced call girl, or an executive secretary who would have sex with her married boss for money. The idea of a committed relationship was not on her radar, especially with the role models she'd had in her life so far. The idea of going to college was not even considered a legitimate way of making a living in her young mind because it was slow money.

Ada gave Cliff money to take care of himself and his kids because his criminal record prevented him from finding work, and his daily alcohol consumption did not help matters. Cliff was much stricter on the kids than Ada had been, by not allowing them to have friends or to go to the places that other kids in the neighborhood went. He was mean-spirited, argumentative, and whipped them for the slightest disobedience. He always insisted that all of his children kiss him on the lips, which made Angela uncomfortable, but she had no choice in the matter. Cliff was not used to having the responsibility of raising children and was very impatient with them. He compounded his poor parenting skills by bringing in his girlfriend, Shirley, to live with them. Shirley wanted to be with Cliff, but knew that could only happen if she tolerated his children. Cliff was abusive to Shirley as well as the children.

Out of rebellion, Angela's brothers were out of control and constantly got into scrapes with the law, exercising lessons from the thugs they had been around at Ada's and also from Cliff. Working for a living was too slow for them, so they teamed up and chose to commit armed robberies. One evening, they planned to rob a dry cleaner. The middle brother would be the lookout while the younger and older brothers went in to collect the merchandise. While in the store, a security guard discovered the robbery and was stabbed and killed by one of the brothers. The brothers took the loot they stole to Cliff's house, where the entire family enjoyed the spoils. They gave Angela a typewriter and a rabbit fur coat that she wore proudly.

A few days after the robbery, a police informant told the police who had committed the crime, and the police arrested the brothers. Because the security guard was an older white man, the severity of the crime increased. The youngest brother received no time, because the older brother admitted to the killing and got the death penalty. The middle brother was accused of being an accessory to the crime and was sentenced and received a lighter sentence. *(The older brother's sentence was eventually downgraded to life, but he later died in prison)*

When Angela was 13, Cliff died from a combination of drinking too much and untreated high blood pressure. Angela was faced with another setback, no mother and now no father, but returning to Ada's house was not an option. Becky had a best friend whose mother was very fond of her, and was also aware of Ada's reputation. The woman wanted to legally adopt Becky, and Ada did not give her any argument, but there were no offers for Angela. Ada gave Shirley money to keep Angela, but caring for Cliff's children was not what Shirley had bargained for. She had wanted him, not his kids, so she did not approach her new single mother role with joy and enthusiasm. She was very mean to Angela, whipping her for the slightest mistakes, so Angela learned to fear and hate her instead of loving her.

Angela escaped Shirley's torture by getting involved in activities at school. She was a good athlete, and became active in track, the drill team, volleyball and basketball. Sports were her only survival tools to mask the pain and loneliness she felt. She was motherless, fatherless, had a grandmother who did not want her, and a stepmother who despised her. She was alone in the world, and anger was her disposition. Angela had never been to church, except to attend a funeral, and did not know that God could be her friend. Because she had seen so many women abused by men at Ada's, and had been abused by her father and stepmother, she made up in her spirit that she would no longer be the victim of any more abuse, especially by men. She decided she only wanted men in her life who loved and appreciated her, and had money. She set out to find some satisfaction.

Two years of living with Shirley was all Angela could take, so she decided to make her move, and make her own mark in life. She met and fell in love with a boy who went to her school named Tommy who was kind to her, and when they were alone, he made her feel like a woman. This fresh new lovemaking thing felt good, and she didn't want to give it up. Tommy even gave her trinkets that made her feel special. He had a gold front tooth, so she wanted to have one too. So, on one of their outings, he took her to get a gold tooth to match his. They were definitely an item.

Shirley didn't like the fact that Angela and Tommy spent so much time alone together and would put Angela on punishment, only for her to run away again. Eventually, Shirley put Angela out because she couldn't deal with her rebellious behavior. Shirley did not understand or care about what Angela had been through, or that she was just searching for some appreciation. Tommy appreciated her.

Tommy's mother took Angela in, and even allowed her and Tommy to sleep in the same bed. She was not the kind of woman to worry over things she knew were inevitable in that she figured they were going to be together anyway, so they might as well do it under her roof. Angela decided that she wanted to have Tommy's baby, and set out on a mission. She and Tommy worked passionately toward parenthood, but it was not to be. They would have lover's spats frequently, with Angela not to be bested. She stayed in her school activities, determined to graduate from high school, and she got an after-school job at a fast food restaurant to pay for her activity fees and uniforms. She did not want to depend on Tommy or his mother to provide for her, just in case they decided they didn't want her around anymore. She had learned the value of financial independence from Ada.

Angela and Tommy eventually moved into their own apartment to have more independence and to start their own little family. With the move away from his mother, Tommy became more controlling and jealous. They seemed to have a fight every other day over the slightest things. One evening, Tommy wanted to show Angela he was the master of the house, and locked Angela out when she came home from school. She had to sleep on the porch all night until he decided to let her in the next morning. This caused her to be late for school, and Angela got detention.

When the time came for Angela to graduate from high school, she was excited and proud of her accomplishments, but she and Tommy had an argument a few days before graduation. Neither he nor his mother attended the graduation ceremony, and only one of her cousins came to cheer for her as she crossed the stage.

She no longer wanted Tommy in her life, since he'd let a little argument keep him from supporting her graduation. She felt embarrassed and abandoned, and it was at this point that she finally expressed her anger with the God she had heard about when she occasionally went to church with Tommy. She felt that God had never done anything for her, because her life had been a string of disasters.

Angela was alone in the world and felt she had had no control over her destiny, since she had not asked to be born into this mess. *Where was God in all of this?* From this point on, she was going to take control of her life and live it on her own terms. She broke up with Tommy after graduation and moved in with her uncle and Aunt Babe (her mother's sister). This stay would be short-lived once her aunt accused Angela of sleeping with her husband, because his clothes smelled like Angela's cologne. Angela tried to reason with her aunt, saying she would not disrespect her house and did not want to have anything to do with her husband. She explained that her husband's clothes smelled like her cologne because his clothes were in the same closet as hers. Aunt Babe still refused to accept Angela's defense and asked her to leave. She was hurt that her aunt would accuse her of such a thing, but there was no convincing her otherwise.

She called Becky, who had gone to Job Corp for training, and she encouraged Angela to go also, so Angela applied and headed to Job Corp. Angela had not forgotten her desire to be an executive secretary, so she saw this as her way to get the secretarial training she needed *(and to be able to sleep with her rich, married boss)*.

The Job Corp campus was in McKinney, Texas, not too far from Dallas, and she would be able to come to Dallas when she wanted. She loved the campus and the freedom, becoming an over-achiever as the fastest typist on campus. She even challenged the instructor to a typing contest, and beat him. She didn't know what the other classmates had on their minds, but she was trying to be the best, to make it to the executive office of some lucky boss.

While at Job Corp, she met Lee, who was very popular on campus, but Job Corp had strict rules against boy-girl relationships, so she and Lee had to be very careful about their relationship. If they were seen together, they could both be expelled. Angela discovered that Lee was a drug dealer and supplied all of the drug users on campus. He had a connection in Dallas and would make drug pickups when he went back and forth to Dallas. Angela saw a business opportunity and started going to Dallas to pick up drugs for Lee, with the agreement that they split the profits, and he teach her how to sell the drugs. She learned quickly and took care of the customers on the female side of campus, and he took care of the male side. Speed (or methamphetamines) was her hottest request, and her locker was her supply cabinet. If anyone refused to pay her, she would beat them up, so she developed a reputation of knowing how to fight. One weekend she and Lee went to Dallas to score drugs, and when their supplier accused Lee of mishandling the money, the supplier tried to kill Lee by shooting at him.

Angela decided that Lee was too dangerous to deal with and gave up dealing drugs for him. She had been warned by the counselors about her relationship with Lee, so they broke it off for a while. She did not want to be expelled. Angela had befriended many people at school while dealing drugs, especially a group of lesbian women. They introduced her to smoking "wack"*(cigarettes or marijuana soaked in formaldehyde).* She became particularly fond of one of her new white friends, Val, who introduced and invited her to the world of lesbianism. Angela's spirit was game for anything. She and Val became inseparable, known throughout the campus as "Salt and Pepper," because Val was white and Angela was black. Val was eventually hired by Job Corp and could not afford to lose her job, and she could no longer be associated with Angela on campus because of her weed smoking and other drug use. They still remained friends off campus, and one of the lesbian women in the group named Minnie began to run with Angela and Val off campus, when they would go to gay bars in Dallas. Minnie and Angela hit it off immediately and became an item, and they looked like salt and pepper too.

Angela and Minnie both became bored with Job Corp and decided to move to Dallas with some of Minnie's other lesbian friends. On one of the trips to Dallas with Lee to pick up drugs, Angela had been introduced to crack cocaine and free basing. From the first hit, the experience took her sense of freedom to a new level, with no limit to her will and wants. From that point on she smoked crack regularly. When she moved in with Minnie, she tried to get her to smoke with her, but after one try, Minnie decided it was not her thing. Angela was hooked.

With the high that crack gave her, Angela was on a high with the love she had for Minnie. It was like no other love she had experienced because it gave her the soft love she needed from a woman, and the sexual satisfaction was a bonus. Angela did not care what others thought about their relationship, because she knew Minnie loved her. Minnie gave her a place to stay and took care of all her needs. Minnie and Angela would frequent gay bars, where Angela would often get into fights. *(Today she still carries a scar on her chin from one of those barroom brawls.)* She was not one to ever walk away from a fight. Minnie was the perfect mate because she was not controlling, and did not mind Angela having relationships with men.

Angela developed a regular sexual relationship with Andy, one of the men who came around frequently to smoke weed. He supplied Angela with the money she needed for her crack cocaine habit, and eventually something Minnie could not provide her with—a baby. Angela wanted desperately to be a mother, to prove that she could treat and love a child like it was supposed to be loved. She would make sure her child knew it was special, which was something she did not experience as a child. Before Angela became pregnant, Andy had a plan to get her pregnant. The two of them would drink E&J whiskey and take Geritol vitamins every day while making love. Angela was willing to try anything to make it happen. Andy was married, and Angela would not be able be a permanent part of his life, but for Angela that was not a barrier because she would be able to have his money and sex without commitment—a win-win situation in her mind. After several "E&J and Geritol" sessions, she finally got pregnant! Minnie was as excited as Angela about the pregnancy.

Angela was overjoyed at the gift Andy had given her, but she did not give up her drug use or worry that the effects of the drugs would harm the baby. She would take her chances when the time came for the delivery that the baby would be clean and sober. She did not want her baby to be the property of CPS *(Child Protective Services)*, but she was hooked so badly on crack that she was not able to stop herself. She smoked crack continuously throughout her pregnancy, and did not go for prenatal care because she feared that the nurses and doctors would report her drug use to CPS. She and Andy would come to blows when he did not do things her way, or would try and push her around. Being pregnant did not cool her temper. In fact, pregnancy seemed to enhance her desire to fight.

When Angela went into labor, she was so high on crack that she did not fully realize she was in labor. She knew it was near time to deliver, and when she thought she might be having labor pains, Andy took her to the county hospital's emergency room. When she arrived at the hospital, her cervix was dilating and she was ready to give birth, so she said a small prayer to God for there not to be drugs in her system or in the baby's system, *and God heard her*. Her sweet brown baby, Dion, was perfect! She was finally a mother to the most beautiful baby boy she had ever seen. *Angela silently thanked God for answering her prayer.*

Minnie loved Dion as much as Angela did, and took care of Angela and Dion when they came home from the hospital. Andy's marriage prevented him from being there for Angela and Dion, but he provided for them financially. Angela did not let Dion's birth keep her from resuming her drug habit. She free-based constantly. She refused to admit that she was an addict, because she saw "crackheads" every day and concluded that she was not "like" them. Minnie kept Dion when Angela was too high to care for him, and soon, Angela started to pick fights with Minnie when she began to try to get her to stop smoking and take care of Dion.

In an attempt to get Angela to quit drugs, Andy refused to give her money to buy them, but she did not let this stop her because there was another way to get the drug money she needed—her body. She was petite, shapely, and pretty, everything she needed to attract men with money. She carefully selected the men she slept with because she did not see herself as a whore, and she wanted to keep what she did out of sight of others.

Angela's drug habit had gotten so heavy that it caused her to betray Minnie by taking the rent money Minnie gave her and buying drugs instead of paying the rent. When they were about to get evicted, Minnie decided she'd had enough of Angela, and she put Angela and Dion out on the street. Angela begged Minnie for another chance, but she knew she had done too much dirt for Minnie to forgive her. Angela found some vacant apartments that she and Dion would call home. They slept on old clothes that she found. They would bathe in service station bathrooms. She took Dion everywhere she went, even to the crack houses. They lived in the abandoned apartment for a few months, until Angela got her Section 8 voucher and got an apartment. This was not the life she wanted for her baby, but she was too strung out to do any better.

In one particular crack house she frequented, she would turn tricks to pay for her drugs, with her baby at her side. One of the other addicts had a "trick" who would come by every Tuesday, and she would take him into the bushes on the side of the house to have sex. One Tuesday, Angela came to the crack house and the other addict was not there to service the man, so Angela decided to take advantage of the situation. She had someone watch Dion while she went into the bushes on the side of the house with the man. He took her to the same bushes he had taken the other woman, and while she allowed him to have sex with her, Angela could see cars passing by and realized they could see what she was doing! Her drug habit had gotten so bad that she was no longer selective about how she conducted her prostitution, and it was at that moment she realized that she had stooped to the level of being a "crack whore." She never knew she could get this low. The call of the crack did not have a moral compass.

She and Dion would walk the streets wherever they needed to go, and she had to be careful not to let CPS catch up with them and take Dion away from her. One day while passing a local convenience store, she slowed down enough to catch a glimpse of herself in the reflection of the glass window. She hardly recognized herself. Angela thought she was looking at someone else, because her face was thin, her temples were sunken in, her eyes were bulging, and her cheeks were drawn in. She had not combed her hair for days and looked so tired and worn, coming to the realization that she was "out there." She looked like the other crackheads she knew and had looked down on. She realized that she was just like them and did not have the power to stop the spiral down.

When Angela got her Section 8 papers to move into her apartment, she was overjoyed at the thought of having a real home for herself and for Dion. Minnie forgave her and moved in with them and helped Angela care for Dion, but she soon moved out because she could no longer tolerate Angela's arguments and heavy drug use. Angela missed Minnie, but she was too far gone to care. She just wanted to give Dion the things she wanted him to have, and to support her crack habit. She needed money, and lots of it, fast, so she called on the business skills she had learned from Ada and established a drug connection to sell drugs out of her apartment. She was soon making enough money to get a small sofa to sleep on and some decent clothing, with enough left over to support her drug habit. If any of the addicts tried to take advantage of her or rob her, she fought them. To comply with Section 8 and explain the money she had, she got a job at the front desk of a local business. Soon her drug habit got so bad that she was using all of the money she earned from her job and from drug dealing to support her habit. Angela's temper and drug use eventually caused her to lose her job, because she came to work high and threatened to shoot her supervisor.

During her drug dealing in the apartment, Angela reunited with some girls she had known from high school who had babies and drug habits, and needed somewhere to stay. Angela was always on the lookout for a fast dollar, and knew how desperation and a drug habit would make people do things they would not ordinarily do. Angela made the girls an offer that she would let them stay in her apartment and arrange tricks for them *(be their "madame"),* and charge each of them for rent, drugs, and protection from any customers who got out of hand. Angela was so strung out that she used the money she was making off the girls to feed her own habit, and did not pay the $14 a month rent. She had stacks of $14 money orders that had not been given to the landlord, because she kept them in case she ran short of drug money and needed to cash them in. She was evicted from her apartment for not paying her rent for five months! The girls, their babies, Angela and Dion were homeless, and Angela was out of business.

With nowhere to go again, Angela, her drug habit, and Dion moved into a house with her uncle *(her father's brother),* her sister Becky, and her cousin. She found out that her cousin was addicted to heroin, and was shooting heroin and speed balls. He would have no competition from her—heroin was not her drug of choice, because she remembered how her mother died from a heroin overdose. During her stay, Angela befriended one of her uncle's married friends named Jessie, who was very kind to her and Dion. He was not into crack but smoked weed heavily. Angela didn't mind him being married, because she enjoyed his company while they smoked weed together. The high from the drugs stimulated their desire for each other, and sex took them higher.

After a few months into their relationship, Angela became pregnant. She was still deep into her crack addiction, and once again her pregnancy did not stop her drug use. She smoked crack throughout her pregnancy, and once again prayed a short prayer to God at the time of delivery that there would be no drugs in either her or her baby's systems. Angela had again not gotten prenatal care, and when she went to the hospital for delivery, she was so high she did not even remember the delivery. Once again God heard her prayer, and no drugs were found. Angela immediately fell in love with her beautiful baby girl Natalie, who was perfect. *Once again, God had come through for Angela, and she would set Him aside until she needed Him again.* She was still angry at God about her past, and could not get past the pain to trust God with the rest of her life.

Angela loved Natalie, but knew that she was too strung out to properly care for her, so at the hospital she gave little Natalie to Becky. Angela held Natalie tight, kissing and crying over her, and then handed her over. Angela did not want Natalie to go into the system, so she felt the arrangement with Becky was best. Becky was glad that Angela had the clarity of mind to give the baby to her and not take the newborn into some unsafe situations. This was not what Angela had planned for her children. She wanted to be a good mother and provider. *If only she could just kick her habit and get on her feet.* Angela kept two-year-old Dion with her, and they would go by and visit Natalie. Dion adored his sister, but Angela knew in her heart that she could not handle being a mother to two small children. Her plans were to get Natalie permanently when she got herself clean and her life straightened out. Occasionally, she would leave Dion with Becky whenever she knew she would be places that were not safe for him, and when she was in jail.

Jessie and Angela fought constantly. Angela won most of the fights, but she was growing tired of Jessie, and he of her. Angela was afraid of guns, so instead she carried single-edged razors in her hair, under her tongue, and in both hands. She could use them in a flash if a situation called for it. Hustling on the streets for her drugs and dealing with shady drug dealers or tricks required her to be in fights constantly. It felt good when she hurt someone else, just like she was hurting inside. *Why should she be the only one in pain?* Between fighting and going to jail for fighting, Angela visited her children. She slept with men to feed her drug habit, but if any of her tricks tried to cross, she did not hesitate to fight or to cut them.

To make regular money, she detailed cars at the car wash and had a regular string of customers. She would often keep Dion with her when she was detailing cars. Some of her customers would give him toy cars to play with while she worked, but if any male customers acted like he was going to disagree with Angela, Dion would ball his tiny fist up and tell them that his mother would cut them if they didn't leave her alone. Men were often amused by the child's comments, but Dion was serious— he had seen it too many times. If Angela got into a fight or cut someone, she would always make sure that Dion was taken to her sister's house before she was taken to jail. She did not want both of them to be taken into custody.

Angela began hanging out with a fellow doper named Slick who understood her, and she him, because they were both out to achieve the same end—drugs, by any means necessary. He was also good company on those lonely nights in strange motels and crack houses. After getting high in the park one evening, they got into an argument about the drugs. Slick pulled a gun and pointed it at Angela's head and pulled the trigger, but the gun jammed! Angela saw her chance, pulled her razor from her hair and cut his throat. He fell to the ground. Blood was everywhere, and she feared she has killed him. She was standing over him, screaming and crying, when he regained consciousness. Holding his throat, he grabbed the gun again. As they struggled over the gun, it went off, and Angela was shot in the leg. Someone heard the commotion and called an ambulance.

When the ambulance came to take Slick to the hospital, Angela protested that she was injured too. The paramedics had not realized that she had been shot, and did not know that she was the one who had cut Slick, so they took them both to the emergency room and put them in beds next to each other. They were laying in the ER, high, crying, and apologizing for hurting each other. The hospital personnel didn't know what to make of them. Angela was treated and released, barely able to walk, when she went back to the hospital and started demanding cigarettes from the hospital staff. To get rid of her, someone gave her a cigarette, and she limped away into the night, back to the condemned apartment in which she had been living. Lonely, alone, and high, she slept through the physical pain, but the spiritual pain was like a raging fire.

After Slick was treated for a few days, the hospital released him and he found Angela on the streets, and they picked up as if nothing had happened. For months they lived in the vacant apartment together, doing their drugs together, and when they wanted to get cleaned up they would go the Salvation Army, pleading that they wanted to get off drugs. They would be given a cot to sleep on and allowed to take a bath.

Angela would frequent "traps" *(drug houses)* to score drugs, and would often get picked up for possession of drugs or prostitution. For one of the drug charges on which she was picked up, the system had become so frustrated with her repeat offenses that she was offered 25 years in prison! Angela broke down in court, crying and swearing to God and to the judge that she would straighten up her act, if he would just give her another chance. *(She decided to call on God again, since he had helped her out with the baby delivery situations. She pleaded in her spirit to God that she would do better, if He would just not let her go to prison.)*The judge gave give her a deferred sentence and put her on probation for 10 years. Angela was released and she celebrated by getting high—still chasing the ultimate high that would perhaps stop the pain in her heart that the past had started. She never found a high to relieve that pain.

One evening Angela and Slick got into a fight, and this time he beat her severely. The only thing that stopped Angela from cutting him with her razors was her fear of going back to jail. However, she was arrested for prostitution by an undercover cop who witnessed the beating, and who assumed that Slick was her pimp. He did not suspect that she was an addict, and during the search he missed the crack pipe she kept hid in her panties. This visit to jail was going to be different from all the others, because Angela was on probation.

She was sentenced to a two-month prison drug rehabilitation program. The judge warned her if she did not complete the program, she would go straight to the penitentiary to serve 10 years. She was genuinely afraid this time, because she had heard stories about things that happened to women in prison. She had only done short stays in jail, and she now had a fear of being beaten or killed in the penitentiary. *She once again called on God to protect her while she was in the rehab program.*

Angela served the two months in rehab, and after her release she went to see her children and quickly went back to the same old habits. She got drunk one night and ran into Slick at a local burger place. They eventually started arguing and got into a fight. Once again he beat Angela up badly. When she heard the police were coming, she had to think quickly. She cut herself with her own razor, hoping it would look like Slick had cut her and she would not be taken. However, instead of jail or a hospital, Angela was taken to a drug detox center.

One evening while in the detox center, Angela left on a pass with one of the residents. He told her he had to pick up some money, and promised to share his "score" with her if she went with him. They missed the required Alcoholics Anonymous *(AA)* meeting that evening, and were considered missing and deemed non-compliant by the program administrator. Angela's non-compliance once again put her at risk for going to the penitentiary. Out of fear, she heard a voice that told her to get drunk and not go back to the detox center. Angela decided to take her chances and run, and pray that she would not get caught.

Something in Angela's spirit was tired of living the life she was living. It was time for a change. She spent the rest of that evening walking by liquor stores and resisting the impulse to drink. She decided to turn herself in the next day and go back to treatment. She was tired of who she had become and what she had to do, day in and day out, to feed her habit. But most of all, she missed her children and wanted a normal life for them and for herself. Angela called Becky to check on her children, and said she would probably be gone for a while. Becky assured her that the children would be fine, and that she just wanted her to get some help getting her life back on track. Little did Angela know that this was the beginning of a new chapter in her life. God was about to collect on the promises Angela had made to Him.

When Angela turned herself in at the detox center, the court ordered her to spend nine to eleven months in a drug treatment facility in Dayton, Texas. Safe-P isn't a regular penitentiary as far as security is concerned. The inmates live in a dormitory-style atmosphere. They wake up at four o'clock every morning to work in the fields. Angela was about to learn about discipline the hard way, and she wanted none of it.

Angela argued with every policy and rule at Safe-P. She was determined to show the others how tough she was by how hard she could buck the system. When the counselors saw how resistant she was to the field labor, they gave her a new assignment moving piles of sand from one location to another with a shovel. During her shovel time she was not allowed to talk, or else she would have to start over, causing her workday to be longer. She was forced to endure the one thing she hated the most—disciplined authority. Until this point, she had always called the shots in her life, and as far as she was concerned she didn't need anyone else to tell her what to do. In her world, if things did not go her way, she would fight. At Safe-P, fighting was not allowed.

The part of the treatment that Angela hated the most was the encounter group where inmates admitted their own faults, and then the group members confronted each other on their behavior. The members of the group would call Angela out on her resistant behavior, and make her apologize to the counselors and others in the group for her bad behavior toward them. Angela hated apologizing for behavior that she felt was justified. *After all, didn't the world owe her something for the rough cards she had been dealt?* She apologized verbally, but not in her heart. After those encounter groups, she felt vulnerable and alone.

After six months of long work hours and encounter groups, Angela asked herself if she really was what the group had labeled her—an addict, a dope fiend, and a crack whore. When she came face to face with herself, she did not like what she saw. This revelation made her more resistant, and she continued to see herself as a victim. According to Angela, the world owed her because it had made her a victim, and she was not responsible. "They" owed her!

During her stay in Safe-P, Angela gave the regular counselor so much trouble that she was eventually called in to meet with the head counselor. He addressed her behavior and admitted to her, "I don't know if you are worth saving." That statement hit Angela like a ton of bricks. She suddenly felt like she was a little girl again, and Ada was telling her she was worthless and not worth her time and trouble. *Had Ada been right all along? Was she really worthless?* None of her family or her friends had once visited her in jail or sent her any money. She began to doubt her self-worth.

With her feeling of worthlessness, Angela became even more defiant and rebellious. She was accused by the group of being a manipulator, and was forced to wear a sign that almost covered the entire front of her body. The sign read, "I am a manipulator." She felt so ashamed, but refused to let the system know that she was hurt. During TV time she was not allowed to watch TV, but had to instead sit under the television and stare straight ahead.

Angela's period of humiliation gave her an opportunity to do something for someone else, which changed her from a manipulator to a motivator. During one of her sessions with the head counselor, he shared that he had a problem with his foot and might need surgery. He made an agreement with Angela that for 14 days he would pray for her behavior problem, if she would pray for his foot problem. Angela had had some brief encounters with God where He had come through, so she was willing to try Him again. Angela sincerely prayed for her counselor every day for 14 days, and her counselor prayed for her. At the end of the 14 days, his foot was better, and Angela felt a renewal in her spirit— she no longer wanted to resist or manipulate. She had heard God's voice speaking to her when she prayed, telling her to give Him a chance and to trust Him with her life. When she saw her counselor's foot healed and her attitude changed, she felt this God thing was a new possibility.

After 11 months in Safe-P, Angela went from being a resistant troublemaker to someone to whom the other women could come for help and encouragement. The counselors saw the change as miraculous. It was a relief for the whole Safe-P staff. The day of Angela's release was one big crying session between Angela and the staff. She could not thank them enough for not giving up on her. She promised to come back one day to help other women in the program. Angela was sent to the Dallas Salvation Army for follow-up transitional care, and there she was allowed to go out daily to look for work, and to visit her children. She was drug tested every day. She truly enjoyed being free, with no drug habit that needed to be fed.

One day, the attendant who did the urine test accidentally got her urine specimen mixed up with another client's specimen, and Angela knew that if her test came up dirty, she would go to prison. She pleaded her case with the counselors and asked to take another test to prove her innocence, but they did not trust her because of her previous bad reputation. Angela did the only thing she knew to do. She prayed for God to straighten the matter out. It eventually was discovered that there had been a mix-up with the urine samples. The client who had given the dirty sample was identified, and Angela was allowed to retest and was found to be clean. *God had continued to be faithful to her.*

During her recovery at the Salvation Army, because God had been so faithful to her, Angela made some solemn vows: to never do drugs or alcohol again; not to date any married men; not to be in any lesbian relationships; not to become involved with any drug dealers; and not date anyone else's man. God had not let her down, and she was not going to let Him down.

When Angela was released from the Salvation Army, she moved in with Becky and was reunited with her children. She felt good to be a clean and sober mother with an appreciation that God had truly blessed her with two beautiful, healthy children. She felt it was her duty to them and to God to be a good mother. For the first time, Angela could embrace their love and love them back. She attended Narcotics Anonymous (NA) meetings daily and returned to detailing cars at the car wash, but this time, she was not carrying the razors or the anger she had carried before. She ran into Slick and he wanted to start their relationship again, but she told him she was clean and wanted no part of that life again. He was still doing drugs and drinking, and he was not ready to quit. Slick respected her decision, but informed her that the door was always open, should she change her mind. It felt good to have the strength to walk away from her past with no regrets.

Angela worked and saved enough money to get herself and her children an apartment, but they didn't have any furniture. They only had each other, and that was enough. Her life was finally on the right track. She actually found a job as a secretary, but her motives for being a secretary were different now. She just wanted to feed her family.

At one of the NA meetings, Angela met a nice man who was serious about his recovery, and they would talk for hours after the meetings about the things that their addiction had put them through, and how they never wanted to return to that life again. Their relationship became intimate, and Angela enjoyed the sober affection that they shared. There was only one drawback to the relationship—this man was married! She had gone back on her vow. *Would God forgive her again, or would God act like the court system and throw her away?* She decided she would work on weaning herself from the relationship after she became more financially stable, but at that moment she needed the money he was providing to help support her children.

One Sunday Angela went to church with him, and she heard a man named Nathan speaking about his battle with his addiction. He spoke boldly of his battle with crack cocaine and how his relationship with God had delivered him from addiction. She was mesmerized by his words and wanted to feel what he felt. She wanted to enjoy the same relationship that Nathan enjoyed with God. She was drawn to him and felt she needed to spend time with him to help in her recovery. She went back to the church, Sunday after Sunday, just to be near him, and to ask him questions. She broke off the relationship with her married friend and pursued a relationship with Nathan, who was impressed with her progress in her recovery. They had a lot in common, and the pursuit became mutual. Angela followed Nathan to different NA groups to hear him speak of his love for God, and she witnessed people's lives changed by the messages he delivered. He was truly the man God had sent to her, and she was proud to be by his side.

After a brief courtship, Angela and Nathan were married in a simple ceremony at Nathan's church. She was truly grateful and happy to be part of a family, her own family. Angela would soon realize that there is more to marriage than passionate speeches; marriage is hard work. She was determined to be a good wife, but found herself getting into unnecessary arguments with Nathan because she did not know how to have a normal relationship. The relationships she had been in, like the one with Slick, involved drug-induced, violent rages, and she did not know how to do sober relationships. She taunted Nathan to see if she could make him hit her first, because she thought that was how all relationships functioned—with violence. If he hit her first, then she would have full reason to cut him or strike back.

Nathan became verbally abusive to counter Angela's taunting. The same man who she had sat and listened to about his love for God would now curse her out on the same evening when they got home. Something was wrong, and Angela didn't know how to fix it. This caused them to break up several times because of the constant arguments. Angela knew how violent her temper could become, and what she was capable of if provoked. She had promised God she would never harm another human being again.

The final straw in the broken relationship came when Nathan forgot Angela's birthday. She was humiliated! All of her life, her family, friends, and boyfriends had failed to acknowledge that she was special, and she was not going to tolerate her own husband doing the same thing. She was determined not to be slighted by him, because he knew her story and what she had been through. He was the last person she expected to devalue her. No apology Nathan could give was enough. She wanted him to feel her pain and disappointment. When Nathan could no longer take Angela's rage, he grabbed her by the neck and began choking her. She fought back and broke his hold. She felt angry enough to cut him, but she remembered her promise to God and walked away from the incident.

Angela realized that she had carried a lot of pain, anger, rage, and other unhealthy behaviors from her past into her present, and that was affecting her ability to have a healthy relationship. She and Nathan mutually decided that the relationship was out of control, and that divorce was their only way out. The divorce crushed Angela, and she was embarrassed and hurt that she had failed yet again. God had brought her a good man, and she had let her baggage get in the way. She and Nathan had developed a wonderful ministry together helping other recovering addicts. They had many mutual friends at church, so they agreed not to interfere with the ministry they had started at the church, and to continue to attend the same church. It hurt Angela to be at church with Nathan and not be able to say she was his wife. They both could see that their pasts had gotten in the way of their futures.

Years after the divorce, Angela has since prayed and reflected on how she does relationships. She wants to stay true to her promise to God and no longer let her past get in the way of her future. She worked hard at becoming the mother her children need her to be—loving and sober. She now champions recovery at every opportunity and delivers her testimony of what God has done in her life, and in her recovery. She also kept her promise to the Safe-P staff and contacted her old counselor to arrange a visit to speak to the inmates. She became a regular speaker at the program to help other women have hope. She encourages them to put their faith in God, to help get them through the hard times.

Angela has since remarried and continues to attend NA weekly, living one day at a time. She continues to minister to other addicts at her church, and works on strengthening her relationship with God. She has been instrumental in assisting many addicts through the recovery process through her commitment to the NA program. She tells addicts how God has personally changed her life, and how He can change theirs, too.

Reflection of Angela's Story

By Rev. Tomeca Richardson, M.Div.

But He said to me, "My grace is sufficient for you, for my power is made perfect in weakness.."
II Cor. 12:9 NIV

Tragedy occurs in our lives when we least expect it, and when we are not prepared. Angela was affected by difficult situations over and over again. It seems as if once she was able to get out of one problem, another one happened. The more she tried to do right, that one bad decision wiped away all the good she had done. Her fight became more difficult each time she tried to do it on her own.

We all have situations in our lives that are difficult to understand; however, it is during those hard times that we need God the most. In the midst of the weight, blindness, and struggle of going through our problems, it is possible to forget that God is there, waiting for our call. Each day it seems that life is too difficult to live and that no one is able to comfort us in the midst of our struggles. It is when we are at our weakest that we need God's help the most. With family and friends around, it is easier to go to them for help, but even when they offer us their best, it may still fall short of what we truly need.

The grace of God is available to give us what we need when those around us fall short. When embraced, the power of God can bring peace to our hearts when we feel like everything is falling apart in life. Angela experienced God's grace repeatedly, and it took time before she fully accepted the help God had been making available to her in the midst of her struggles. God's grace often protects us from suffering and even death, when death is what we deserve. Alternatively, His grace delivers us when condemnation is our verdict, and others salvation when we are spiraling out of control.

Even as tragedies blind, God is there, waiting to make things clear for us. Once God has shown us mercy and we see a break in the clouds, things become clearer to us than they have ever been before. This newfound clarity rushes through the doors of our hearts in the form of forgiveness, peace, wisdom, and the ability to live and to love again. We no longer hide who we are, but we confront ourselves, even our imperfections. This open and honest look at who we are helps us to become who we were created to be.

Angela accepted God and the grace that God offers to us all. She vowed to no longer let her past get in the way of the grace, love and peace that God had in store for her. God's grace is great enough to care for us in our moments of weakness, in order that we can be made strong.

Asking God for help may seem difficult at times, but that moment when we finally ask, it is just what we need, just when we need it. We all have regrets in our past that we wish we could do over. Even though we cannot undo the past, we can make new decisions about our future. Once Angela embraced God's grace, she never looked back. She knew she had been redeemed.

As we take each day at a time, just know that God is there and is able to give us all that we need. It is impossible to be too far away from God. He is just a cry away.

"Hannah: the First Lady"

Story by J. Harris

Reflection by Pastor Brenda Carradine

In life, there are many "first" opportunities to celebrate: your first steps as a baby, your first tooth, your first kiss, your first car or your first child; just a few examples. You cherish the first; the new, the beginning. Just as in the White House the President's wife is crowned "The First Lady," the pastor's wife is often referred to as a "First Lady." There is a prestige that goes with the First Lady title that is given a special place of honor and respect in the church, and in some cases her very own parking place. A First Lady is expected to be a strong pillar, and to support her husband in ministry, no matter what.

Congregation members observe every move the First Lady makes and often try to imitate her, and at times even envy her. She sets an example and a tone for the other women in church, but her own needs are rarely ever considered or acknowledged. The needs of the church, her husband, and her children all come before her own needs. This can often lead her to feel isolated, and to suffer in silence.

There is often a silent code for a First Lady when abuse is involved. These women are dedicated to the churches, to God, and to their husbands' ministries, and they feel guilty about potentially exposing their husbands' flaws. Theological questions get in the way, for example: *"What will happen to the church? Will exposing the pastor's abusive behavior cause the church members to lose faith or to fall away from the church? What will happen to this man of God? Will God hold me responsible for his fall? If my husband loses his job as pastor, what will happen to my own children, and how will we survive?"* Many First Ladies remain silent, because they feel the stakes are too high in exposing the abuse.

There are many wounded and broken women who are victims of abuse in these sacred relationships, and silence only perpetuates the pain. In order for First Ladies to experience help, and for their husbands to get their help they need, these injustices must be exposed. Women like Hannah must step forth and challenge this code of silence. To give a voice to other First Ladies who have been victims of abuse, Hannah comes forth to share her experience. To see Hannah now, you would never imagine that she has experienced such sorrow in her life. She is smart, confident, beautiful, and successful, and her very essence is that of a survivor. No one would know that she was once at the breaking point of life, struggling to keep body and soul together.

Hannah found herself wrestling with the decision to finally end her 12-year marriage to one of the most popular ministers in the Baltimore area. Theirs had been a marriage built on lies and deception, and she had taken all she could stand. She wanted out in order to move on, and for the sake of her own sanity. Broken-hearted and afraid, she now had to trust God with her life as she never had done before. She had to completely lean on God for her own survival and that of her child, because she had nothing and nowhere else to go. She had been totally dependent on her husband for support. As her mind raced, trying to make plans for the future, she reflected on where her trouble began. *"How did my life come to this? Where did I go wrong?"*

Hannah and her two brothers, Matt and Clay, were born and raised in Brooklyn, New York. They spent their childhood being passed between their widowed father, Rev. Cane *(not his real last name),* a Baptist preacher, and Rev. Cane's spinster sister, Rachel. Growing up, Hannah's life was safe, orderly, and religious. Her aunt made sure she and her brothers went to church every Sunday and said their prayers every night. Hannah's father, fondly called Rev. C by the members of his church, was the pastor of one of the largest African American Baptist churches in the New York area. *(The Baptist Church her father pastored gave Hannah the spiritual grounding she would need to survive the tough times to come.)* He was dedicated to his congregation, and was often at the church or seeing after his large flock at funerals, weddings, preaching, church members' family crises, and hospital visits. He did not have much time left over for family household details.

Rachel stepped in to manage the children and the house when his wife passed away after a bitter eight-year fight with breast cancer. Aunt Rachel seemed to have the children in attendance every time the church doors opened. Often, Hannah and her brothers would not see their father at all until Sunday in the pulpit, and would listen attentively to his sermons as if he were a visiting preacher, just to stay familiar with his voice. Other kids often envied them because they were the children of such a dynamic preacher, but had no idea what little time they spent with him.

The highlight of childhood for Hannah and her brothers were summer vacations. They knew that for two whole weeks each year, they would have their father's undivided attention. They could talk to him, be hugged by him, get familiar with the scent of his cologne, and just be themselves with him. Rachel took a break from the family during that time by visiting her sister and cousins in Chicago. During those two weeks they would go to Charlotte, North Carolina, and rent a beach house. They spent time living like beach bums. Hannah's grandparents on her mother's side lived in Charlotte, but they never stayed with them when on vacation.

The children would have a designated evening to visit their grandparents, get gifts, get and give hugs and kisses, take lots of pictures, eat a meal, and then go back to their beach house. It felt like Christmas in July. The grandparents often complained that they did not get to spend enough time spoiling their grandchildren, but Rev. C insisted that he spend as much quality time as possible with the children, since taking a break from ministry was rare for him. In retrospect, Hannah wondered if perhaps seeing his in-laws reminded their father of his wife, and if he could not bear to see the pain in their eyes.

Hannah always thought that her parents had made the oddest couple, because Reverend C was tall (6'3), very dark skinned and thick, and her mother was light brown skinned with strong American Indian features and a tiny frame, and she was barely five feet tall. They had been college sweethearts, and the love they had for each other was deep and real. Hanna's mother taught her what the role of First Lady entailed. No matter what problems arose at the church, her mother never wavered from having Rev. C's shirts freshly laundered, his suits and robes cleaned and pressed, and making sure he had a freshly pressed handkerchief in his inner suit pocket. Hanna's mother had even grown accustomed to an occasional late-night crisis call from church members. After her mother passed, Rev. C would often tell Hannah that he would never remarry because, "Heaven broke the mold when they made your mother. These women nowadays don't' know how to be wives, they're just in it for the show." She could sense his loneliness, and he seemed to pour himself into the ministry as a distraction.

Pastoring a 2,000-plus member congregation was a full-time job, and then some. There were times when Hannah's mother had gone to numerous doctor appointments, chemotherapy, and frequent hospital stays as she fought cancer that Hannah and her brother stayed several weeks with the grandparents. Those times were often filled with anxiety and longing for their mother. *(Rev. C often told Hannah that she reminded him of her mother because of her long black curly hair, long black eyelashes, high cheek bones, and flashy white smile.)*

Early on in life Hannah knew she was different, and not just because of her Black American Indian appearance, but because she was very intelligent, too. With long black braids hanging down her back, and her dark brown skin and high cheekbones, she was often teased by the other children at school. They called her "red skin" or "black Injun." She often went home from school crying and wondering what she had done to deserve such cruel treatment. Her appearance was beyond her control

In the fourth grade, Hannah tested higher than the other kids in her class, and her teachers recommended that she transfer to the ASPIRE Program for gifted students. Her brothers were one year and two years behind her, so she set the standard for the Cane children. Her brothers would eventually follow in her footsteps in the gifted program.

Brains and beauty, a combination that should have been Hannah's ticket to popularity—but instead, it became a source of isolation. The ASPIRE program pulled her out of the regular classroom and placed her in another part of the school building. The ASPIRE students even had their own lunch period. This only gave the other children more ammunition to tease her. Hannah decided she would have to live with the criticism. Her only satisfaction was being intellectually gifted.

When Hannah was in the eleventh grade, she was accepted to Harvard at the age of 17. She had done all of the work required to complete high school, and had taken advanced placement classes for college when she was only a junior. Even though she was a freshman in college, her high school allowed her to participate in senior activities as if she were in the senior class. Hannah saw going to college as an opportunity to get out from under the strict rules of her father and her aunt, and finally live! Rev. C was very proud of Hannah, and he expected her to be the first doctor in their family.

Hannah's academic success had netted her a full academic scholarship for her undergraduate degree, with the potential for more scholarships to cover her medical school expenses. She decided to be an oncologist. After seeing her mother suffer and die of cancer, she wanted to be a part of the treatment and cure for cancer, and to hopefully prevent anyone else's mother from dying of the disease. Tolerating the teasing and isolation in her high school had finally paid off with her shot at medical school. Her father, aunt, brothers and church members sent her off to school in grand style with a huge sendoff party. They gave her everything she needed for her dorm room, and for her college experience. Her father had committed to send her an allowance each month to make sure she did not want for anything. Hannah was grateful for the opportunity and looked forward to being out on her own.

Hannah's arrival at Harvard University in Cambridge, Massachusetts, was a scary but exciting experience. She wondered if she would be teased by the other students, or be able to fit in and make new friends. She just wanted to be accepted and appreciated for who she was. She cherished being at Harvard and living in the dorm, free from the noise, distractions and curfew. One of Hannah's ASPIRE classmates, Ann, had graduated from high school a year before her and was also attending Harvard, and lived in an off-campus apartment. She invited Hannah to move in with her and share the rent and the expenses. Ann was into the party scene, but that was not Hannah's flavor. Rev. C agreed to let Hannah move with Ann on a trial basis, on the condition that she would keep up her grades up. Hannah was excited to have such freedom, even though she did not care much about partying. She just enjoyed being able to make her own decisions.

Hannah had been exposed to drinking and smoking weed from some of the neighborhood youth who attended their church when she was younger, but she knew she did not fit into that crowd. The late night parties and loud music at Ann's apartment interrupted Hannah's studies, so she decided to get a part-time job and her own apartment. She thought she would be able to manage using part of her scholarship money. Since she was away from home, she no longer felt obligated to go to church either.

When she lived with Ann, Hannah went on her first date with a junior premed student named Damon. Hannah was impressed with Damon because he was such a nice, respectful young man, and the son of a Methodist preacher. The Methodist experience was slightly different from the Baptist experience that Hannah was used to, but she welcomed the change. She started to attend Damon's church and they studied the Bible together. The people at the church thought she and Damon made a perfect couple, and that they would possibly get married someday. Damon's parents loved Hannah and thought of her as a daughter.

As the relationship progressed, she noticed Damon's behavior changing and found out that he was forging her checks and stealing things from her apartment. When she confronted him about the theft, he broke down and admitted that he had a crack cocaine habit. She was shocked! She wondered how she could have missed that flaw in him. Just when she was about to belong to a solid family, she thought, this had to happen. Hannah had no choice but to file charges against Damon for the thefts, and he was convicted and sent to jail. His parents, of course, were embarrassed by the incident.

Hannah experienced her first heartbreak and breakup in the worst way. *Was love really worth all of this?* She later found out that this was not Damon's first bout with drugs. Hannah struggled with whether Damon had chosen her because she was naive and an easy target, or if he really cared for her. The answer would have to remain with him. She realized that in the worst of situations, good things can happen. At least her relationship with Damon had led to her getting back to church. She had found her way back to Christ. Her renewed relationship with Christ would bring her to, and carry her through, some even darker times to come.

The breakup did not keep Hannah from going to the Methodist church and the young adult Bible classes. No one blamed her for ending the relationship with Damon. Ed, the young adult Bible class teacher, was a tall, handsome, dynamic young preacher, and Hannah enjoyed his class. She had been badly hurt by the relationship with Damon, and Bible study was the one place she could find some comfort. Ed consoled and counseled her after the breakup, and she felt gratitude toward him for his concern.

Hannah rededicated her life to Christ, and Ed performed her re-baptism. She wanted a second chance for Christ in her life. She did not realize that Ed's attraction to her was more than that of a counselor, until one day he showed up at her apartment to ask her out. *How did he know where she lived?* She trusted him and agreed to the date. He took her for a long drive in the hills, where they spent the entire day walking and talking. Hannah appreciated and needed some special attention, and she found herself attracted to Ed. He was very charming and witty. She needed someone in her life who would help her forget Damon, so she agreed to see more of Ed, as much as her studies would allow. She told him that her studies came first, and he agreed not to interfere.

When the members of the church found out that Hannah and Ed were dating, a huge scandal erupted. Ed was seven years older than Hannah, and the church leaders felt it was inappropriate for the youth pastor to date one of his younger students. It was too late— Hannah and Ed had fallen in love. After six months of dating, Ed asked Hannah to marry him. Hannah was swept off her feet. Because the church disapproved of the relationship, the leadership refused to let them get married at the church, and Ed also lost his position as the youth pastor. What a way to start off a new chapter in life. Hannah took Ed home to meet her father so that he could ask for her hand properly. Hannah's father told the couple that he strongly objected to the marriage because of the age difference between them, and he felt the relationship would distract Hannah from her studies.

Hannah begged her father to trust her decision and told him how much she loved Ed, and Ed promised to take care of Hannah and to support her goal of finishing medical school. Rev. C saw that his daughter was hopelessly in love, so he reluctantly agreed to let her marry, and performed the ceremony in his home. He had always dreamed of giving a big wedding for his daughter and of walking her down the aisle, but this would have to do. Aunt Rachel cried loudly during the entire ceremony. *You would have thought someone had died.* Her brothers were just excited about having a big brother.

In Hannah's heart, she wanted to have her own family, where she finally felt she belonged. With Ed, Hannah felt like a woman, and she wanted to do whatever she could to please him. They were in marital bliss. To support them, Ed got a job working construction, and Hannah poured herself into her studies to secure their future. She felt she was the luckiest woman in the world, with the man of her dreams in her life. How wrong the church folk, her father, and Aunt Rachel had all been about Ed. If they could only see how happy she was!

Swisssssh! Hannah felt the wind from Ed's hand pass her face as he swung at her. *What was going on?* It was not yet a month into their marriage. They were driving down the street, having a discussion, and Ed suddenly swung his long arm, with his big hand on the end of it, at Hannah's face. She ducked, and he missed. She screamed in shock, "Did you try to hit me?" She had no idea what had set him off. He yelled at her that he did not want to hear what she had to say, and that whenever he told her to shut up, she needed to be quiet. She did not know how to respond to him. She had never seen or even heard her parents have an argument, and certainly did not expect this from her husband. Not wanting him to explode any more, she did as he said— she became silent. Later that evening, Hannah called her cousin and told her about the incident. Her cousin told her to pack her things and leave him immediately!

How could she leave? She had not even been married a month! She could just hear her family and the church folk saying, "I told you so!" It would be too embarrassing to leave now, so she decided to stay and make it work. Maybe Ed's violence was caused by Hannah being inexperienced as a wife by spending so much time studying. She decided she would work harder to make him happy.

When they got home after the incident, Ed told her that they needed more money, and she would have to quit school and work full time. Getting into a prestigious university like Harvard was a major achievement, and now he was asking her to walk away from her once-in-a-lifetime opportunity. Her life was becoming a blur. She had been an ASPIRE student, but was not savvy enough to figure this situation out. Her academic classes had not prepared her for how to handle an angry husband and a troubled marriage. She wanted peace, so she agreed to quit school for the time being, and got a full-time job at a credit card company.

When Hannah told her father she was quitting school, he was furious and afraid she would lose her scholarship. He contacted the dean at Harvard and begged him to hold her scholarship for a year, until she got settled into her marriage. The dean agreed to hold her money for a year, but after that, she would lose everything if she did not return to school. Rev. C told Hannah about the dean's decision, and Hannah was grateful for the extension. She told her father that the year would give her time to settle into being married and for them to get on their feet.

Hannah confronted Ed about his anger, and he said that he wanted her to leave him alone. He offered no explanation as to why he was so angry at her. Hannah decided that Ed may have blamed her for him losing his position at the church. As the days and weeks went on, no matter what Hannah did or said, she could not make her new husband happy. The following month they had another big argument, filled with more yelling and screaming. Any little thing Hannah did caused Ed to become angry. He stormed out of the house and did not come home for three or four days. Reality began to set in for Hannah—marrying Ed had possibly been a major mistake. While Ed was gone, Hannah cried out to God to please fix whatever was wrong with their marriage. She was so troubled that she could not eat or sleep.

When Ed finally came home, Hannah met him at the door with tears, demanding an explanation of his whereabouts. He calmly told her that he had spent the time away with an ex-girlfriend. Hannah went wild yelling and crying, letting him know how much he had hurt her. Ed picked up a Bible that was nearby and slapped her across the face with it. The blow sent her small frame flying halfway across the room. She knew she had to get away before he killed her. She called her dad, crying uncontrollably, begging him to come and get her. He told her to call the police, and that he was on his way. Hannah felt she could get this resolved without the police; she just wanted out of there.

She gathered her things and sat near the window for hours waiting for her father. When she saw her father's car drive up, she ran out to the car. Ed did not bother to stop her or offer any explanation to Rev. C, who had gotten out of the car and was yelling at Ed to come and face him like a man. Hannah begged her dad to get back into the car and just drive away. Rev. C was angry and wanted to fight Ed for hitting his daughter, but he honored Hannah's wishes and got into the car. As they drove off, he told Hannah how he had seen countless women being abused by their husbands, and it never ended well. He pleaded with her not to go back, explaining that it would only get worse. He stressed, "I raised you better than this!"

Hannah quit her job and moved back home for four months. Her brothers didn't ask a lot of questions when they saw her crying. They were just glad to have her home. Hannah needed time to think things through and consider whether she had really given her marriage a chance to work. *Perhaps school and Ed's unemployment had been too much strain on the new marriage?* During their separation, Hannah sought counseling about the violence, because she felt she needed some spiritual guidance other than that of her father. He was too close to the situation. The counselor advised Hannah that she had good reasons for a divorce and recommended that she seriously consider divorcing Ed, because the violence would only escalate. Hannah thought divorce seemed like the cheap way out, and thought about her parents being married for years and making it work. She wanted that same stability.

While they were separated, Ed called Hannah daily. He told her how much he loved and missed her. He told Hannah how sorry he was for what he had done and how he wanted his wife back, and reminded her that they were a family. She decided she wanted to stay in the marriage and work out their problems. *Later, Hannah would find out that while they were separated, Ed had moved to Philadelphia and worked at a church there. He had later been dismissed from the church staff due to allegations of an affair with one of the church members.*

Hannah was determined to make this marriage work, and to be the best wife she could be. Rev. C reluctantly drove her back to Boston and told her to call him if she needed him. His heart broke to see his child suffer like this, but Hannah was a grown woman and she was in love. She was able to get her full-time job back, and Ed got another job working construction.

Hannah soon became pregnant and was so excited to become a mother. She vowed to always be there for her children, and to provide them with a solid home. Ed was excited about the baby and resigned from hitting her while she was pregnant, even when his temper flared.

One evening when they were arguing, he raised his hand to hit her but she reminded him that she was pregnant, and he stopped. On another occasion, Ed had become angry and threatened to hit her with an iron. Usually when they argued, Ed would disappear for days at a time, and would return with no explanation of where he had been. Hannah knew he had been with another woman, and this only brought on more arguments. Hannah hoped and prayed that the new baby would help Ed settle down and be more loving.

When their daughter Sarah was born, Ed was a proud, loving, and supportive father. He wanted Hannah to stop working and be a stay-at-home mom. For a few months after Sarah's birth, they were the ideal family, and Hannah forgot about medical school. She was focused on being a good mother and wife. Rev. C, his sons, and Aunt Rachel would come visit Hannah's little family. Ed usually found some other place to go during their visits. Aunt Rachel would just hold Sarah and quietly cry, and Hannah would say that everything was all right. Rev. C reminded Hannah the extension on her Harvard scholarship was almost up. Hannah said she would give the school a call to see if it could be extended, and told her dad not to worry. Rev. C was still worried about Hannah for many reasons.

Soon after Sarah's birth, Aunt Rachel died suddenly, and Hannah took the loss very hard. Hannah knew she had broken the heart of the woman who had given up her own life to raise her and her brothers. That strong influence in her life was now gone, and she missed her Aunt Rachel dearly.

At this point, Hannah realized how her struggles with her marriage had driven a wedge in between herself and her relationship with her family, and her brothers were growing so fast, she was missing seeing them grow up. The family gathering for the funeral was refreshing and filled with lots of tears and hugs, and she felt like the prodigal child returning home. Ed did not feel comfortable around Hannah's family, so he did not attend the funeral.

After the family gathering, Ed drove up to Rev. C's house and blew the horn so Hannah would to come out, yelling that it was time for her to come home. When she did not come out immediately, Ed began yelling and cursing for her to hurry. Hannah was humiliated, and went to the car, and tried to explain to him that she had not seen her family in a long time and that she wanted to spend more time with them. Right there, with her father and brothers watching, Ed got out of the car, grabbed Hannah, and began slapping and hitting her on her father's front lawn! Hannah screamed and cried in pain and humiliation. She had not wanted her family to know how she was being treated at home. Rev. C called the police, pulled Ed off Hannah and threatened to kill him. Ed jumped into his car and was gone by the time the police arrived. Rev. C and her brothers begged Hannah to stay with them, but the next day, Hannah and Sarah took the train home to Ed. Rev. C called Harvard to see if Hannah's scholarship had been extended, and the dean informed him that they had not been able to extend it beyond the first year. Hannah could return at a later time, but would have to find another funding source. Rev. C was crushed, and called Hannah with the news. Hannah could hear the disappointment in her father's voice, but she was in a fight for her dignity and her life. School would have to wait until her marriage was stable.

It seemed that after Sarah's birth, Ed's violent attacks were less frequent but more intense. He no longer cared if he left marks on Hannah's body that were visible to the public. One evening after coming home from one of his weekend ventures, Hannah confronted him about his habit of not coming home, and Ed took a heavy object and struck her across the face with it, leaving her bleeding profusely from a large gash above her eye. The blow sent her reeling, and left her almost unconscious. Ed left the house with her bleeding on the floor, with little Sarah crying nearby. Hannah managed to gather herself up and called a cab to take her to the hospital, with Sarah in her arms.

At the emergency room, little Sarah could sense that something was wrong with her mother. Sarah cried and clung to her mother. The nurse let Sarah sit on Hannah's chest while they stitched her head wound. As she looked into Sarah's face through her tears, Hannah felt ashamed to be her mother. She wondered if trying to keep her little family together was worth this shame. The hospital social worker asked if she wanted to pursue charges against Ed, but Hannah refused and left into the night with Sarah still clinging to her chest.

The next day, Hannah went to see her counselor and told her about the incident. The counselor told Hannah that because of the sheltered, protected environment in which she was raised, she did not have any coping skills to deal with Ed's unstable personality. The counselor recommended that Hannah end the marriage before she or her child were seriously injured or killed. Hannah appreciated the advice, but opted to keep trying to save her marriage. She did not want to fail at anything else. She had dropped out of Harvard and lost her scholarship, and she did not want to be a failure at marriage too. She would stay with Ed and try even harder to be a good wife.

Shortly after her Aunt Rachel's passing, Hannah found out she was pregnant with her second child. Ed's temper flared this time. He not care that she was pregnant. During one of their arguments, he pushed her down the stairs in their apartment and seemed unconcerned as she lay there, almost unconscious. Drowsy from the fall, Hannah begged him to call an ambulance because she was hurting and having contractions. Ed panicked and called an ambulance, but left before it arrived. When the ambulance arrived, Hannah was more responsive and told them she had accidentally fallen down the stairs.

In the trauma suite at the emergency room, the doctor told her that the fall had caused her to go into labor and that she might lose the baby. Hospital volunteers kept little Sarah entertained while the doctors attended to her mother. Hannah was only three months pregnant, and the possibility of the baby surviving was slim. The medical staff worked feverishly to stop the contractions and the bleeding, but to no avail. They asked Hannah if her husband was coming to the hospital. Hannah covered for Ed and said he was visiting relatives out of town. The nurse called the chaplain to be with Hannah in recovery, after the procedure to remove the fetus was completed.

As the chaplain visited with Hannah, she prayed with her and told her that their conversation was confidential. She asked Hannah point blank, "What really happened with the fall?" Hannah could not believe her direct question. *Had she said something under anesthesia to let on that Ed had pushed her?* Hannah tried to remember what she had told the paramedics. The chaplain assured her that she was not there to pass judgment, but only to help her get through this crisis. Hannah suddenly had a flood of emotions and began to pour out her heart and the story of her and Ed's

115

relationship. She told about the beatings and about Ed's temper, and how he had pushed her down the stairs. She felt she had failed at yet another thing—motherhood. This made Hannah cry even harder as she thought of losing her baby. *How could Ed do this to his own child?* For the first time, she felt hatred toward him.

The chaplain sat quietly and listened attentively as Hannah poured her heart out. She was experienced in ministering to women who had lost their babies. After Hannah had emptied her thoughts, the chaplain asked her if she was going back home to Ed. Hannah thought long and hard, because she knew she needed time to recover from the miscarriage and that Ed would not be supportive. She told the chaplain that her father was a minister, and asked her to call him and let him know where she was, and that she was all right. The chaplain called Rev. C and told him that Hannah was in the hospital and was stable. Rev. C wanted medical information, so with Hannah's permission, the doctor explained Hannah's medical condition to her father. Rev. C offered to come get her, but Hannah chose to go home to Ed instead, because she felt Sarah needed a mother and a father in her life.

Hannah called Ed, and he came to the hospital to get her and Sarah. No words were exchanged between Hannah and Ed as they were given instructions by the hospital staff regarding Hannah's care. When they had driven a few blocks from the hospital, Ed asked, "What did you tell the doctor about the fall, and are the police coming for me?" Hannah assured him that she had told them it was her fault, and that she had not spoken to the police. She did not tell him what she had told the chaplain; that was confidential.

During her three-week recovery Ed was very attentive and helpful. Perhaps Ed feared she would go to the police about the fall. Ed told Hannah they should try for another baby as soon as possible to help her get over the miscarriage. Hannah was afraid that Ed would cause her to have another "accident," but she did not dare tell him about her fear. She agreed to have another baby sometime later in the future.

As soon as Hannah was able to return to work, Ed's temper and weekends away from home returned. Hannah had her hands full with Sarah, grief, Ed, and work. Ed made a point not to fight with Hannah in front of Sarah, but behind closed doors, the slapping and hitting continued. Ed had gotten a position as youth minister at another church. Hannah saw that fatherhood was causing Ed more stress. She was tiring of the beatings.

Hannah's counselor again recommended that she leave Ed and expose him to the congregation where he worked, explaining that the exposure could force him to get help. The counselor felt Ed had bipolar personality disorder, and that he needed to be on medication. Hannah felt that exposing Ed might expose her too, and suggest that she was not a good wife. She thanked the counselor, but decided once more that she just needed to try harder. The counselor pointed out, "I see that you keep trying, but is Ed trying too? You are not the only one in this marriage. He has to do his part to make it work." Hannah buried that thought in her heart.

Ed applied for and was hired as senior pastor of a growing Baptist church in the tough inner city of Miami, Florida. The area was drug infested, and the gang wars there were heated. The search committee that hired Ed felt that a young, dynamic pastor was what they needed to relate to the community. Hannah felt that a change in environment might help their marriage, and because she was so determined to keep her little family together, they packed up their car and moved to Miami. She prayed to God that the change would help Ed focus on ministry and stop the violence.

Hannah told her father about the move, but only after it was done. Rev. C was devastated because he had witnessed Ed's violent temper firsthand, and he was afraid for Hannah and Sarah to be moving more than just a drive away. He feared getting a call in the middle of the night saying that Ed had killed his daughter. Hannah cried on the phone as she told her dad not to worry about her. The strain of worrying about his baby girl, raising two growing boys alone, and pastoring was taking its toll on Reverend C.

Hannah truly felt that God had orchestrated the move to Florida to help Ed become mentally and financially stable, and less stressed about money. At the new church, Hannah would be the "First Lady," and surely that would change how Ed viewed and treated her. Hannah, Ed and Sarah stayed in the church parsonage, which was small but comfortable, and was just two streets away from the church, easily within walking distance. The church members were very welcoming and went out of their way to make sure their new first family was comfortable. Hannah made some lifelong friends there.

A few weeks after the move, Hannah found out she was pregnant again. She was excited and fearful. She did not want to lose this baby; she felt it would destroy her. At this point, Sarah was completely potty trained. Two babies would be a challenge, but Hannah was determined to cover all her roles—wife, mother and First Lady. Hannah missed her dad and brothers, but felt she was where God wanted her to be.

Ed had finally gotten Hannah away from her family and from them meddling in his business. Ed seemed to settle down in Miami, and he was actually kind to Hannah during this pregnancy. He had never apologized for pushing her down the stairs during the last pregnancy. It was as if not beating her during this pregnancy was a sort of apology. Hannah gave birth to a healthy baby girl and named her Rochelle, because she wanted her to have part of her Aunt Rachel's name. She was so proud of her two beautiful daughters, and of the fact that they had her American Indian features. Sarah loved her new sister and called her "Shelly." Ed proudly showed off his new family addition, and dedicated her in a ceremony at his church. The congregation had come to love and respect Ed and Hannah. Ed had been instrumental in promoting peace between the gangs in the area and decreasing the violence in the community. Many of the gang members would attend the church. Hannah started a youth ministry that embraced and affirmed local troubled youth. Hannah was truly their First Lady in name and deed.

Hannah felt a sense of pride when she was addressed as First Lady, and she thanked God for the move to Florida and for the peace she was experiencing in her marriage. She felt God had answered her prayer to save her marriage. She thought about what she had sacrificed to save the marriage: medical school, living near her dad, and motherhood. She felt she had made the right choice by staying with her husband and making her marriage work, and realized that her faith in God had carried her through.

A few months after Rochelle was born, Ed began to start arguments with Hannah, slapping and pushing her around again. He had not changed, so Hannah spent more time in prayer and worked on deepening her faith in Christ. Her life with Ed had taught her about the potential dark side of being married to a pastor, and about the silent role she believed she had to play as a pastor's wife. She found herself sitting in the church audience, admiring his sermons, knowing he had hit and slapped her the night before. She had learned how to apply her makeup to hide the bruises. She found herself saying, "Amen!" with the rest of the crowd. Oh, how he could preach, and how the members looked forward to his sermons.

Hannah realized that as a pastor's wife, she had to maintain the image of a loving and supporting wife to her husband. She was to be a shoulder for others to lean on, and she had to put herself and her needs last. Whatever pain or humiliation she suffered behind closed doors, it was not the congregation's business. She had taken the First Lady's unwritten oath of silence.

At the fellowships for area pastors and their wives, Hannah often looked at other pastors' wives and wondered if their marriages were similar to hers. If they were suffering, they did not dare discuss their issues, for fear of exposure—for themselves and their husbands. Hannah realized that if she exposed Ed, the congregation would be greatly affected. Those members who were weak in their faith would suffer the most. The ministry to the youth was dear to Hannah's heart, and she could not risk that ministry being destroyed. She kept silent for the sake of the congregation. She loved her husband, and he was her weakness.

The congregation loved Ed's preaching style and his charm, and their numbers grew to more than 500 as his popularity in the area grew. Hannah was behind the scenes balancing their two girls, Ed's temper, and the needs of the growing congregation. Their lives were in a very delicate balance, and one mistake would send the whole thing toppling down. It was Hannah's responsibility to keep up the front of the happy pastor's wife and loving mother, and at the same time sweep all of her troubles and pain under the rug. Hannah eventually confided in one of the deacons about Ed's beatings, hoping that he would go to Ed, man-to-man, and help him. The deacon suggested that Hannah expose Ed, and then leave him, but he did not offer her any financial support if she left Ed. She had no money and no job, so she felt she had no choice but to stay. Soon, rumors started that Ed was sleeping with one of the young female members of the church. The young lady was a student in the college Bible class group. Hannah was no stranger to the rumors about her husband; she knew Ed was guilty. It would do no good to confront him about the rumors, because that would only cause an argument, and then denial, and finally the inevitable violence to which she had become accustomed.

The church leaders held a meeting and spoke to Ed about the rumors about the young lady, and he denied them. One of the church members who had befriended Hannah told her that the student had come to her, bragging about the affair with Ed. Hannah knew it was true, and she was so humiliated. Again, she questioned her ability as a woman to satisfy her husband. *Why was he always seeking other women's beds? Wasn't she woman enough for him?* She felt like a failure as a woman, and as a person.

The majority of the church leaders wanted to dismiss Ed, but instead they offered to pay for him to receive counseling for his problem. He charmed them and verbally committed to counseling, and thanked them for the chance to be a better man and husband. The leaders quietly asked the young college student to relocate her membership, and sent Ed to a spiritual retreat center in the area for counseling.

The church leaders did not offer Hannah any help besides moral support, in case she decided to leave Ed. She informed them that this was not the first time this had happened, and that she would keep their advice in mind. They still did not offer her any financial support in the event that she did decide to leave Ed. Yet again, she decided that she had to try harder to be a better wife and lover to her husband. Hannah's faith in God had weakened because God had failed to fix her marriage, and He had not protected her from Ed's violence. *Where was God in this mess?*

When Ed came back from his two-week long retreat/counseling sabbatical, he was more attentive toward Hannah and their girls. His sermons seemed to be more riveting, and his popularity grew. It seemed that all was forgiven. Hannah wondered if Ed had been delivered from his demons *(as he tried to deliver others from their demons)*. Under Ed's leadership, the church had a food pantry, clothes closet, gang intervention program, prison reentry program, and a medical clinic. The impact of the church on the neighborhood could be seen in the lives of the families that came to the church for help.

With Ed's improved attitude and involvement in community politics, Hannah considered going back to school. The University of Miami had a well-respected premed program, and she could take some of her classes online. Hannah talked to Ed about her desire to return to school. She stressed the fact that if she was a doctor she would be able to earn more to support the family. Ed thought about the financial aspect and agreed to let Hannah begin school with two classes. Hannah hired a sitter for the girls for the days she would be in classes. It felt good to be in the academic environment again, and she found that she had not lost her edge. She was sharp as ever. Her professors noticed how quickly she learned, and Hannah had the highest test scores in class.

Ed seemed to be a changed man. He did not start any arguments or bother Hannah while she was studying. She finally seemed to be pulling it all together. Rev. C was glad to hear that she had returned to school, although he still missed his daughter and she missed him. Ed had made it known that her father was not welcome in their home, and he had not allowed Hannah to visit her father for the past two years they had been in Miami. She did not want to get Ed angry, or for the beatings to start again, so she did not press the issue of visiting her father.

Hannah taught Sunday school and mentored the youth while raising her own children and going to school. After just one semester, Ed started to pick arguments again and said that the girls missed her, and that she needed to be home more to care for their needs and his. She tried to remind him of the end results of her studies; a doctor for a wife. One Saturday when Hannah was preparing for an exam, Ed interrupted her and said she needed to watch the girls, because he had to run an errand. Hannah gave the girls books to read so she could finish studying. The "errand" Ed ran lasted all night. She did not see him until he showed up at church on Sunday.

When they got home after church, Hannah confronted Ed about not keeping his commitment to the church leaders to be a better husband. Ed slapped her hard across her face and told her to never question his comings and goings. Hannah's worst fear was now a reality that Ed had not, and would not, change. She had more things to worry about, like finishing the semester. She now realized that she HAD to finish her degree and get into medical school. That was her ticket away from Ed to independence, and being able to take care of her girls.

The violent attacks from Ed decreased in frequency, but their intensity increased even further, just like they had the first time they resumed. His method of attacking her became more and more unpredictable. She never understood why he hated her, but he refused to let her leave. Through it all, she completed the semester with straight A's and made the Dean's list. She was committed to finishing her degree.

During the summer break, the elders hired an intern to help them with the summer youth program at the church. The young man stayed with Ed and Hannah in their spare room, and also helped out with the girls. Hannah welcomed the presence of the intern, and hoped that having an adult male in the house would help to decrease Ed's violent attacks. Hannah decided to throw Ed a surprise birthday party, so she called all of their friends for help in making the party arrangements. To make sure no one was left out, Hannah asked Ed about a particular male friend of his. Her intention was to see if this was someone she should invite. Ed reacted in a totally bizarre manner. He began questioning her, why was she was asking about this man? In the midst of trying to explain that she was planning his surprise party, Ed accused Hannah of cheating. He then went to the closet and came back with a shotgun! She did not want the intern to know they were fighting, so she desperately tried to calm Ed down.

Hannah was crying and pleading for her life as Ed put the shotgun to her head. All Hannah could think of was what would happen to her children. Suddenly, he began choking and beating her, until she almost passed out. Ed sat on the side of the bed all night with the shotgun, watching her crying in a heap on the floor. She was so thankful to see the sunrise. God had spared her life another day. She never knew if the intern had heard the altercation, because he did not intervene. Now Hannah was really afraid that Ed would kill her. He had never threatened her with a gun before, and she feared that the next time he snapped, he could kill her. She seriously considered leaving him, but she needed an escape plan.

Again, rumors began to circulate about Ed's possible involvement with a staff member at the church. Hannah was all too familiar with these accusations, and knew all too well what would follow next—they would have to move. She really liked Miami and the wonderful people she had met. There she had partnered with one of the members named Beth to feed the homeless, and to work with the young women in the church. Hannah could see the impact their ministry was having on the neighborhood.

She was respected as their First Lady. People from all walks of life, homeless, millionaires, and everything in between, found a place to worship at their church. It truly looked like heaven! One Sunday, one of the deacons called Hannah aside and told her about the accusations against Ed, but she would not speak on behalf of her husband because they had been down this road before. She had tried to get help for Ed, and he had vowed to change his ways. When the deacons called Ed into the meeting, Ed denied everything. This time, Hannah really wished the charges would be false, because she did not want to see all of the hard work they had done in the community abandoned.

The church leadership dismissed Ed from his position. This dismissal hurt Hannah in a new way, because she truly loved the members of the church, and she had made some lifelong friends there. The church members were hurt and disappointed when the leadership announced Ed would no longer be their pastor, and Hannah did not confirm or deny the accusations against Ed when members asked why they were leaving. She explained by saying they were getting another church assignment. They had to move out of the parsonage and into a small apartment with the money they had saved.

She was growing tired of Ed's pattern of affairs with women at the different churches, and she knew that with this dismissal, he would become even more violent. Hannah was planning to go back to school in the fall, but with Ed out of work, she found herself relying on the church's food pantry to feed her own family. She was embarrassed as the former First Lady coming for food, but she needed help, and this was no time to be proud.

With Ed out of work, it did not take much to set him off. Hannah did everything she could to keep him happy, but nothing seemed to work. He complained about the amount of sex he was getting or not getting. He complained that the kids were getting on his nerves, the bills were too high, or the food wasn't cooked right. There was no pleasing him, and the hitting continued. Ed finally found a part-time position at another church in the area as a youth pastor. Hannah wondered how long it would be before the accusations began again.

Hannah was trying to maintain their only vehicle during this crisis. It was the only transportation they had to get the girls to and from school and activities, and her to school. One day when she was calling repair shops to get estimates on brake repairs, Ed saw her on the phone and accused her of cheating on him. She tried to hand him the phone to speak to the repair shop, but he would not take the phone. He pulled a gun from the drawer and made her sit at his feet for about 30 minutes while he preached to her about the duties of a wife, and how she was not a worthy wife. He said that he should kill her. She was thankful that the girls were at her friend Beth's house, because she did not want her children to see her dead body. She knew that she needed to keep her head about her and plan her escape. She kept her eyes on the bedroom door. She knew she had to get out of the room, or else he really would kill her this time. As his "sermon" grew more intense, he put the gun to her head and threatened to pull the trigger. She prayed to God to protect her as she made a run for the door, but before she could reach the door, he hit her on the side of the head with the butt of the pistol. The blow dazed her, and blood gushed from her head. She immediately knew she needed medical help.

It no longer mattered what she had on, and what her title was—Hannah was a First Lady running for her life. *Where were the church members on whom she had tried so hard to make a good impression?* Only God could save her. Her mind raced back to her dad and her brothers in Baltimore, and to all of the church leaders and counselors who had told her years ago to leave Ed.

Hannah had tried to be a good wife—she really had. All she wanted was a family she could call her own. With only a housecoat and no shoes on, Hannah ran out of the back door and down the alley, screaming for help. Ed was standing in the alley, cursing and screaming for her to come back home. As she ran, she kept waiting for a hot bullet to pierce the back of her head. Hannah ran to a neighbor's house and beat on the door, crying and pleading for help. The neighbor answered the door and saw she was bleeding and needed help, but would not let her in, but called the police. As Hannah hid in the alley waiting for the police to arrive, Ed took the car and left. When the police finally arrived and took her back to the house, they took her statement. This time, Hannah was filing charges. This was no accident.

Hannah called one of the deacon's wives who she had befriended, and asked her to take her to the hospital. It would be humiliating to let others see how she really lived, but the time for pretense was over; Hannah needed help. The deacon and his wife arrived on the scene to find a blood-covered, weeping, sobbing Hannah, not the First Lady they had seen on Sundays. They took her to the emergency room to get stitches and took her home. Hannah called Beth and informed her of what had happen, so Beth picked her up and took Hannah and the girls to a hotel and made sure they had food and were safe. Hannah had no money or means to support herself, because Ed had controlled the money and had spent every spare dime she could save on his own pleasures. *What would she do after this night was over?*

That one night alone in that hotel room, with her girls in bed with her, changed Hannah's life forever. She first thanked God for sparing her life and the lives of her children. She knew that her children were at risk of becoming motherless, and if not for any other reason, she had to get out of this madness for their sake.

All of the love that Hannah's parents had poured into her came back like a warm flood. How she missed her mother and daddy. Perhaps her search for a place to belong and the need for a family of her own had driven her to this point. She had done everything in her power to make her marriage work, but she had failed. She had always excelled at everything she had done in the classroom, but real life was not so easy. *What else could she have done differently to make it work?* At this point, God spoke to her heart to reassure her that He was with her, protecting her. Her gut reaction was one of anger toward God. "Why am I in this mess? Where were you, God, when guns were being drawn, and when fist were flying?" She pumped her tiny fist at God and shouted through tears, "Where were you?" In a deeper place, God spoke to Hannah's heart saying, ***"I should be first in your life. When I am first, all things are added after that. 'First Lady' is just an earthly title—I need to be first in your heart. I come before your commitment to marriage, to school, to jobs, to anything else. I come first! Anything that comes before me must be moved. If I am to bless you like I want to bless you, and if you are to be loved like***

you truly need to be loved, you must put me first!"
With this revelation, she laid face down on the floor, and with endless tears she asked God for forgiveness and rededicated her life to Him.

At that moment she realized that since she had met Ed, he had become her heart, and she had given God her leftovers. God now wanted her heart back. Ed had programmed her to think he should be the source of her happiness, and if she was not happy, it was her fault. Ed refused to take responsibility for his own misguided actions. Hannah was now ready to put God first, and to hear what He wanted her to do. She needed God to breathe and to survive. God's message to her was clear: *"Leave, enough is enough. Leave! Ed's actions are not your fault. I have greater things in store for you."*

Suddenly, Hannah jumped to her feet and cried out, "Home, I've got to get home to heal!" Hannah called Beth and told her she needed help to get home, so Beth paid for their room for a week and brought them food while Hannah got her affairs in order. Beth came by every day to make sure they were safe. This gave Hannah time to think and pray about what her next steps should be. It was her time to surrender to God, and to let God take control of her life, because she was tired of the fighting, the beatings, the arguments, the put-downs and embarrassment. Just tired.

Hannah called her dad, and he sent her money to come home. Beth went with Hannah to the house to get their things and load the car. Ed had left the car and gone into hiding, but they did not know if he would come back to check the house. They hurriedly packed the car, bought groceries for the trip, and then Hannah and her girls headed to Baltimore. Home!

Home was just what Hannah needed, and Rev. C embraced her when she arrived, almost smothering her.

129

He had missed his child, and he thanked God she was home safe. Her brothers almost tackled her when they saw her get out of the car. Hannah and her brothers picked up being siblings again and became inseparable. The 14-hour drive had been worth every mile. After a few weeks, Rev. C helped Hannah and the girls get settled into an apartment. Ed had isolated her from her family for years, and she wanted to see them and tell them how much she loved and missed them. Hannah missed that closeness. Sarah and Rochelle got to know their uncles and their grandfather again, and they would often spend the weekends with Rev. C.

One weekend when Hannah and the girls had come to visit Rev. C, Hannah put the girls to bed, and she and her father sat on the porch and shared a bowl of fruit. They made small talk, and then Hannah opened up and shared with her father the horrors she had been through with Ed. She had become so accustomed to keeping the sad details of her marriage secret that it felt good to finally talk about all that she had gone through. Rev. C's heart ached for his baby girl and all that she had endured. This was not what he had wanted for her. Hannah felt good to be safe and loved in the company of her father.

Rev. C helped Hannah get a part-time job, and Matt and Clay helped look after the girls while she worked. Hannah wanted to go back to school, but realized she had been through a lot. She had to withdraw from the college in Miami, because returning there was not yet an option. She needed professional help to sort through all of the emotions she was experiencing. Rev. C helped her get professional counseling to begin to put the pieces together.

Hannah's counselor helped reassure her that Ed's behavior was not her fault. She helped Hannah see that the weakness she had for Ed was tied to her feeling of disconnection after her mother passed away. Her father had not always been there for her as a child after her mother's death, and this led to feelings of abandonment. In her marriage, Hannah had tried to create a world where she felt someone was responsible for her well-being, that she felt was lacking growing up. Those words set Hannah free to begin to find her place in the world.

Several months after Hannah returned home, Ed began to call and say he missed the girls and that he wanted her to come back home. Rev. C was angry about Ed's calls and pleaded with Hannah not to believe that Ed had changed. "Once an abuser, always an abuser," he told her. Ed spun a tale of how the Lord had been working on his heart, and that he had really changed. He wanted her to give him another chance to be the kind of husband and father he should be. Hannah's most recent memory of Ed was of her head laid open and bleeding, but she also remembered how sweet, kind and loving he could be, and she was lonely. Hannah took into consideration that Ed said he had found a girlfriend, but that she meant nothing to him. Hannah was who he wanted in his life. Hannah processed the information, and filed separation papers that mandated Ed pay child support.

Ed made sure he paid his child support and talked to the girls each night. They missed their father. Ed continued to call and tell Hannah how much he loved and missed her. *The real question now was, did she miss him?* She had experienced some peace during the last few months away from him, and she enjoyed the healing and peace of mind. Hannah told Ed she needed time to think about returning to Miami, so Ed flew to Baltimore to see them for a few days. Hannah saw how much the girls missed their dad, and she considered returning to Miami, for their sake.

After a year of being away from Ed and his control, she had learned to survive on her own, and realized how strong and smart she really was. Being a single parent was not easy, but it felt good to be able to hold her own. Most of all, she had learned to put God first, instead of Ed. She knew if she went back to Ed, and he started with his old ways, she could leave him and survive. Ed called daily, and finally, Hannah agreed to go back to Miami. She took a leave of absence from her job instead of quitting, in case things did not work out. Rev. C begged her not to trust Ed, and feared that Ed had planned to kill Hannah and he wouldn't be there to protect her.

Hannah assured her father that this reconciliation would be different from the others—it would be on her terms. She made Ed understand that she would not tolerate any more fighting, and that if she felt uncomfortable with his behavior, she would leave and never come back. She would also stay in her own place before moving in with him. Ed was elated to have Hannah and the girls back in his life and agreed to her terms, and even agreed to help her with the first and last months' rent. Ed flew to Baltimore, packed up the car, and drove his family back to Miami. *A new beginning?* After Hannah and the girls drove off with Ed, Rev. C cried and prayed for his child. He felt he could help the people in his congregation but was helpless to help his own child.

When they arrived in Miami, Ed informed Hannah that he did not have the money for her apartment, and that she and the girls would have to stay with him until he could get the money together. She had trusted him to keep his end of the bargain, and he had already started to act like his old self. She and the girls had nowhere else to go, so they had to stay with him. The money for the apartment rent never came.

There was a difference in Hannah this time. She had gotten a taste of independence, and she liked that feeling. She wanted her own money, so she went job hunting. She was a fast learner and had no trouble securing a job at a hospital. She began saving for her own apartment.

Hannah was determined to never have to rely on Ed for food or shelter again. Hannah re-enrolled in the University of Miami, and this time, they offered her an academic scholarship because of the grades she had previously made. The scholarship money was enough to cover her tuition and books, and there was even some left over for living expenses. She and the girls had their own apartment, but would occasionally stay with Ed. Hannah was not ready to move in with him totally, and she was not going to blow her chance at medical school again. She was a star student, making all A's, and she had offers for scholarships to attend medical school when she completed her undergraduate work.

For about eight or nine months, Ed did well with his temper. He kept the arguments to a minimum. Hannah could now disconnect herself from him easily and go to her own place when she felt uncomfortable. She found out that he started back seeing his girlfriend again, and was determined not to put herself through that again. She confronted Ed about the girlfriend, and the arguments started. This time, though, Hannah didn't wait for the hitting and slapping to begin. She gathered the girls, left Ed's apartment, and went to her apartment. Ed followed her in his car, forced her to pull over, and tried to force her into his car. For the first time, Hannah fought back! Ed had never seen this Hannah before. A passerby witnessed the incident and called the police, and Ed left the scene before the police arrived. Hannah went to her apartment and stayed up all night watching over her girls, vowing to protect them to the death.

Hannah now had her own money and her own place where she called the shots. Times were tight, raising two growing girls on her own, but she was now living life on her terms. She remembered her talk with God, promising to always put Him first in her life. God was removing the blinders from her eyes and showing her who she really was, the way He saw her—gifted and blessed, the very things Ed had not honored.

Hannah called Ed and told him that after 12 years of marriage, she wanted a divorce. He threatened to take the girls away from her if she divorced him. He knew Hannah did not have the money she needed to fight for custody of her children. Ed continued to call and harass her, threatening to take her girls away if she did not come back to him. He would even come to pick up the girls, and threaten to hit or harm her if she didn't come home to him. With every abusive word, Hannah got stronger, and her weakness for Ed decreased. He even spent the night occasionally, but her desire for him was gone, because he was no longer first in her life. She had begun to see him for who he really was.

Ed came over one Saturday evening and spent the night. The next morning, he got up to go to church, and never came back. He left a note on the bedside table saying he wanted the divorce too. He later called with threats to take the girls from her in the divorce. Hannah just wanted the whole thing behind her, but she didn't have the money it would take to fight him. She remembered God's promise to be there for her, and she went into prayer mode.

Hannah's biology professor could see that she was troubled, and he called her into his office to see what was wrong. She confided in him about her 12 years of being in an abusive marriage, and about wanting a divorce and custody of her children. She shared that Ed was going to fight her for the girls. Her professor did not hesitate to get on the phone with an attorney he knew who handled high-profile divorces. He personally gave the attorney a large sum to fight her case. Hannah was speechless! This man who hardly knew her was willing to do this for her. That was nobody but God.

Hannah's professor confided in her that he had lost his daughter years ago due to an abusive relationship that she had been in; her boyfriend had beaten her to death and had hid the body. Years passed before she was found. He had always promised that if the opportunity ever availed itself, he would help another woman get out of a violent relationship. Hannah was touched by his kindness and could not thank him enough.

The attorney worked swiftly on her behalf and asked Hannah if she was willing to give up child support for her freedom and custody of her children. The attorney informed her that the law required her to ask for child support, but they would only ask the minimum. Ed was now jobless and broke, so Hannah only requested the bare minimum amount of child support. She just wanted out.

When Ed got the agreement, he called to threaten her. If he did not get custody of the girls, he would come over and beat her face in! Hannah had had enough of his threats. She slammed her hand down, and for the first time she challenged him, saying, "Bring your ass over! Come on, right now! I'm not afraid of you anymore. You have pulled guns on me, cut me, beat me, humiliated me—what else could you do to me that you haven't done before? Kill me? Bring it on! One of us is going to leave here dead! BRING...IT...ON!" Ed did not come. The next day, Ed signed the papers. Sixty days later, the divorce was final—12 years of marriage was over.

Hannah was no longer the First Lady, and she was all right with that. God was now first in her life, and He had made all of the crooked places in her life straight. God had blessed her with intelligence, and now she had confidence. She continued in school and excelled, finishing her undergraduate degree in three years with a 4.0 GPA Summa Cum Laude.

Rev. C retired and became a frequent visitor to see his grandchildren. Matt and Clay were finishing high school and getting ready for college. After college, Hannah applied for Harvard medical school, and was accepted! She had been restored to her destiny at the school where she had started. Rev. C now had his family back. Hannah thrived in school and on her own. Medical school residency was four long years, but Hannah graduated and eventually became one of the leading oncologists on the East Coast. Hannah learned how God can restore and heal when you put Him first. God is merciful, and later blessed Hannah with a loving, supportive husband.

When asked what her message would be to other First Ladies or pastors' wives, Hannah said, "First Ladies feel as if they can't be transparent or tell others that they are hurting. They have the burden of the members of the church being hurt, the ministry being hurt, and souls being lost if they come forth about their own personal situations. There is no recovery system in place just for women in these situations. There should be resources for women in all situations who are trying to escape that will help them reach safety and start over. If you are being hurt in your relationship, get out! You cannot minister to anyone if you are not around. God *will* take care of you. Just put Him first."

Reflection of Hannah's Story

By Pastor Brenda Carradine

"To console those who mourn in Zion, to give them beauty for ashes, the oil of joy for mourning, the garment of praise for the spirit of heaviness; that they may be called trees of righteousness, the planting of the Lord, that He may be glorified."Isaiah 61:3

In spite of the many difficulties we face in life, God defines us as the daughters of Zion and the plantings of the Lord. The burden of managing "titles of notability" often complicates our sense of self-perception. Nevertheless, the principles our parents and elders taught us as little children challenge us to err on the side of righteousness.

Hannah, the First Lady, was overwhelmed by a dangerous kind of love as words of condemnation and shame trapped her behind a wall of silence. However, the day came when Hannah no longer allowed abusive circumstances to impede her need for true love and security. The church, in all its pomp and formality, could not protect her from the attacks that haunted her in the night. She had to look within herself for the dignity and significance she once found in her relationship with God. The fear and uncertainty that once guided her decisions now give way to joy and peace. For the Lord has declared, through the pain and the tears, that enough is enough!

Hannah, "Lift up your head, and see the power of your worth." You are fearfully and wonderfully made, and no trophy or title can define your wealth. God has turned your mourning into dancing, and given you beauty for ashes.

"Carolyn"

Story by J. Harris

Reflection by Min. Neisha Strambler-Butler

To look into Carolyn's pleasant face and see the light in her eyes, you would never dream of the tragedies her eyes have seen. It almost makes you wonder if you are being deceived. But deceptive, she is not. She tells her story with ease, because she is sure that the Lord sustained her through it all. Carolyn's story tells of how negative and harmful generational spirits can be transferred from one generation to another if they are not confronted. If you do not recognize those spirits, you will continue to walk in them, generation after generation, suffering the same sorrow as your ancestors. Telling her story and recognizing those spirits led to Carolyn's deliverance.

Carolyn's beginning was much like many Southern black families in America, taking a little and making just enough. She was born in the Texas Panhandle. Her mother, Velma, her stepfather, James, and her four siblings moved to Dallas, Texas, when she was two years old. Perhaps they were in search of a better life from their dusty existence, or maybe Carolyn's mother saw Dallas as the "promised land" for herself and for her family.

Velma had come from a large family and was the oldest of twelve children. Velma was running from some destructive spirits, but she did not realize that wherever you go, you must take yourself and all of your baggage with you. Carolyn later found out that Velma's father had worked her and her siblings like farm hands in the cotton fields and demanded that the cotton be free from trash and dirt. If their work did not meet his expectations, he would pull up cotton stalks and use them to beat his children fiercely. Velma suffered from asthma and often had asthma attacks from the cotton dust, but her father was unsympathetic toward her condition, and would beat her for passing out from her asthma attacks. Velma became silent and distant whenever she was asked to share more of her past. Carolyn also discovered that Velma was raped as a young child, but had been too afraid to tell anyone.

Velma was so anxious to leave her father's house that she went to another violent man, Carolyn's father, who once beat Velma so severely that she miscarried. Velma never received any counseling or therapy for the trials she endured, so she just suffered through it, internalized it, and then passed it on. The era Velma came from did not understand or believe in therapy, and in most black communities, it was an unwritten rule at the time that if you had a problem, you worked it out in the privacy of your home, or prayed it out yourself. As a result, Velma's emotions were bottled up and later expressed in the relationships closest to her—her children. She believed that only "crazy" people went to the "head doctors."

The move to Dallas proved to be anything but promising for young Carolyn and her siblings. Her stepfather was kind to them and loved them as if they were his own. Velma had always worked hard at various jobs. She worked as seamstress, housekeeper or nanny, doing what she could to make sure her family had the best she could offer, but Velma seemed to break under the strain of moving and adapting to a new environment.

She began to drink heavily. She worked steadily through the week, but on the weekends, the peaceful household would turn into turmoil. When Velma was drunk, no one was spared from her violent rages—not even her husband, James. No matter how violently Velma attacked him, James never struck Velma back, and peace only came when she passed out. It hurt Carolyn to see her stepfather treated so cruelly.

James did everything he could to make Velma happy. He even had a nice three-bedroom home built for her in the Oak Cliff section of Dallas. Surely, a new home should make any woman happy, and after they moved into their new home, Velma seemed to be at peace and she stopped drinking. However, this peace only lasted a few months, and Velma began drinking on the weekends again, and the arguments, beatings, and fighting resumed. As time wore on, James could no longer tolerate Velma's violent behavior, and he left the family. Carolyn was crushed, because the one stable and safe part of her life was gone.

After James left, the family's condition went downhill quickly. Velma began drinking more, and she began to abuse Carolyn's oldest sister, beating the girl for no apparent reason other than that she was available. Carolyn and her other siblings dared not intervene out of fear of becoming part of the whipping party. When her older sister could no longer tolerate the treatment, she went off to Job Corp, and Velma started to beat the next oldest child, until she too became old enough to go to Job Corp and left.

With Carolyn's two older sisters gone, Carolyn knew she was next in line for Velma's abuse. To avoid being beaten, Carolyn would often hide in the closet on weekends with her younger sister and brother, until her mother either sobered up or passed out from drinking. Carolyn could hear Velma's drunken voice calling for her. She knew that a whipping was waiting for her. Carolyn would often remain in the closet from Friday night until Sunday night, when Velma would finally pass out, and then she'd come out to find food.

To escape the madness, Carolyn would occasionally slip out of the house to visit a church in the neighborhood. She loved going to church and seeing the people there having a good time and enjoying themselves, and it helped her to forget what was waiting for her at home. If Velma found out she had been to church with "those crazy people," she would receive a severe beating. This did not keep Carolyn from remembering what she had heard, seen, and felt at church. The family moved several times after James left, each time to a smaller place, and Velma's drinking becoming worse.

Velma made Carolyn drop out of junior high at age 14 to take care of her four- and five-year-old sister and brother, because she said she could not afford a babysitter for them. The school's truant officers would come by and ask her why she was not in school, and all she could say was that she had to take care of her sister and brother. After a while, they stopped coming by or caring. Carolyn wanted to go to school with her friends and felt trapped with the responsibility of caring for her siblings, but she did not want to leave her sister and brother at home alone. Often, there was no food in the house to eat, and when they did eat, it was only once a day. They survived mainly on peanut butter and jelly sandwiches or stale chips. Velma had one boyfriend after another in her life who used her for her money. They would wait until she passed out from drinking, and then take the money out of her purse.

Carolyn recalled one boyfriend who was around longer than the others. She described him as "The Devil Himself." When Velma was drunk, he would try to fondle

Carolyn and her younger sister, but they would fight him off. He would give Carolyn his sneaky laugh and say, "I'll get you next time; just wait." When Carolyn and her sister told Velma, their protector, she did not believe them. He would be in the background loudly proclaiming his innocence. "The Devil Himself" openly demanded money from Velma for marijuana and other pleasures, leaving next to nothing for the children. Carolyn's baby brother attempted to fight him whenever he saw the man approach his sisters, only to get slapped around by the man.

One day when Carolyn was running errands, the boyfriend succeeded in his advances and molested Carolyn's baby sister, but the child was too afraid to tell anyone. A few days after the incident, Carolyn noticed that her sister was walking with her legs far apart, and she had a bad body odor. When Velma was not home, Carolyn took her sister down the street to a neighbor she had befriended and asked her to examine the girl. The neighbor saw that the child needed medical attention and recommended that Carolyn have Velma take her to the emergency room. When Velma came home from work, Carolyn told her what had happened to her sister, and what the neighbor recommended.

After cursing the woman out, Velma finally took the child to the emergency room, where it was discovered that she had been sexually molested and had contracted syphilis and gonorrhea. They treated her for the diseases, but Carolyn never knew if justice was served against the molester. After the hospital visit, Velma came home and cursed out "The Devil Himself" and made him move out. Carolyn and her siblings were relieved, but in his place would soon come another character just as sly. The children were always in harm's way.

Carolyn had a lot of responsibility for such a young girl, caring for herself and her brother and sister. She had to wash their clothes by hand in the sink, and prepare what food she could find for their once-a-day meal. There never seemed to be enough food because of Velma's drinking and giving money to her men friends. Carolyn and the children used laundry soap to bathe with, because there was nothing else available. If the house was not spotless when Velma came home, Carolyn would be blamed and whipped. Carolyn had no life of her own.

Carolyn became very good at braiding her sister's hair, and people in the neighborhood began to pay her to do their hair. She would hide the money from Velma and use it for food for herself and her siblings. One day during the summer when Carolyn was 15 years old, she agreed to braid a young man's hair who lived in the neighborhood. Velma was at work, and her sister and brother were away from home visiting friends. She had braided his hair before. He lived on her street, and had not given her any reason to be afraid of him, but this time he brought two of his friends with him. Carolyn knew them from the neighborhood too, and they had always been nice to her.

On this day, the boys had plans that included more than hair braiding. The boy who was having his hair braided began to make sexual suggestions toward Carolyn, and Carolyn politely declined his advances, saying she was not interested. He continued to pressure her about having sex with him, but she stood her ground. Suddenly, his mood changed and he grabbed her arms, threw her to the floor, and began to tear her clothes off. She fought back, but the other two boys joined him and held her down. She fought with all she had for her dignity and her body, but the more she fought, the more they beat her. Each of the boys took turns raping her as the other two held her down. She cried and screamed for them to stop, but her pleas fell into the hot summer air. She heard them laughing as they held her down and raped her. They treated her like she had no feelings. When they were through, they left her on the floor in a heap of bloody shame and despair. Their last words were, "If you tell anybody, we will kill you!"

A million things raced through Carolyn's mind as she lay on the hard floor, beaten, bruised, and bloody. *Was this her fault? Why wasn't she more careful? Was it something she said that made them think she wanted to have sex with them? What would Velma say?* Her whole life had been changed in just a few moments. Her virginity had been taken, and there was nothing she could do about it. Carolyn had wanted to wait until she was married to have sex, and now that choice was taken away. She had taken pride in being a virgin, and now that was ruined.

Carolyn was still fighting the air after the boys left. She could not stop crying. She became aware of the pain her body was in when she saw her bruised, bloody and swollen private parts. Her clothes were torn and bloody, and she knew she had to get some help. Her mother was not an option. She remembered the neighbor who had helped her sister, so she decided to go to her. She did not care about the death threats from the boy because she felt dead already. She could not think clearly enough to worry about her clothes or her appearance; she just wanted the pain and bleeding to stop.

She wrapped herself in her robe, walked barefoot to her neighbor's house, and told her what had happened. The woman immediately put her into the car and took her to the emergency room. The hospital contacted Velma at work to get permission to examine Carolyn, and she consented, but did not come to the hospital until later. To collect evidence, Carolyn had to undergo further humiliation and pain by having her private parts examined and photographed by strangers at the hospital. The hospital staff was very kind to her during the examination and explained that they were collecting evidence against the boys who had attacked her. Carolyn wept silently as they did their job, and her neighbor stayed with her and held her hand.

When Velma eventually arrived at the hospital, she did not even bother to thank the neighbor for helping her daughter, and instead accused the woman of meddling in her business. Velma was furious with Carolyn for letting this happen to her, and blamed her for letting the boys into the house when she was not home. Carolyn pleaded with Velma that these were kids from the neighborhood who had come before to get their hair braided, and that she had done nothing to provoke them.

Velma refused to see Carolyn's point of view and continued to blame her for what had happened to her. To add insult to an already sad condition, Velma called her names like "whore" and "slut." Carolyn was devastated and felt so alone. With much persuasion from the hospital social worker, Velma finally agreed to file charges against the boys on Carolyn's behalf. The hospital social worker assisted them in filling out the paperwork and in filing aggravated rape charges. Carolyn had to relive the entire rape by telling the social worker and lawyer what happened. Velma listened, but still would not support Carolyn. At home, Velma continued to call Carolyn names and to tell her it was her fault. Carolyn was crushed by her mother's lack of compassion and the fact that she did not believe her.

During the trial, Carolyn had to meet her attackers face to face again, and had to again recall those dreadful moments of the rape in front of the world. The testifying was almost as humiliating as the rape. Carolyn was asked very explicit details about the rape by the attorneys. They used words that she felt offensive, like "penis" and "vagina." At the end of the trial, each one of the boys was found guilty and sentenced to eight to nine years in prison. The scars and results of the rape would be lifelong, but at least some form of justice had been served. Carolyn was proud she had stood up to her attackers.

A few months after the rape, Carolyn noticed that she was gaining weight and was not able to keep her food down in the mornings, but dismissed it as a virus. About four months later, she began to feel movement in her swollen belly. She did not know why her body was changing, and again sought help from her neighbor about the matter. The neighbor took her to a clinic in the neighborhood, and Carolyn was informed she was going to be a mother! She was stunned and had no idea what was involved in pregnancy and in giving birth. She understood that the life she was carrying was innocent, and that she needed to protect that innocence. She knew what it was like to not be protected and cared for. The next horrifying step would be to tell her mother.

When Carolyn got home, she told Velma about the clinic visit and about the pregnancy. She wanted and needed her mother's support, but instead Velma hit the roof! She told Carolyn that her pregnancy was not her problem. She vowed she was not going to take care of her and some "rape baby." Velma remained true to her word. She refused to buy Carolyn maternity clothes, and did not care if she ate or not. She treated her as if she did not exist.

The isolation and verbal assaults from Velma were almost too much to bear. All Carolyn could do to console herself was to recall the songs she had heard in church, and how they sang of God being a good God in times of trouble. *Would this wonderful God be her God after what happened to her?* She would eat what was left over after her brother and sister ate. The neighbor would occasionally offer her a meal. Carolyn had no maternity clothes and had to try and cover her large belly with her too-small clothes. Velma did not even seek prenatal care for Carolyn.

When Carolyn's labor pains started, she was frightened, and afraid to tell Velma. She was not sure what labor was and what to expect, so she went to her neighbor and told her that she was having stomach cramps. Her neighbor told her she was in labor and drove her to the hospital. The entire labor and birthing experience was foreign, painful, and frightening to her. This was a time when a girl really needed her mother. Instead, when the neighbor called Velma, she refused to come to the hospital. Once again, the neighbor stayed with Carolyn and held her hand through the pain.

Carolyn had never experienced pain like this, and she was afraid she was dying. She kept calling on the Lord to help her. When she finally saw the face of her beautiful son, the pain, the rape, and the humiliation no longer mattered. He was so tiny and helpless, and he was the most beautiful baby she had ever seen! She could not believe that her body had created this wonderful creature. She chose to name him Adam, from the Bible. Adam was innocent, and in her heart Carolyn resolved to be the best mother in the world. Unlike how Velma had been toward her, she wanted to protect Adam from all of the hurt and pain in life. As she rocked Adam's small, warm body in her arms, she prayed to God to make something good come out of this painful situation. Velma never visited Carolyn while she was in the hospital.

The nurses at the hospital taught Carolyn how to care for Adam, and gave her the basic supplies that they give to all new mothers. Carolyn's neighbor picked her and Adam up from the hospital and took them to Velma's house. Returning home from the hospital with her beautiful infant son was a lonely experience. Velma refused to help Carolyn care for the baby, and she would not buy milk or diapers for the baby. She referred to Carolyn's baby, her grandchild, as "the rape baby," and she still insisted that Carolyn babysit her sister and brother. Carolyn blocked out the names Velma called her son, and she saw Adam as her baby boy who she dearly loved. He did not have a choice about how he entered this world, but God had given him to her, and she would give her life to protect and care for him. Carolyn would occasionally take Adam to the neighbor for help, and the neighbor gave her diapers and instructions about how to care for him, bathe him, and love him.

Carolyn tore up old sheets to use as diapers when she ran out of the disposable diapers. When she took Adam in for their follow-up visit, a social worker at the clinic helped her to sign up for WIC *(Women, Infants, and Children program)*. This allowed her to get milk, cheese, cereal and other necessities for herself and Adam. WIC was like an answered prayer, and Carolyn was overjoyed to receive the much-needed help. She and her sister and brother celebrated moving up from peanut butter sandwiches to cheese sandwiches, milk, and cereal. Steak and potatoes could not have been more welcomed.

Being shoeless in the summer in Dallas can be cruel, but that is how Carolyn found herself. Velma's withdrawal from her position as mother and provider meant that she would no longer buy Carolyn shoes, clothing, or anything else that she needed. Carolyn had outgrown her last pair of shoes and had none to replace them. Occasionally her brother would pass on a pair of sneakers that were too small for him, and she would wear those for a while.

Carolyn loved Adam dearly, but she was just not able to provide for him. When Adam was five months old, the only clothes she had for him were the same newborn t-shirts and receiving blankets that he came home from the hospital in, and she had no money to buy him any other clothes. She washed his little wardrobe with her hands to keep it clean, and carried him with her wherever she went. Another neighbor noticed her walking the streets each day with no shoes on and with the baby in her arms, and asked her if she had any shoes. When Carolyn said no, the neighbor gave her some used shoes she had that were her size. When Velma saw Carolyn with the shoes, she asked her where she had gotten them. Velma went to the neighbor's house and cursed the woman out for getting involved in her family's business. Carolyn was so grateful to get her feet off the hot concrete that Velma's rage did not matter.

On one of her walks with Adam, Carolyn walked by the Boy's and Girl's Club, and was delighted at what she saw. There were teens her age having fun, laughing and enjoying life. She wanted so badly to be in a place where people laughed and were happy, instead of living in constant arguing and chaos. When Carolyn asked Velma if she could become a member of the club, along with her younger brother and sister, Velma scolded her and screamed, "No!" Carolyn pleaded with Velma that the club would be a way for the kids to get out of the house and be with other kids their age, and that it was free. Velma cursed her, and still said, "Hell no!" Carolyn was only looking for some form of joy in their lives.

Carolyn continued to take her walks by the club, stopping to look in, but could not be part of the activities. The social worker at the club saw Carolyn looking in one day with Adam in her arms, and asked her if she got a check for the baby. *(She probably noted the shabby condition they were in.)* Carolyn told her she did not know anything like that existed, so the social worker invited her in and assisted her in signing up for Welfare Assistance. Carolyn could not believe that this help had been available to her all along, and Velma had not bothered to tell her. Through tears, she thanked the social worker over and over for her help.

Carolyn watched for the mail daily to intercept the check before Velma saw it. When the check came, she hurried to cash her $65 check at the nearby corner store. They told her that with the next check, she would have to have a social security card. She had never obtained a social security card and did not know how to get one, so she went back to the social worker and got help obtaining cards for herself and for Adam. She spent her first check buying clothes, diapers, food and shoes. She was so proud that she was finally able to provide something for him. When Velma saw the new things and found out about the check, she demanded Carolyn give her over half of the check each month to cover her living expenses; lights, water and shelter for herself and Adam. After Velma's cut, this left Carolyn with only about $20 to $25 a month. And, if it wasn't bad enough that Velma took her money, Carolyn had to watch Velma give that money to one of her current boyfriends while Carolyn looked on.

Carolyn loved Adam with all of her heart, and she wanted him to have a better life than she had, so she saved every penny she could to devote to him and his well-being. One day, Velma delivered the most devastating blow yet when she said, "You and your baby have to get out of my house. I can't take care of ya'll anymore." Carolyn cried, "WHY?" Velma stated that her current boyfriend did not want to take care of Carolyn and Adam along with Velma's children too. He had given Velma a choice between him and the money he was giving her, or Carolyn and her baby. Velma chose him. Carolyn begged and pleaded with her mother to reconsider, and promised to get a job to help out. She was willing to do whatever it took to keep a roof over her baby's head. Velma told her that she did not have any choice, because she needed the help that her boyfriend was giving her. With a straight, cool face, Velma told Carolyn that she and Adam would have to find somewhere else to live.

Sixteen years old, a new mother, and alone and confused, Carolyn sought help from the one person in the community who was known for helping other people, a woman named Ms. Amy. Ms. Amy was a beacon of light and had children of her own, but was known for being a loving person who would help anyone in need. Carolyn gathered her and Adam's few belongings, went to Ms. Amy's, and explained her situation, and asked if she and Adam could stay with her for a while until she could get on her feet. Ms. Amy immediately said they were welcome to stay as long as they needed to stay, at no charge. Carolyn thanked God for providing her and her baby a place to stay.

At the time, Carolyn had no idea that being evicted by Velma was really a blessing. Ms. Amy prepared a room for them and took the time to teach Carolyn how to care for Adam properly. She made sure they had good food and clothing. For the first time since Adam was born, Carolyn felt like a real mother. Velma found out where Carolyn was staying and came to Ms. Amy's home, accusing Ms. Amy of meddling in her business. Velma proceeded to give Ms. Amy pointers on how she thought her daughter should be raised, but did not invite Carolyn to come back home with her. Ms. Amy let Velma have her say, and continued to care for Carolyn and Adam.

The thing Carolyn appreciated most about living at Ms. Amy's was going to church. She joined the church and was baptized, and Adam was also dedicated to God in front of a crowd of witnesses. At church, Carolyn and Adam were able to be among people who were positive and accepting. She would later find that her relationship with God would carry her further than any welfare check or man ever could. She and Adam stayed with Ms. Amy for nine wonderful months, and Ms. Amy cared for Carolyn as if she was her own daughter. Carolyn wanted to go back to school, but she was too old and had fallen too far behind to attend junior high classes. She knew she needed to get her GED after she got on her feet, but it was just a matter of time and opportunity.

During the time of her stay with Ms. Amy, Carolyn met a young man named Terry who was a friend of one of Ms. Amy's sons. Terry liked Carolyn a lot, and she liked him, but Carolyn knew that at the age of 17, and in her unstable condition, she was not ready for a serious relationship. She did want to get married someday and to provide Adam with a good father and a loving home environment, but she did not want him to grow up in a home filled with fear, violence, and hatred. She knew that Adam's circumstances were special, and that it would take a special man to accept the two of them. When Terry came by, he bonded well with Adam, and this made Carolyn like him more. He took special interest in her and helped her apply for and get her first job at a fast food restaurant. She was so proud to be making money and taking care of Adam, and that she was able to give Ms. Amy money for babysitting while she worked. Her minimum wage job was like a gold mine to Carolyn.

Terry and Carolyn started to date under the watchful eye of Ms. Amy. Carolyn occasionally snuck home to visit her brother and sister when Velma was at work. She often found them with little or no food in the house, no clean clothes to wear, and living in a mess. She brought them food or prepared a good meal, washed their clothes and gave them baths, knowing she had to be gone before Velma got home. She had taken care of them for so long that they referred to her as "Mama."

After the nine-month stay with Ms. Amy, Carolyn moved in with her older sister, who had returned from the Job Corp. She was sad to leave Ms. Amy, but she knew she had to work toward moving out on her own. She had learned some valuable lessons from Ms. Amy about how to be a good mother and a good woman. Carolyn and Terry continued to date for about two years before the relationship became more serious and began to involve sex. Carolyn appreciated the fact that she was able to choose to have sex this time. She had shared things about her past with Terry, and he was very patient with her.

Carolyn became pregnant with her second child, and when Velma found out that she was pregnant again, she came to the sister's house and gave Carolyn, Terry, and her sister a good cursing out, but still did not offer to take Carolyn back because Velma's boyfriend still did not want her there. Carolyn cried many nights with the pain of her own mother choosing a man over her own daughter and grandchild.

With the birth of another child, Carolyn wanted to be married, but the relationship was not holding up. Terry was there for the birth of their daughter, Maya, and was very supportive, but they began to grow apart and went their separate ways. Carolyn's sister helped her to care for the new family addition while Carolyn continued to work at the restaurant to make sure Adam and Maya had what they needed. On her off days, she would take the children to the park and to church, because she wanted them to be around positive people and activities involving other children. She still went by to check on her sister and brother and bring them food, as Velma was still drinking and not caring for the children. Carolyn feared for their safety but was not in a position to help, other that coming by occasionally.

About a year after Maya was born, the postman in the neighborhood, Darren, noticed Carolyn and began stopping by to see her. He was ten years older than Carolyn, very polite, and would always ask her sister for permission to visit. Carolyn went to Ms. Amy and asked her advice about dating an older man. Ms. Amy knew Darren and felt that Carolyn dating a more mature man would be good for her. Darren did not approach her with the proposition of sex, and was genuinely interested in her and her children. He brought Carolyn food and anything else she and the children needed, took them out to eat at nice restaurants, taught her how to drive, and helped her get her driver's license. Carolyn saw in him the qualities a husband should have, and because Darren was older and more experienced, he taught her about life. He helped her get her first apartment, but he did not want to move in with her. She enjoyed his company, and the things he did for her and the children, so much that she wanted him in her life permanently. They discussed marriage, and Darren agreed that they would get married when the time was right.

Nine months into the relationship, Carolyn began feeling very lonely and isolated in her new apartment. It felt like she was living her life in isolation from love and affection. She convinced Darren to move in with her, and for the first time in her life she felt like she was part of a real, normal family. She cared for her children and Darren as if they were married, and she felt like a real

155

woman and mother. Darren loaned her his car to go and look after her brother and sister, but she would not invite him to meet Velma. She knew Velma's lifestyle and was afraid that Velma would be drunk, and that the house would be a mess if she took him there. She was embarrassed for him to know her mother lived like that.

Carolyn and Darren were together for two years before she took a chance and let him meet Velma. Finally, one evening when they were driving around, and after much provoking by Darren, she took him to see her mother. Just as she had expected, both Velma and the house were a disaster! Carolyn had to pick things up off the floor and out of chairs to find Darren a place to sit. The same mean boyfriend who had kicked Carolyn out was still there, and showed his displeasure at Carolyn and Darren's visit by slamming doors and going into the back room without speaking. Velma shook Darren's hand but did not say much. She almost seemed jealous to see how well Darren had taken care of Carolyn. Carolyn kept the visit short, and Darren never questioned her about visiting her mother again. Velma found out where Carolyn lived and occasionally came to visit. During her initial visit she gave Darren a good cussing for being older and for living with her daughter, but Velma still did not ask Carolyn to return home. Carolyn and Darren eventually learned to ignore Velma's outburst.

Carolyn and Darren's relationship lasted 11 and a half years. During that time they had two additional sons, Isaac and Marcus, but still no wedding. Carolyn had finished cosmetology school and worked for a salon in the mall, and because Darren was a good provider, she only worked when she wanted to. Life was good. While cleaning the house one day, Carolyn found an empty syringe with a needle and had no idea what to make of it so, when Darren got home from work, she confronted him about it. She asked him if he was on some type of medication. She was concerned that he might be ill and keeping it from her. He told her he was on a medication of sorts, but after further questioning, he finally admitted that his "medication" was heroin.

Carolyn was very naive and had never heard of heroin, so she asked him what it was. He told her it was an addictive drug, and that he had to have it or else he would have the shakes. When he said that, she recalled him occasionally going into states of chills and tremors, but she thought he was coming down with a cold or something. Darren always kept a big bowl of candy at the house, which was for the sugar cravings caused by the drug. *(She had thought that the candy was for the children)*. When he educated her on the fine points of heroin and the use of it, she was shocked and felt very foolish. He said he had been using heroin long before they had met, and he had managed to keep it a secret from her all the years they were together.

This new revelation about Darren made Carolyn do some serious thinking about their relationship. As much as she loved him, Carolyn decided that Darren was not the man for her, because she did not want any type of drugs around her children. She immediately broke off the relationship. Darren sincerely apologized for not being up front with her about his drug use, but he was not yet ready to quit. Carolyn and her children moved out and went back to live with her sister. She found herself sad and lonely again, but knowing that her children would not be around drugs was enough comfort. She now had her cosmetology skills and would be able to feed her growing family. She still longed to be a wife and have a normal family, but it never seemed to work out for her.

There were many times that Carolyn wondered how she could have been so blind to Darren's addiction. *Was she so desperate to have a normal life that she overlooked his problem?* Carolyn decided to give relationships a break and instead concentrate on working and raising her children. She was appreciative that Darren had raised her standard of living, and she wanted to maintain that for her children. She only wanted the best, but earning minimum wage and feeding four growing children did not always add up, so she would have to live with her sister until she could get enough money saved to move out on her own.

About a year after leaving Darren, Carolyn became acquainted with a gentleman named Mack who came to the salon to get his hair cut when he was in town. He would only let Carolyn cut his hair. He told her about his job driving trucks nationwide, and how he was a deacon at his church in East Texas. The company he worked for was based in East Texas, and he would occasionally come to Dallas and pick up loads. Having just gotten out of a painful relationship, Carolyn was not anxious to get into another one, but Mack did not hide his feelings for Carolyn and was persistent in asking her out on dates. She shared with him what she had recently been through with Darren, and he said he understood her reluctance to get into a new relationship. Carolyn was determined that the next man she became involved with would be her husband, and Mack was looking and acting like good husband material.

Carolyn and the children lived with her sister another six months, until she qualified for Section 8 housing and was able to get her own place. Mack visited regularly when he came to town and was becoming more serious about Carolyn becoming his wife. He seemed committed to being a good husband to her and a good father to her children. After about six months of being pursued, Carolyn felt she had finally gotten it right and said yes to Mack's proposal.

After she said yes, Mack told Carolyn he wanted them to get married in East Texas by his uncle, who was a minister there. He also wanted Carolyn and the children to move to East Texas with him. Carolyn was very reluctant to move away from her family, and had only met a few members of his family. When Mack had previously taken her to visit East Texas, she had briefly met his mother, but wanted to get to know her better if she was going to marry her son. Mack had explained that his mother was only 50 years old, but looked much older because she had become ill as a result of some poor lifestyle choices. She lived in a trailer house, and Mack seemed to be the only one of his siblings who took an interest in her care. The fact that Mack cared for his mother made Carolyn admire him even more.

Carolyn and Mack had a whirlwind marriage at the church in East Texas, with his uncle presiding over the ceremony, and he began moving her and the children's things from Dallas on the same day. Carolyn was shocked when she realized that Mack had not planned for them to move into their own place, but instead, with his mother. She did not like the living arrangements at all and voiced her displeasure to Mack, but his comment was, "You are my wife now, and a wife needs to follow her husband."

Carolyn soon discovered that Mack's mother was a bed-bound incontinent invalid who required total care, went to dialysis three times a week, and was losing her sight because of diabetes. Now it became clear to Carolyn why Mack always kept their visits to his mother brief, because he knew she was in such bad shape. Mack's sisters would not have anything to do with their mother because of the cruel way she had treated them as children during her years of alcohol and drug abuse. Mack had not really wanted to be responsible for his mother, but the check his mother received went to him, and the use of her trailer made it tolerable.

When Mack met and pursued Carolyn, he had already been devising a plan about how he would be relieved of the day-to-day care of his sick mother and still be able to keep her disability check. When Carolyn arrived at the trailer, she immediately became Mack's mother's primary caregiver. She felt angry and betrayed because she had fallen for Mack's deception. She not only had to care for her own children, but now she was responsible for this sick woman. *How did she not see this coming? Was she so desperate to have a husband that she had looked past all the warning signs?* She decided she would make the best of this sad situation, because she did not want to see Mack's mother suffer.

Carolyn had to totally take care of the woman by bathing her, changing her diapers, and transferring her from the chair to the bed as if caring for an infant. The woman had ruined her body due to years of constant drinking and drug use, and Carolyn could only imagine if this would one day be Velma's fate. Mack's mother eventually developed gangrene in one of her legs due to a diabetic foot ulcer that would not heal, and the leg had to be amputated. The woman craved clay dirt, and she made Carolyn go in the fields to dig the dirt, bring it home, and bake it for her to eat, to help control her constant diarrhea. Carolyn resented Mack and felt totally betrayed.

Mack, Carolyn, and the children attended the church where Mack's uncle was the pastor, and almost everyone who attended the church was related to Mack. His family did not approve of him marrying a woman with a "ready-made" family, and would often come to their house complaining and causing disturbances about how Mack's mother was being cared for; but none of them ever offered to care for her themselves. During all of this transition, Carolyn discovered an even darker side to Mack—he was extremely jealous, controlling, and manipulative. She found that the sweet, loving, kind man she had met and married would become her worst nightmare.

Carolyn needed an outlet from caring for her invalid mother-in-law, so she began directing the youth choir to feel part of something positive. Mack became very jealous of her being in front of the church with her legs visible. He made her lower the hem of her dresses all the way to the floor. Mack felt she was having too much fun being in front of people, patting her feet to the music while she directed. He forced her to resign from directing the youth choir. Carolyn hated the control he had over her, but she was trying to be an obedient wife. However, some of the things Mack was demanding were just wrong. Carolyn and the children were not allowed to buy new clothes, and the clothes they did have were from garage sales or thrift stores.

Mack often came home from work and, for no apparent reason, started arguments. Carolyn would try and ask what she had done to cause him to be so angry, but he could not give a reason. He would just begin hitting her or pushing her around when he was angry. Carolyn fought back, but he was stronger. *In the past Mack had been an amateur boxer and knew how to use his fists.* The kids hid in their rooms during the fights, which became more frequent, louder, and more violent. Mack's mother could not help because of her condition, so could only yell out, "Mack, stop it! What are you doing to that girl?" The fights were so bad that the kids would drop what they were doing, run to their rooms and close the doors when they heard Mack's car drive up to the house. Mack was so jealous and insecure that he would often accuse Carolyn of having another man. She would try to assure him that there was no one else in her life but him, but still Mack's accusations and abuse would go on for hours.

Carolyn never knew what mood he would be in when he got home. She was a nervous wreck. She began eat for comfort, and her weight increased from 150 to nearly 250 pounds. Some days Mack would come in cheerful and calm, but that was always short-lived. Something would come on the television, or the food would not be cooked to his liking; anything unexpected, and he would go off. Many times, it was the interference of Mack's family members that would start his screaming, accusing, cursing, and fighting with Carolyn, so she suggested that they move out of his mother's house and get their own place in the hopes that it might resolve the fighting, but Mack would not hear of it. His answer was, "This is my mother's place, and I can stay here as long as I want to."

Carolyn wanted out of the exhausting role of caring for her sick mother-in-law, and out of the marriage. Carolyn convinced Mack to allow her to get a job and arrange for a home care aide to come in and care for his mother. She was able to get a job in a hair salon nearby. She was very good at her job, and her employer and her customers liked the work she did, as evidenced by the big tips she would receive. She was so tired of the abuse from Mack and she wanted out, but she knew she would need enough money for bus tickets for herself and the children to get back to Dallas, so she hid her tip money between the mattresses. Mack made her deposit her paycheck into their joint checking account, and then would withdraw most of the money. Carolyn and Mack were constantly being threatened with eviction for not paying their rent on time. Mack would send Carolyn to negotiate partial payment of the rent with the landlord. She could not figure out what he was doing with the money, because he did not smoke, drink or use drugs, but most of the time they did not have enough food in the house because he had taken all the money from the account. Carolyn figured this was just another method to control her and keep her from leaving him.

Mack was so jealous that he would often sit all day at the salon, staring at Carolyn's customers and the other workers. This behavior went on for several weeks, until one day Carolyn's boss called her in and said that they liked her work, but that her husband's actions were making the customers and staff uncomfortable and they would have to let her go. This had been her one chance to earn enough money to get away from Mack, and he had ruined it for her. After being fired, Mack came to pick her up, and she confronted him in the parking lot about it being his fault that she had been fired. This caused a huge argument, and with everyone watching, Mack beat Carolyn up right there in the parking lot! She was so embarrassed and humiliated when she noticed that her former co-workers had seen the fight. She had tried to fight back, but Mack was too strong. Carolyn's former boss came to her rescue and offered to call the police, but Carolyn would not let him, fearing it would only make matters worse.

The next day, Carolyn went to the salon to apologize to the salon manager for the scene. Several of her co-workers offered to kick Mack's butt for her. She confided in the manager that her rent was two months behind, and she and her children were facing eviction, and that she really needed her job to support her family. What she did not tell him was that she had to hide her purse under her mattress to keep Mack from stealing her tips. Mack had even disallowed her to get the mail from the mail box, in case her family tried to send her money. If they did, Mack would intercept it and keep it. The salon manager gave her money for two month's rent, even though Carolyn begged him not to. He felt sorry for having to fire her, and he wanted to help her as much as he could. She could do nothing but thank him repeatedly through her tears.

After she had lost her job because of Mack, their arguments became more frequent, until one evening when they were having one of their typical arguments and she mentioned she wanted out of the marriage. Mack went wild and started pushing, hitting, and choking her. Her children watched in terror, and screamed at Mack to stop hitting their mother. He took a big swing and caught Carolyn on the chin, causing her to fall backwards and hit her head on the floor. She almost lost consciousness. When she tried to get up, he leaned over her and started punching her in the stomach with all of his power, and repeatedly kicked her in her back. With each blow, he reminded her that he would never allow her to leave him. He would kill her first.

Mack then did something he had never done before—he pulled a gun on her! She didn't even know he had a gun. He lifted her to her feet, stuck the gun against her side and told her, "Bitch, don't you know I will kill you before I will let you leave me?" Her children were helpless to defend her, and she was helpless to defend herself. She began praying to God in her spirit to stop Mack from killing her. She could not bear to think of her children witnessing her death and being motherless, with no one to care for them. All she could do was cry and beg him not to kill her. After about 30 minutes of watching Carolyn struggle and beg, Mack took the gun away from her side and continued to remind her that he would never let her go, never! He warned her that there was nowhere in this world she could go where he would not be able to find her.

Because of the beating she had suffered, Carolyn had constant back and jaw pain, but Mack would not allow her to go for medical attention. She felt trapped. In the days to follow, Carolyn slipped into an even deeper depression, and again her only comfort was eating and sleeping, with her weight increasing to over 300 pounds. She made sure her children were cared for and tried to be a good wife, but she was not able to please Mack. The slightest thing angered him, and the fighting would start over again.

One Christmas, Carolyn wanted the children to have some type of joy. She recalled how as a child living with her mother, they never had a Christmas tree, so she wanted her children to have one. She went to a Christmas tree lot and bought the cheapest tree she could find. It was a sad-looking little tree, but it was better than nothing, so she brought it home and let the children make little homemade ornaments out of things they had around the house. Mack came home, saw the tree and became furious. He yelled, "I don't want that mess in my house!" He tore the tree apart and threw it out in the yard. He did not allow the children to have Christmas gifts or Easter baskets. Mack had become a tyrant. He began demanding trivial things, such as Carolyn not being able to wear nail polish or makeup, and the children not being allowed to watch their favorite cartoons on television on Saturdays. Carolyn and the children were Mack's prisoners, and he enjoyed the fear and control he had over them.

Carolyn had been in East Texas for almost five years, and her children were growing up. Mack had made sure she was isolated and did not have any contact with her family in Dallas. She noticed a change in her 14-year-old, Maya, becoming very outspoken and argumentative. This was not her normal personality, but Carolyn chalked it up to her being a teenager. Maya and Mack began to get into arguments because Mack threatened to hit the boys, and Maya challenged him, and he backed down. When the arguments started between Mack and Maya, Carolyn would hear Maya say, "I'll tell, I'll tell!" Carolyn asked Maya what was it that she would tell about, and she would give Mack a quick glance and say, "Nothing." Carolyn would repeatedly ask her daughter to open up to her and tell her what was causing her to act out, but Maya would not give her an explanation.

One day, the argument between Mack and Maya escalated until Maya told Carolyn the secret was that Mack had touched her breast, and this made Carolyn furious! She didn't care if Mack attacked her. She needed answers, so she fearlessly confronted Mack about the issue, and he laughed it off as just an accidental brush against the girl's breast that Maya had blown out of proportion. Maya eventually agreed that maybe she had made too much of the incident, and Mack looked on in approval as Maya defended him. Carolyn urged Maya to let her know if anything inappropriate had happened to her, and that she could always come to her, so Maya agreed and her behavior problems seemed to improve after that encounter. Carolyn kept a sharp look out for anything inappropriate between Mack and Maya, because she remembered "The Devil Himself" molesting her sister. She would risk death to defend her child.

Several weeks after the "breast" incident, Mack came to Carolyn with much concern, and with his typical loud gestures, said that he thought Maya had been with a boy. He said, "I think that girl has gotten herself pregnant!" Carolyn was shocked! She knew all of her children's friends and had never noticed Maya having any particular interest in boys. She asked her sons if they had noticed any particular boys hanging around, and they said no. She confronted Maya, who began crying, saying that she could be pregnant. Carolyn became numb and could not believe that her baby could be pregnant. She thought she had been aware of her children's friends and those close to them. *How could she not have seen this coming?* She asked Maya who the father was, and Maya just withdrew and cried.

Carolyn took Maya to a doctor to have her examined, and it was confirmed that the 14-year-old was pregnant. Carolyn wanted to know who the father was because her daughter was under the age of consent to have sex, making this a criminal matter. Carolyn knew all too well the plight of a pregnant 14-year-old, remembering her own rape at the same age. She became sickened that the same thing could be happening to her daughter. Carolyn and Maya discussed abortion options with the doctor, but the abortion option was thrown out because Maya was too far along in her pregnancy for a safe abortion. She would have to go ahead and have the baby, and either keep the baby, or put it up for adoption.

Mack was insisting that Maya tell them who the father was. He wanted to approach the boy's parents and force them to take some responsibility for the baby. There was one young man at school who Maya sometimes had conversations with, as a friend, and Mack made her give him the boy's name. Mack flew off the handle and went to the school, found out what classroom the boy was in, and called the boy out in front of the class. He accused the boy of getting his step-daughter pregnant, and demanded that he be responsible for the baby. It was an extremely embarrassing moment for Maya and the boy, so Mack arranged a meeting with himself, Carolyn, Maya, the boy, and the boy's parents. At the meeting Mack was ranting about how the boy should be forced to take care of the baby and possibly go to jail, because Maya was underage. The boy kept repeating to his parents that he was not the father, and had not done anything wrong. The boy's parents were very apologetic for their son's possible actions and said that they would do the right thing to help care for the baby.

During the remaining months of the pregnancy, Carolyn was worried about how they would be able to care for the baby, since they were barely making it now, but she did not want her grandchild to be put up for adoption. Mack was still making the money disappear. Carolyn made sure Maya ate properly and went for prenatal care, but Mack and Maya were still getting into occasional arguments. Carolyn wanted to work, but knew it would only cause more fights with Mack, and lead to her to getting fired again.

When Maya was eight months pregnant, Carolyn noticed she was in pain and not feeling well, so Carolyn took her to the hospital and, after being examined, was told that Maya was in labor. The doctor informed Carolyn that Maya's blood pressure was dangerously elevated and this was going to be a very risky delivery. To complicate matters, Maya's water had broken earlier that day and she had not realized it, so the birth would have to be a painful dry birth. The doctor said their hospital was not equipped to handle such cases, and Maya would have to be taken to Dallas by helicopter for emergency delivery because her condition was life-threatening for her and the baby. Mack was out on the road in the truck and could not be reached. Carolyn was frantic at the possibility that her daughter could lose her life and begged the hospital staff to let her ride in the helicopter with her daughter. Their policy would not allow non-medical personnel to fly with them; she would have to drive.

Even though Carolyn had not spoken to Velma in the last few months, when she called to tell her about Maya, Velma seemed to actually miss her and asked what she could do to help. Carolyn was in a crisis and had no time for past feelings to get in the way. She needed her mother to meet her at the hospital. Carolyn hurriedly loaded the boys and a few things in the car, and also called her friend Deb to meet her at the hospital. Carolyn did not know that this crisis would be her escape from East Texas. God makes ways out of our painful circumstances as only He can. Carolyn drove as fast as the car would go without regard for her life, or the life of the children in the car. She was like a woman possessed. A highway patrolman stopped her because she was going over 100 mph. She explained the emergency to the officer, and showed him the paperwork that the hospital had given her. The officer called ahead to other patrolmen and told them she was coming through, and not to stop her. The officer begged her to slow down to avoid killing the other children in the car. She slowed to 100 mph, and the officer followed her all the way to Dallas with his warning lights on.

The two-hour drive took only an hour and fifteen minutes. The patrolman later told her that he followed her to keep her from hurting herself and others on the highway. All Carolyn could think about was that her child needed her and could lose her life. When Carolyn arrived at the hospital, Velma and Deb were waiting there, and the doctors had taken Maya into the delivery room. Maya was frightened, screaming, and fighting with the doctors and nurses. The whites of Maya's eyes were dark because her blood pressure was so high. Carolyn stayed with her and calmed her down enough for the hospital staff to give her the care she needed. They had to insert tubes into the uterus to provide fluid for the baby to be delivered, and had to give her medication to bring her blood pressure down. After a long and difficult labor, Maya delivered a healthy baby girl. That beautiful baby was the only joyous thing that had happened out of the tragic situation, leaving Carolyn and Maya exhausted.

After the delivery, Maya began crying uncontrollably, and Carolyn tried to comfort her and explain about hormone imbalance after giving birth. When Velma saw the baby, her face dropped with shock, and she asked Carolyn, "Did you see the baby?" Carolyn said that she had seen the baby, and said how beautiful the baby was. Velma again asked, "Carolyn, look at the baby!" Carolyn again looked at the sweet face of her granddaughter and saw nothing wrong. By this time, Maya was crying louder, saying, "Mama, I'm sorry. I'm so sorry!" Carolyn was totally confused. She asked Maya, "What are you sorry for?" She was just glad that Maya and the baby had survived. Velma again asked Carolyn to take a close look at the baby, saying, "Can't you see that baby looks just like him?" Carolyn finally saw what her mother had seen; the baby looked just like Mack! Suddenly, she absorbed why her daughter was crying so——why she was saying she was sorry—remembering the arguments between Maya and Mack. It all came together in one terrible crash! Carolyn demanded the truth, and Maya finally cried out, "He raped me, Mama! That's his baby! He told me if I told anyone, he would kill all of us!"

Carolyn began to have a smothered feeling, like a sense of panic. Suddenly she took off running down the hall and was unaware that she was running, or where she was going. Finally, someone from the hospital staff caught her outside before she could run into the street. Carolyn did not remember how she got there. All she knew was that her heart was broken into a million pieces, and she was confused and angry. She just needed some time to absorb what had happened over the last few minutes, months, and years. Her mind flashed back to how Mack had brushed off the incident of "accidentally" touching Maya's breast, to Maya's change in behavior after she became pregnant, how Mack had been so aggressive, trying to find out who the father was and trying to bring the boy to justice, how Maya must have suffered in silence, just like she had done when she had been pregnant with Adam. How she had been totally unaware of what Mack had done to her daughter because she was so wrapped up, dealing with his abuse toward her, and how Maya had almost died trying to bring this child into this world—his child!

For the first time in years, Velma showed compassion toward Carolyn, and held her in her arms as if she finally understood Carolyn's struggle and what she had been through all of these years. Velma offered no apologies for her mistreatment of Carolyn, just recognition and empathy when she said, "I'm sorry about this. I know how you must feel." Carolyn melted into Velma's arms; it was just what she needed. It was sad that their reunion and reconciliation had to be under these circumstances, but it was better late than never.

Carolyn's daughter was now a rape victim, just like she had been. All she could say, over and over, was, "Oh, God, how could you let this happen?" All of these emotions and feelings had just come to a head, and her soul could not bear any more. Maybe that's why she had taken off running, trying to catch up with her soul. Somewhere in her flight, God caught her and spoke peace to her. She suddenly felt that somehow things would work out. She couldn't see it now, but she had to draw on all of her faith and hold on tight.

Carolyn finally stopped crying long enough to process what her next steps should be, so she went to Maya, who was still a bundle of tears, and consoled her. She reassured her that no one else would ever hurt her again, and vowed that Mack would pay for what he had done, and that what happened to her was not her fault. Carolyn informed the nurse caring for Maya about the rape, and said she wanted charges filed on Mack immediately. The nurse got the social worker, Child Protective Services (CPS), and the police involved. Carolyn gave them all of Mack's work information, and said he was possibly making a delivery to Missouri. Within hours, the highway patrol had located him on his way back to Texas. They pulled him over at a truck weigh station, confiscated his truck, and took him to jail.

Carolyn knew that she and her children could no longer go back to East Texas. She was grateful to God for delivering them out of that horrible situation. After several hours, Carolyn finally got Maya settled down enough to tell her and the CPS worker about everything Mack had done to her. Maya told of how Mack had forced his way into her room and made her have different types of sex with him (vaginal, oral and anal), and how he had threatened to kill her, her mother, and her brothers if she told anyone about it. Carolyn explained to Maya that Mack was using the threat as a control mechanism, and that once she spoke her truth, the threat would be over, and justice would be served.

After Mack was arrested, Carolyn told Maya that she might have to testify against him. She asked Maya if she felt strong enough to handle the trial, and Maya said she was ready to do whatever it took to make him pay for what he had done to her. She wanted and needed justice. The most important thing for Carolyn at that moment was caring for Maya and for her new grandchild, so she called her sister to see if they could stay with her for a while. Carolyn knew that Mack would come looking for her at her mother's house. Her sister gladly agreed, and after a week at the hospital, Maya and the baby were released.

Mack's uncle, the preacher, led a campaign to get Mack out of jail. His family had gotten the bail money and bailed him out of jail within hours of his arrest. Carolyn could not believe that the church members were supporting him in this crime. She told her children that they would never return to East Texas, and the children broke down with tears of relief. They shared their stories about things that had happened to them during their time in East Texas. They told of how Mack's mother hadn't allowed them to watch television, to go outside, or even to eat any food, and of all the ways she had been mean to them. Their stories angered Carolyn even more. She became concerned about how angry Mack would be about being arrested, and wondered if he would come after her and the children. She recalled the threat he made, that he would never allow her to leave him. The CPS case worker helped Carolyn get a protective order against Mack, which stated that he could not come within 100 feet of her or the children.

Mack did exactly what Carolyn had anticipated he would do—went looking for her at Velma's house. He told Velma that Carolyn was his wife and that he had come to take his family home, because their place was with him. Velma finally spoke up for Carolyn when she told him that he dare not enter her house insisting that Carolyn go back with him, after what he had done to her and her children. She cursed him with all she had, then called the police. Mack left Velma's house before the police arrived, but not before he threatened to kill Carolyn before he would allow her leave him. Velma called Carolyn and told her what Mack had done, but Carolyn had faith that God would protect her, not just that little piece of paper alone. Mack had proven that he had no respect for the protective order by coming to look for her.

Carolyn's friend Deb had witnessed Maya's ordeal at the hospital, and Carolyn later confided in her about the threat that Mack had made about not allowing her to leave him. Deb told her that she owned a gun and would come over every day to see how she was doing. She vowed to take care of Mack if he ever showed up. Carolyn had a true friend in Deb.

Carolyn needed to get their things from East Texas, so Deb volunteered to go with her, pistol in hand. Carolyn checked with Mack's job to confirm he would be at work and away from the house before going to East Texas. When she and Deb arrived, Carolyn was so frightened that her bones felt like jelly when she entered the house that had been her torture chamber for five years.

She feared that Mack would walk through the door at any minute and kill her, so she and Deb quickly collected what they could carry, with Deb's pistol drawn. They managed to make it back to Dallas without any incidents, and Carolyn enrolled her boys under assumed names in a school near her sister's house. The CPS worker made daily visits to check on Maya and prepare her for the trial. When the baby was two months old, Maya enrolled in school, and Carolyn babysat. Deb also came by every day *(with her pistol)* to check on Carolyn.

Carolyn and her children's presence caused problems for her sister and husband, so Carolyn took a chance and asked Velma if she and the children could temporarily move in with her. The old boyfriend was gone, and thankfully Velma agreed, because her new boyfriend said he did not mind them staying there. Carolyn was not planning to stay long, and she had outgrown the need for her mother's shelter she'd had when Adam was a baby.

Soon after they moved to Velma's, Mack returned to Dallas with his sisters, the preacher, and his sick mother in the car. He demanded that Carolyn give his car back, so Carolyn called the police, and then called Deb. Carolyn knew she had a right to the car, because she had been making the payments. When the police arrived, Carolyn showed them the protective order. All the while, Mack yelled about wanting his car. The police asked Carolyn to show proof that she had been making the payments, and she produced the receipts. The police informed Mack that Carolyn was allowed to keep the car, and that he was under arrest for violating the protective order.

While the police handcuffed Mack and were putting him in the car, Deb drove up. When she saw Mack, she hit the gas pedal, narrowly missing Mack, and ran over the front yard fence! She got out of her car, waving her pistol and cursing, and the police almost arrested her too. The police questioned Deb, but she convinced them that she had "accidentally" hit the gas instead of the brake, so they let her go with a warning on safe driving. After the police left, Deb later told Carolyn that she was trying her best to run over Mack, and would not have felt bad if she had.

Because Maya's rape occurred in East Texas, the case had to be tried there. Carolyn had to take Maya and the baby to the East Texas medical examiner for DNA testing. Deb was not able to go with her, so Carolyn and Maya traveled without escort. The trip was short, and fortunately they did not to run into Mack or any of his family members. The next trip to East Texas would be for the trial, and each time Carolyn traveled there, she feared for her life. When the DNA results came back, they confirmed that Mack was the father of Maya's baby. This only increased Carolyn's hatred for him.

When the day for the trial finally arrived, Maya was nervous and tearful all the way to the courthouse. Carolyn was afraid that Maya would not be strong enough to give her testimony. Mack's entire family and some of the church folk were in the courtroom to support him, filling up most of the seats. They wanted to give the judge the impression that Mack was a fine, upstanding, well-respected Christian member of the community.

Carolyn and Maya felt intimidated because no one was with them besides Deb, who could not take her gun into the courthouse. Mack's uncle, the preacher who had married them, testified that Mack was a wonderful, loving Christian father and husband. He said that there was no way Mack could have committed the horrible crime he had been accused of.

Family member after family member testified about what a wonderful person Mack was. Carolyn was worried that the judge believed the lies. Then suddenly the judge said, "Enough of this! Let's hear from the victim." Maya took the stand and bravely, through occasional tears, told about how Mack had come into her room for over a year and forced her to have vaginal, anal, and oral sex with him. Maya said Mack had threatened to kill her mother and brothers if she told anyone about what he had done. To make the case solid, Maya's attorney presented the DNA report indicating that Mack was the father of Maya's baby, supporting Maya's testimony. The judge believed Maya and sentenced Mack to 10 years in prison for statutory rape. Carolyn felt a sigh of relief, and she and Maya clutched each other, crying and thanking God for justice.

Mack's family was outraged and started yelling and screaming that Mack was innocent. They actually did not believe that Mack would be convicted. After the trial, the preacher approached Carolyn, not with an apology, but with a sly grin. He said, "I can't believe that boy would do that." She could not believe how casual his statement was, or his lack of compassion toward her daughter. Carolyn did not dignify his statement with a response. She let the judge's verdict speak for itself. *(The preacher later went on to become the leader of several other churches in the area).* Mack served only four of his ten years in prison, and Carolyn's divorce was finalized while he was in prison.

Carolyn knew she could not stay with her mother forever, but she was too afraid to go out into the world on her own. Deb helped her get set up with Section 8 housing again. Carolyn did not even have the $50 required for the apartment deposit, so Deb took her to the neighborhood store and purchased her a money order for her deposit. Because of the protective order and history of abuse with Mack, the apartment complex listed her under an anonymous name.

Carolyn was able to get an apartment that was large enough for her, the boys, Maya and her grandchild. In spite of all the times that Velma had refused to allow Carolyn to move back home, she and Velma had grown close during the last few months, and Carolyn did not want to leave. Velma was not drinking as heavily; the years of drinking were beginning to affect her health. Even after Carolyn moved into her own apartment, Carolyn went to visit Velma every day. Carolyn enrolled her children in school and kept her grandchild while Maya was in school.

Carolyn had an uncontrollable fear that when Mack got out of prison, he would find her and make good on his threat to kill her. She told the manager at the housing project about her situation with Mack and asked if she could get some protection. The manager connected her to a private investigator who would keep track of Mack's location. Carolyn was deathly afraid to leave her apartment during the day and only ventured far enough away from home to transport her children to and from school, to visit her mother, and occasionally to go to the corner store for food. After all the years of abuse and stress Carolyn became depressed and could not sleep or eat, and her weight dropped to 95 pounds. She would keep the curtain tightly drawn at all times, and would get up every hour on the hour to make sure the doors were locked.

One evening, after the children had gotten home from school, Carolyn allowed them to go outside and play. She usually never let them out, but the weather was nice that day, and she did not want to punish them because of her fears. She was watching out the window while they played when she noticed the outline of a man coming across the apartment complex that looked exactly like Mack, headed toward her apartment! She panicked and wondered if it was her imagination, but the man was the same height and build, and walked exactly like Mack. She was convinced it was him and that he had found her, so she went into attack mode.

Carolyn turned off all of the lights in the apartment, closed the windows and doors, got the pistol that Deb had given her, and crouched low to the floor. She crawled upstairs to make sure it was secure, then crawled back downstairs. She felt she could hear the sweat as it popped out on her forehead, and every nerve in her body was on alert. Her hearing was extremely sharp, and she was ready to empty the gun clip toward any little noise. She lay down on the floor on her stomach where she could see the front and back doors, and kept both hands on the gun's trigger. She could hear her heart beating rapidly, and her every breath as it went in and out of her lungs.

Time seemed to stand still. Carolyn decided that it was a kill or be killed situation. She made up her mind that if Mack knocked on her door or tried to come in, that she would shoot through the door and empty the .357 Magnum clip into his body. She crawled on the floor with the gun ready to fire at either door. She had to anticipate any move he would make, because she knew he would not stop until she was dead. She heard the footsteps approach front the door, and then she heard them walk past the door. She slowly crawled to the window and saw the figure pass by. It wasn't Mack!

Just then, her children turned the knob to the back door to come in from playing outside, and there Carolyn was with a gun in her hand. If she had not realized that the man was not Mack, she would have shot her own children as they walked through the door! If the man she thought was Mack had knocked on her door by mistake, she could easily have emptied the clip into him. She broke down in a heap on the floor, crying and feeling helpless that Mack had turned her into a wounded animal. Mack was not even there, yet he controlled her emotions enough to make her want to kill another human. The young man who had passed through her breezeway had no idea how close he had come to death that day.

After the incident, she called Deb and told her everything that had just happened. Deb instructed Carolyn to take the clip out of the gun, and she would come and get it. Deb realized that Carolyn was much too depressed and emotionally unstable to have such a dangerous weapon in her possession. When Deb arrived, Carolyn handed over the gun to her without argument, because she realized that she was out of control. She kept thinking that she could have killed her children, had they touched the door one second before they did. She needed help, but she was afraid, and didn't know where to get help.

A few days after the incident, Carolyn got a visit from CPS. They were investigating a tip that Carolyn was possibly abusing her children, because one of her neighbors had said that they never saw her come outside, and that her kids never came out to play with the other kids. Carolyn willingly let the case worker visit with the children, and she inspected the refrigerator to prove that there was plenty of food in the house. She told the case worker about the abusive situation she had recently come out of, and the fear that her abuser would still try to kill her or her children was the reason for the children not going outside. The CPS worker was satisfied that the children were safe, but concerned about Carolyn's mental status.

There was an organization in Carolyn's apartment complex that connected families with available resources they needed. One of the community workers came by to visit Carolyn to see if she had any needs, and let her know they offered GED classes. Carolyn mentioned that she was very interested in completing her education but feared leaving the house. The community workers would come by weekly to see Carolyn and to challenge her to come to class. Carolyn finally took a good look in the mirror and realized how she had let herself go. She had been so depressed and had not cared for herself, until she hardly recognized herself because of how thin and worn she looked.

Because Carolyn was so thin and poorly nourished, she had contracted pneumonia twice since moving to the complex, and her hair was brittle and had fallen out in patches, so she kept her hair tied up in an old scarf. Her clothes were ragged and too big for her because she had lost so much weight. She could not buy new clothes for herself, because there was no money left after she bought the children's clothes for school and clothes for her grandchild. She wanted to start going back to church, but was too afraid to leave the house and ashamed of her appearance. She had an old Bible that she had brought with her from East Texas, and she would read it daily and pray that God would help her create a better life for her children.

When Carolyn received her next welfare check, she went to a second-hand store in the neighborhood and bought herself some nicer clothes. None of the clothes matched, but they were not rags. She bought a wig and some cheap makeup, and began to pull herself together.

Carolyn wanted to get her GED, but she knew she needed to leave the house to get it done. When her children saw their mother all "dressed up," they were excited, and she was excited too.

One morning after Carolyn saw the children off to school, she gathered up her grandchild and walked through the door at the community center. The community worker gave her a big hug and told her how glad she was that Carolyn taken the step and come to class. Since Carolyn had only completed the seventh grade, she had lost a significant amount of memory about things she had learned earlier. The instructor informed Carolyn that she tested on a fourth grade level for reading and math , and she would have to relearn a lot of things. The road to getting her GED would be long, but not impossible. She was a little discouraged, but eager to get back the education that had been denied to her. What her mother had denied her, and Mack had tried to beat out of her, she was determined to get for herself.

The community center that Carolyn attended provided free babysitting while she attended GED classes. She made new friends in class. The people at the community center were so impressed with Carolyn's kind spirit and work ethic that they offered her a part-time job driving the van to pick up other students for class. She accepted the job and didn't look back. She worked hard for five years to obtain her GED, and she appreciated every test she had to take to prepare—it just made her study harder.

Carolyn eventually was hired as a community worker who went out into the community to reach out to people like her. She's a walking, talking, breathing testimony of what your faith in God can do. She went on to complete medical assistant training and has plans to become a registered nurse.

Reflection of Carolyn's Story

by Min. Neisha Strambler-Butler

"Now the Lord is the Spirit, and where the Spirit of the Lord is, there is freedom." 2 Corinthians 3:17

I see Carolyn's story as a tale of "From fear to freedom." After reading Carolyn's story, I found myself experiencing a rush of different emotions all at once. I was shocked and saddened by all the abuse that Carolyn endured, angry at the folks who abused her, and elated that she became a living testimony of just how good God is. Perhaps the most overwhelming emotion I experienced was awe. I was in awe of the strength that God gave Carolyn to rise above such terrible ordeals she endured. Only God could provide the fortitude Carolyn needed in order to live through these kinds of terrible tribulations, and to ultimately triumph over them—only God.

In many ways, Carolyn's story is similar to Biblical story of the Israelites. In the book of Exodus, God delivered the Israelites from the cruel bondage of the Egyptians, but it took them 40 years to fully realize it. The Israelites were out of bondage, but the bondage wasn't out of them. Likewise, Carolyn escaped several abusive situations, yet she was still held captive in her mind by the abuse that had plagued her. Long after her last abuser had been placed in prison, Carolyn was still imprisoned by fear.

The good news is that God delivered Carolyn, just as he delivered the Israelites. Indeed, His grace and mercy liberated her from the fear and the abuse that held her captive all of her life. He moved her from fear to freedom, and that freedom provided Carolyn with the life she so richly deserved.

That is what I love about God—He is a God of freedom. He came to set the captives free *("He has sent me to proclaim freedom for the prisoners and recovery of sight for the blind." Luke 4:18b)* and hasn't stopped liberating people since. He can liberate anyone from anything. There is no situation or scenario that is too complex or messy for him to handle. Carolyn's story reminds us of God's supernatural power and His supernatural love.

"*Olivia*"

Story by J. Harris

Reflection by Rev. Dr. Marjorie Hamilton Scott

IF YOU CAN IMAGINE ANGELS CRYING, then imagine Olivia's tears streaming down her face as she remembers her painful childhood. In the depths of her despair, God sent angels to cover her, to love her, to protect her, and to rescue her. Olivia's story is not unlike the stories of thousands of other women in America. The one difference is that she chose to share it.

Many Hispanic families have migrated from Mexico to America in search of a better life. Often, these female immigrants become victims of their "leaders" and become trapped in a whirlwind of abuse and suffering. They survive in a world where language barriers exist and cultures clash. Their children can also become victims, and the vicious cycle repeats itself generation after generation.

Olivia's prayer is that by telling her story, immigrant women who feel trapped and afraid will know that they can take steps to save themselves and the next generations. Olivia was traumatized by what is called "secondhand abuse," which means that children witness the abuse of a family member, and are sometime affected by what they have experienced. Olivia's desire is to raise awareness of the severity of trauma that this secondhand abuse could have on a child, and that it has almost the same effect as if they were abused firsthand.

Both of these witnesses are affected long term, and often times lifelong.

Tiny, graceful, and gentle are everyone's first impressions of Olivia. She is shy but sophisticated, and unafraid to take a stand for justice. She is well educated and her soft words are articulate, with only a hint of her Spanish accent seeping through. From a distance she appears to be a tiny teen, but her outward appearance is misleading. Inside, there is a fighter and a survivor. Her venture from Mexico to America is a tale of survival within itself. Her life in America is a tale of how she went from victim to victor.

Olivia was only five when her father, Manuel, made the decision to bring his wife, Anna, and their six children to America to find work and more money to support his growing family. His work as a ranch hand in Reynosa, Mexico, did not pay enough to feed his growing family. Manuel ruled his family with an iron fist, and what he said went. If anyone, wife or child, disobeyed or angered him, he dealt with them severely. On the dangerous streets of Reynosa, Manuel learned about life the hard way. There was an unwritten code of fight or die, and let no one push you around.

Manuel was one of 13 children, and when the hard work and abuse from his father was too much to bear, he ran away from home at only nine years old. Being one of 13 children in a poor family, no one came looking for him. Fighting every day for his manhood, scraps of food, or begging for change from tourists was his way of survival. Life had not been kind to him, so he did not see the need to be kind to others. Manuel tried his hand at different jobs just to keep food in his belly, but his internal anger always expressed itself outwardly, and he would eventually be fired.

As a teen, Manuel was influenced by some older men to try working as a ranch hand. He was comfortable with horses and cattle, because they did not try to defy him or betray him once he tamed them. He realized that working with animals put him in control, so he perfected his craft as ranch hand. Manuel considered the job as a bonus, because the ranch gave him a place to sleep and one meal a day, which was much better than what he got on the streets. The older ranch hands schooled him on how to drink hard at the end of a long, hard day's work, and on what women could do for him. The alcohol helped him escape his personal pain, and the pleasure he received from the women in the taverns soothed his rage. He didn't have to love them to get pleasure from them. The streets had not taught him how to give or receive love.

When Manuel was old enough to marry, and felt he could be a good provider, he looked for a wife. He knew he did not want a saloon woman, so he sought out one of the young church girls in town who had not been "another man's woman." Manuel met Anna at a church social and admired her beauty and quiet spirit. He decided she would do to take care of his needs and pass on his blood line. He had heard the older men on the ranch talk about how they "trained" their wives to stay in their places, and how Manuel must do the same if he was to call himself a man. He was not sure he loved Anna, because he did not know what love was. His instincts told him he needed a steady bed partner during those lonely nights, and someone to bear his children. He envisioned eventually using his children as laborers, and that someday they would have their own ranch. Perhaps his children would grow up to be prosperous and even take care of him someday. During their courtship, the 15-year-olds took long walks and were carefully watched by Anna's parents and others in the community. Anna had never had a boyfriend, so she was swept off her feet by Manuel and his promises of a wonderful life as his wife. After a six-month courtship, Anna's father agreed to allow her to marry Manuel. The simple ceremony was held in the chapel of the Catholic Church with lots of well wishes to the couple as they set out to establish themselves in society.

Anna was quiet and innocent, and had been taught that her responsibility in life was to marry and have children to establish her status in the community as a woman. Because she was a woman, higher education was not discussed as an option for her, so she only completed the fifth grade. Since she was raised in the Catholic Church, she tried to encourage her new husband to attend church in order to have God's blessings on their marriage and their children, but Manuel could not see where God had done him any favors, so he refused to attend. God had not been there to spare him the beatings from his father, or to protect him from the cruelties of the dangerous streets, so as far as Manuel was concerned, God was not a necessity. His heart was hard, and after they married, he forbade Anna to attend church or to visit her family. She was his wife, and therefore his property, and she would do as he said, or else.

Anna and Manuel lived on the ranch in a tiny shack, and their family quickly grew. The pressure of too many mouths to feed on a ranch hand's salary wore on Manuel, so he prepared to move his family north, to America. One of his fellow ranch hands put him in contact with a "coyote" *(a person who illegally smuggles humans across the border for money)* who could help get him and his family across the border from Reynosa into McAllen, Texas. By this time, Manuel and Anna had four small children, all under the age of 10. Olivia was the youngest of the children at three years old. Her older sister lived with Olivia's aunt while her parents worked on the ranch. When it was time for Olivia's family to leave for America, her aunt would not let Anna and Manuel take the child. She had become too attached to the baby, because she had no children of her own *(she wanted to be a mother too)*. Anna and Manuel begged the aunt to return their child, but she would not let the girl go.

When the day arrived for Olivia's family to leave for America, Manuel had run out of time to continue the argument. He told the aunt he would be back to get his daughter after the family was settled in America. Anna's heart ached for her child. That would be the first of many heartaches Anna would have.

Manuel saved up and paid the Coyotes $50 per family member, a total of $250, to take them across the Mexico/Unites States border. They met the coyote at an isolated place outside of Reynosa in the dead of night. Olivia and her siblings were sleepy and did not know what was going on, but were obedient to Manuel's instruction to wake up and walk. The coyote packed them into the back of a pickup truck with a camper that was carrying a load of building supplies. Some of the children cried because of the cramped space, but Manuel sternly warned them to be quiet or else, and the crying cease. The ride in the back of the truck's cramped quarters was rough and took several days, because they had to make frequent stops to look after the children. Anna had brought water and all of the food she could scrape together. They rode across the border at the border check point with no problems.

After they had crossed the border, the coyote unloaded them in an isolated area near McAllen, Texas, and disappeared. They never knew the coyote's real name and never saw him again, as he headed back to Mexico to bring another load of humans. The family lived on the bare necessities they had brought, and slept in parks and in wooded areas until Manuel found a ranch that gave him work. He rented a small, one-room house for his family to live in on the ranch property. The ranch owner did not ask questions about his citizenship, but was only concerned that Manuel was an experienced ranch hand. The pay was poor and the family's living conditions were inhumane, but Manuel knew he could not complain, or else he and his family would face deportation.

The American dream the coyote sold him of living in a big house and making lots of money was proving to be a lie, but they considered themselves fortunate, because they were not as poor as they had been in Mexico. They were constantly aware of the immigration officials who would occasionally searched the ranches for illegal immigrants. To stay ahead of immigration, the family moved from ranch to ranch at least once a year, and because of the frequent moves Olivia and her siblings struggled in school. Spanish was the only language spoken in their home, but at school they were expected to learn, speak and understand English. Olivia did so poorly in school that she was eventually placed in special education classes for slow learners.

Life at home did not help Olivia in coping with the learning difficulties at school. Manuel was becoming unbearable with his heavy drinking and fits of rage aimed at Anna. If the food was not on the table when he walked into the house, he slapped Anna around. If his food had too much salt, or wasn't the right temperature, he would beat her. Sometimes he beat her for no reason, drunk or sober. Olivia and her older sister, Nadia, tried to do what they could to help their mother with the chores and cooking in hopes that it would keep Manuel from beating their mother. If any of the girls interfered when he beat Anna, he would hit them too, or push them out of the way. Manuel only scolded Olivia's brothers and never hit them. He laughed and talked to them, took them fishing, and made sure they ate first when it was time to eat. Life for Olivia and her sisters was full of isolation and disrespect. Manuel made it clear that they had no voice in how the house was run, and he rarely had any conversation with them. The only time the girls heard from him was when he was displeased with them. All of the communication to the girls from Manuel came in the form of being slapped or pushed out of the way.

Olivia did not sleep well at night for fear that Manuel would come home drunk and start beating Anna for no reason. She lay awake at night listening to the arguments, followed by the sound of slaps, Anna's screams, and furniture being overturned. Olivia could only cry herself to sleep and wish that her mother would gather the children together one day and leave Manuel behind to fight with himself. Anna felt trapped because she was pregnant again, Spanish speaking, illegal and totally dependent on her husband for money. *Where could she go with four children, and one on the way? Who would provide for them?* Manuel had taught her that it was useless to fight back, because he showed them how strong and mean he could be.

Manuel saved enough money to get the family a car. It was not even a decent car, just a broken-down piece of junk. The family had been in America for five years and had become skilled at staying one step ahead of immigration by moving frequently. One evening, Olivia's 14-year-old brother, Juan, took the family car for a joy ride and had an accident. When the police questioned him, he had no insurance or identification and could not speak English. They suspected he was in the country illegally.

The police in the border towns had a reputation of being very intimidating toward illegal immigrants. They would use threatening tactics to get them to reveal where other illegal immigrants were located. The police told Juan that if he would tell where the rest of his family was, they would let him go, and if he did not tell, they would take him to jail and he would never see his family again. Being a child, he did not know what to do, so he told the police where his family lived. The immigration officials made a visit to Olivia's home, took them all into custody, and deported them, including Juan, back to Mexico that same day. Manuel was angry with Juan for revealing the family's location, but he did not beat him. The family was taken to the Mexico-United States border and let out on the Mexico side.

The family walked the long road back to the ranch in Reynosa where they had lived years before, to see if Manuel could get his old job back. Jobs were scarce, and he could only pick up part-time work. The family lived in an abandoned, empty house with no furnishings, no plumbing and no food. Anna's relatives in Reynosa shared what little they had with them, and Olivia got a chance to see her oldest sister who had been left behind in Mexico with her aunt. It was a strange meeting, because after five years the sisters were strangers to each other. Anna cried when she saw her daughter and begged her sister to let her stay with the rest of the family, but Anna's sister would not let her go. Too much time had passed, and the aunt was the only mother the child knew. This would be the last time Olivia would see her sister, and her sister would never realize the blessing of being left behind.

After five weeks, Manuel still had not found enough work to feed his family and he decided to take another chance again to get the family back across the border to America. He did not have money for the coyote, so he risked doing it himself. He waited until it became dark and took his family to the bridge where the cars crossed the Rio Grande River from Mexico to McAllen. The water was deep and swift, and crossing would be dangerous, especially for small children and a pregnant woman. With Manuel in the lead, they all grabbed onto the chain link fence and monkey-walked along the outside ledge of the bridge, eventually inching their way to the American side of the border. If any of them had fallen, they would have drowned, because none of them knew how to swim. Olivia's greatest fear was that her pregnant mother would fall and be killed, leaving them with her father. However, they all arrived safely, and the family hitchhiked their way to San Antonio, Texas, where Manuel found work as a ranch hand on several farms in the area.

The ranches that Manuel worked were so close in proximity that on one occasion, Olivia and her siblings enrolled in one school, and re-enrolled in the same school when they moved. Olivia continued to do poorly in school, mostly due to the stress of her home life. Manuel continued to abuse Anna, even while she was pregnant. When it was time for Anna to have the baby, the family could not risk going to the hospital for fear of getting deported. Manuel took Anna to a lay-midwife *(patera)* clinic, paid the fee, and left. Many of the illegal immigrant women used *pateras* to deliver their babies and to have the births registered as legal United States citizens.

The clinic labor room was a cot with a thin curtain around it, and minimal sanitation was provided. Anna was used to Manuel abandoning her to give birth, because he felt it was not a man's place to be at the birth of a baby. This child was a baby boy, and was underweight because of Anna's poor nutritional status and the tremendous stress she was under, but fortunately was healthy otherwise. After the birth, the *patera* allowed Anna to rest for a couple of hours, then Anna had to yield her bed to another illegal mother in labor.

Olivia and Nadia helped Anna care for their new baby brother and prepare food for the family for the next three weeks, until Anna was stronger. Manuel still demanded his dinner on the table on time, even in Anna's absence. Olivia would daydream about running away, but felt guilty when she thought of how she needed to be there to protect her mother. Manuel ordered Anna not to ever leave the house without him, and he went wherever with her. Olivia and Nadia tried to go with Anna when their father took Anna out to protect her from a potential beating. The family went to church together about once every three to four years. Perhaps it was Manuel's way of repenting for his actions, but he would go back to his usual abusive tactics afterward.

With Manuel's increased drinking, his beatings of Anna became more frequent, and Olivia became even more depressed. When Manuel drank, his behavior was unpredictable. One evening when he was drunk, he came walking through the house completely naked! Anna tried to cover him and told him not to behave like that in front of the girls, but he swung at her and said, "This is my house, and I'll do whatever I want to do!" Olivia and the other children were shocked and embarrassed, but said nothing. Soon after that incident, Olivia's 17-year-old brother moved out on his own, with no explanation other than he couldn't take it anymore.

One evening on the way home from the grocery store, Anna and Manuel got into one of their typical arguments, but this argument was more intense. Manuel was driving the ranch truck with Nadia between him and Anna, and Olivia was in the bed of the truck. Olivia did not hear what the argument was about because she had learned not to care enough to listen. *What was one more argument?* When they got home, Olivia noticed Manuel's expression had become darker, and Nadia was not her usual happy self, but instead was quiet and withdrawn. When Olivia asked Nadia what was wrong, she became teary-eyed. Olivia had never seen her like this and demanded that she tell what had happened. Finally, Nadia collected herself enough to tell her what the big argument had been about. While they were driving home, Manuel had pulled out his penis and demanded that Nadia touch it, with Anna sitting right there looking! Olivia began to question Nadia more intensely about whether Manuel had ever made her touch him before, and Nadia became very quiet and did not answer. Nadia's silence spoke volumes, and Olivia knew then that she had to leave and take Nadia with her.

Olivia knew Nadia was not lying, because she knew personally what Manuel was capable of; she had once caught him looking at her while she showered, and he had made her feel dirty when he stared at her. He never apologized for intruding on her privacy. It was intentional on his part. Olivia dreamed of him touching her and looking at her, but she could not tell if the dreams were reality or not. Her mind would not let her open that door.

A few days after the argument in the truck, Olivia noticed Manuel constructing some type of weapon out of coat hangers. It was as long as a rifle, and had a thick handle on it. His eyes were bloodshot from heavy drinking, and he had a dark and evil look on his face. Olivia felt in her spirit that he was going to do something bad to Anna when she saw him put the weapon in the truck, and then told Anna to come with him to the store. Olivia told Nadia about the weapon, and they knew that one of them needed to go along on this trip. They begged Manuel to take them along, but he just pushed them aside and shouted, "No!" Manual and Anna were gone from that afternoon until about 1:00

a.m. the next morning. Olivia and Nadia held hands and held each other close while their parents were away, fearing that they might never see their mother again.

When Olivia and Nadia heard the truck drive up, they ran to check on Anna and found that Manuel had almost beaten her to death. Anna could hardly walk, and she had several huge, black bruises and deep gashes all over her body. Blood was everywhere! Olivia and Nadia helped Anna into the house and cleaned and dressed their mother's wounds. When Anna finally stopped crying, she told the girls that Manuel had taken her to the local landfill, dragged her from the truck, and beaten her as if he were insane. He beat her continuously for hours. Anna felt he had taken her there to kill her. She had to stay conscious to stay alive, because she knew that if she passed out, he would kill her. When she did not pass out, he threw her back into the truck and brought her home. Olivia knew then that she would either have to leave home, or kill Manuel. She began plotting his murder. She would put rat poison in his beer and serve it to him. They would all be rid of him forever, and he would never hurt them or their mother again.

Olivia was bitterly angry with Manuel for what he had done to Anna, but she was also angry with Anna for staying with him. *Why did she continue to stay and take his abuse?* She could have called the police and had him arrested for what he did, but she was too afraid of what he would do when he was released. She also feared the deportation of her family. Manuel had brainwashed her and trained her to believe that he was her only hope for survival.

After this last beating, Olivia decided that she could no longer live at home. She shared the details of her home situation with her teacher. She wanted to move out, and asked her teacher if she knew of any place she could go. One of her teachers, Mrs. Madison, was married and had three sons, and offered her home to Olivia. She had always wanted a daughter and said Olivia would be the daughter she never had. They arranged for Olivia to come home with her after school one evening, and once she was at Mrs. Madison's home, they would contact the authorities. Olivia went home and put a few items of clothing in her backpack, and told Nadia she was leaving. Nadia decided to stay home to try and protect Anna. The next day after school Olivia went home with her teacher, and it was not until late that evening that Olivia's parents realized she had run away. For the first time in her life, Olivia felt safe with her own room and her own space. Mrs. Madison did everything to make her feel at home, but because of Olivia's bitterness toward her father and toward males in general, living with three boys was difficult. Olivia would often pick on Mrs. Madison's youngest son, who was only seven years old. Olivia focused her anger on him by constantly picking fights and lashing out at the boy. Mrs. Madison was patient and gave Olivia time to adjust, but her son was suffering unnecessarily at the hands of Olivia.

After about three weeks of living with Mrs. Madison, Olivia was asked to leave because of her abusive actions. Olivia felt bad about her behavior toward the boy. She knew what it felt like to be abused, but she could not stop herself. Mrs. Madison contacted Olivia's parents, and they picked her up. Manuel was very polite to Mrs. Madison and apologized for any inconvenience Olivia may have caused her. Manuel was quiet on the drive home, and for two days he did not say anything to her about running away. Olivia knew that the punishment was coming, but didn't know what or when it would be.

About a week after Olivia returned home, Manuel came home with the same expression he'd had when he had taken Anna to the landfill. He looked straight through Olivia with blood-red eyes, and she knew she had to leave that day, or else Manuel might kill her. Suddenly a thought came to Olivia—she asked Manuel to take her and Nadia to the skating rink. At first he said no, but after some persistence, he agreed. He said he would be back to get them, and they agreed to be ready when he returned. Olivia told Nadia that escape was now or never, and asked Nadia if she was running away with her. Nadia thought about it, and again decided she needed to stay and protect Anna and the other children. Olivia said she would never be back, and the sisters hugged and cried in each other's arms. (*To this day Olivia feels guilt for leaving her other siblings unprotected, but she knows that she would not have survived the beating Manuel was going to give her. She will always have visions of Anna's body after her beating.*)

From the skating rink, Olivia called some of her close school mates and told them she was running away that day. They were already familiar with what was going on with Manuel and were willing to hide her out. With only the clothes on her back, Olivia stepped out on faith and desperation. The mother of one of her friends picked her up from the skating rink and took Olivia to her home. Her friends loaned her clothes and shoes to wear to school, and she would stay with one friend for a while, then move to another friend's house. Manuel began asking around, trying to find out where she was, but her friends would say they had not seen her. Manuel would not go to Olivia's school, possibly out of fear that there would be a Child Protective Services investigation, and he and his family would be deported again.

One of Olivia's friends had an aunt named Abby who was a recently retired widow and lived alone. The friend told Abby about Olivia's situation and that Olivia had no permanent place to live. Abby generously took Olivia, which began a new chapter that would change Olivia's life forever. When Olivia met Abby, who was in her 60s, Olivia liked her instantly. Abby was a small-framed, graying white woman. She was soft spoken, with a quick smile and gentle warm eyes. Abby lived in a small modest home that was comfortable and welcoming. Olivia had her own room, even though she owned very few items. Abby's only source of income was a pension from her deceased husband, and her Social Security benefit. Olivia and Abby agreed to split the housekeeping tasks, and Olivia was more than willing to do her share around the house. She thanked Abby and God for a safe place to stay.

After Olivia had settled into her new surroundings, for probably the first time in her life, Olivia slept soundly. She did not have the stress of being awakened during the night to the sounds of her mother and father fighting, or of her father's drunken rages. With this peaceful sleep came dreams that she had never had before. She began to have nightmares about Manuel standing in her room, and in her own bed! The dreams were fuzzy and seemed so real. They would begin with Manuel's finger over his lips, whispering, "Shhh, don't tell anyone," then he would move away from her. She could not tell if he was leaving her bed, or if she had witnessed him coming from her sister's bed. *What did this mean?* Night after night, she had this same reoccurring dream. She did not want this to be true, so she continued suppressing the thoughts and concentrated on her school work.

Abby and Olivia went to church every Sunday. Olivia found that she enjoyed the services and seeing the people singing and smiling. The songs and sermons made Olivia realize that she needed a relationship with Christ to complete her life. Through weekly Bible study and youth group activities, she began to grow spiritually while being challenged to face her past. One evening during a reflecting exercise at a youth retreat, Olivia came face to face with the trauma that she had been through in her young life. She had a spiritual experience that urged her to let go of the anger, bitterness and hatred she had for her father, in order to have a true relationship with God. Those emotions were holding her back and causing her too much pain. She made a decision to step out on faith and allow the Spirit of God to take control of her life, and fill the empty places in her heart to begin healing. This experience took her breath away and helped her to see that every step of the way in her journey, God had His hand on her life. At that retreat, she surrendered her life to God and to Christ. Surrender felt wonderful, and she rejoiced that she was finally free!

Olivia thrived in Abby's haven. Her English and grades improved, and she was no longer labeled as a slow learner, but was actually found to be among the brightest students in her class. All she needed was a loving, caring environment. Manuel and Anna eventually found out where Olivia was living, and came by occasionally to see how she was doing. Olivia made it clear that she was not going back home, and Manuel did not challenge her. Olivia missed her mother and Nadia so much, but knew that this was the living situation for her. Anna would not speak about it, but Olivia knew Manuel was still beating her; she could see the bruises. Olivia wanted to tell Anna about the nightmares she had about Manuel in her bedroom, but did not know how to begin. She wondered what good it would do anyway.

Abby helped Olivia to obtain her American citizenship. After she completed high school, Abby encouraged Olivia to go to college. Olivia loved learning new things. Abby helped Olivia apply to college. She was accepted at the University of Texas (UT) in Austin with the goal of becoming an attorney. Olivia had no fear about going forward, and there would be no looking back to the past.

At UT, Olivia met a wonderful Christian man, Daniel, who later became her husband. Throughout their relationship, Daniel helped Olivia continue to grow spiritually. Olivia wanted their relationship to be transparent, with no secrets, so she opened up and told him of her journey to America, and about what her home life had been like. Daniel prayed with her and for her, and vowed to love her regardless of what had happened to her. Olivia confided in him about the dreams, and he suggested that she see the university counselor about them.

However Olivia felt embarrassed about the possibility of someone knowing her secrets. It was not until her emotional state started to affect her relationship with Daniel that she agreed to get help. Counseling helped Olivia deal with the trauma and guilt from her childhood, and the abuse she'd witnessed between her parents. It also helped her understand that living under the day-to-day stress and threat of abuse had caused her to suppress her emotions and to disconnect from her feelings. With the counselor, Olivia began to open many of the emotional doors she had closed, and healing took place.

Olivia is determined to face her past, the abuse, the fear, and the drama head-on. She will always love her mother for sacrificing her happiness and safety in order to protect and sustain Olivia and her siblings. Olivia and Daniel were married after completing college, and they now have their own family. Olivia works as an immigration attorney in San Antonio, and Daniel has his own dental practice.

Olivia is finally able to visit her parents, but views them very differently, especially when she sees how

Manuel's health has been affected from the years of drinking. Olivia has replaced the anger and rage she held for him with compassion. Because of his health, Manuel is no longer a physical threat to Anna, but Anna refuses to leave him. Olivia is a strong advocate for women and children who have been abused and who face deportation, because she can honestly say, "I know how you feel." She credits her survival to a loving God who kept His loving hand on her. She has dedicated her life to being a true servant of Christ in all that she does.

Reflection of Olivia's Story

By Rev. Marjorie Hamilton Scott, Ph.D.

The story of Olivia, from childhood to a young adult, through a heavy and difficult season, is one of amazing strength, courage, and survival. The strength of a person is found deep inside, and not in the shallow human eye. Olivia's strength is personified through her ability to endure and persist until her situation changed for the better. Strength is defined by Webster's dictionary as "the ability to obtain a moral or intellectual position firmly." In the Bible, one finds examples of physical strength in characters like Sampson in the Old Testament, and spiritual strength like Paul in the New Testament.

It is wise to train like athletes to gain physical strength and stamina, and like people of faith who glean from the amazing strength of God. In physical training, the hard work manifests itself visually in one's physique and stamina. Manifestation in spiritual training builds character, dedication, love, and emotional stamina. Olivia did not have the resources or setting to train physically, but the amazing strength of God buried deep within helped her persevere and not grow weary, until a brighter season in her life emerged.

Courage is another attribute of Olivia that enabled her not only to endure, but to speak up when she needed help. When she could not vocalize her need for help, her courageous acts or acting out prompted those around her to come to her assistance. Life has obstacles that can hinder or prohibit one from overcoming or moving beyond. Olivia demonstrated courage that would not allow her to accept, or to adopt the abuse she witnessed or experienced into her own lifestyle. God never leaves one alone in any given situation. Divine intervention is available through accessing spiritual resources like prayer, study, and worship, and by those who are the willing feet and hands of God, with the compassion, experience, and resources to help.

An angel of God came to Mary in Luke 1:35 and said *"The Holy Spirit will come on you, and the power of the Most High will overshadow you."* The Holy Spirit is the power of God, which is available to everyone who believes in God and every human being who searches for a Higher Power. Olivia was overwhelmed, and she had no other choice but to look beyond herself and her circumstances to obtain the power she needed within, to overcome her circumstances and survive. God is so amazing in giving humankind the choice to seek the One who is omnipresent *(ever present),* omnipotent *(all powerful),* and omniscient *(all knowing).* The human search for God is prompted from a place deep within for the knowledge, power, and companionship of God.

Olivia survived the turbulent and troubled childhood of abuse, and she grew and developed into a strong young woman of God. Her experience, strength, and courage will inspire many others. Olivia's presence is the lighthouse for others who are troubled, confused, scared, or experiencing overwhelming life circumstances. The amazing power of God will guide them to the lighthouse where refuge, love, and strength abide.

"Katherine"

Story by J. Harris

Reflection by Rev. Ella McCarroll

LIFE WILL NOT BE WITHOUT ITS PROBLEMS and struggles, but how we handle them often determines how we are defined. We can look back and say, "I should have handled this or that differently," or say, "If I had it to do all over again, I would do it like this or that." Whatever our decisions in life, if we are followers of Christ, he will see us through our decisions. That is the foundation that Katherine has based her life on—that God will see her through whatever He has placed in her path. Her story is one of courage and strength that could only come from her faith In God.

The all African-American Acres Home addition of Houston, Texas, was not an easy place to grow up in, but one aspect the residents had in common was a sense of community—a village. Neighbors supported one another through thick and thin. Everyone knew everyone else's family and their business. Children felt protected and watched over by people in the community. Children went to the same schools and the same churches. This is the type of community that Katherine's mother, Norma, brought her up in. Norma was an only child and had always wanted a big family. She finished high school and soon after met and married Katherine's father, Clay. Norma was young, naive and beautiful, and Clay moved

Norma to his farm in South Texas, where she was satisfied being a farmer's wife.

The marriage soon began to fall apart after Norma became pregnant with Katherine. Norma knew that living on a farm in South Texas with no medical care was not the environment she wanted to have her first child in. She tried to convince Clay to get her proper medical attention, but they were poor and he felt it was an unnecessary expense. His mother had given birth to 15 healthy children on that very farm, and she did not have prenatal care, and he felt Norma didn't need any either. So, a very pregnant Norma packed her bags, headed down a dusty road toward town and the train station, and went home to her parents in Houston, where Katherine was later born safely. After two years of attempting to work out the marriage issues long distance, the couple divorced.

Norma found the only type of work a single black woman in those days could find—as a domestic worker for wealthy white families. She worked hard to support her and Katherine because Norma loved her baby girl, and only wanted the best for her. She often did without to make sure Katherine had the things she needed. She pleaded with Clay for support that rarely came, and because of his anger with Norma for leaving him, Clay wanted no contact with Norma or Katherine. To Norma, the thought of him not wanting to get to know their beautiful daughter was painful and would prove to be a place of pain for Katherine throughout her life. Norma was lonely and found herself in another relationship that did not work out, but left her with another mouth to feed, a baby girl named Cheryl. Norma had always wanted a large family, but she had not intended to bear that burden alone. She wanted Katherine and Cheryl to have a father and a stable home.

When Katherine was ten years old and Cheryl was six, Norma met Will. Norma had long black hair, caramel colored skin and natural beauty, and Will fell for her instantly. He was a hard worker and said he was willing to include Katherine and Cheryl as his own. This was what Norma wanted for her children—acceptance and stability. When Katherine was 11 years old, Norma and Will married, and he did not want Norma to work any longer, so she became a housewife. It did not take long for she and Will to get started adding to their family. Katherine soon became the oldest of six kids with the addition of her four brothers. Norma was a strict disciplinarian, and was quick and stern in the disciplining of her children. Will was also strict and very frugal, watching every penny that came into the house and criticizing anything that he considered waste. This frugality often caused conflict between him and Norma, especially when their growing family had needs to be met.

Norma had been raised in the United Methodist Church, and she started her children out the same way. She knew that introducing her children to God would take them further than she ever could. Will did not always go to church, but he also did not stop Norma and the children from going. Will was a "jack of all trades" and hustled hard for his money, doing various jobs like tearing down old houses, cleaning out incinerators, and other odd jobs. He used Katherine and her siblings as free labor, and worked them hard.

Will worked hard and played even harder. On the weekends he would drink, smoke tobacco and hang out with his friends. Will had accepted Katherine and her sister Cheryl as a package deal when he married Norma, but was not warm or loving toward them. His sons, on the other hand, were treated differently. He took the boys on outings and left the girls behind.

One day Will took his sons fishing in Galveston Bay and allowed the boys to play near the shore while he was fishing on the ledge. A large tide came and pulled Katherine's six-year-old brother Mike out into the deep water. The boy screamed for help, and a fisherman in a nearby boat saw him and tried to pull him out of the water, but the current took Mike under and he drowned. Norma was stricken with grief and would always blamed Will for letting the small children play too close to the water without adult supervision. Will did not want to accept responsibility for his son's death, so he blamed Katherine's older brother, Jackie, for the accident. From that day on, Will was physically cruel to Jackie, and pushed the blame for Mike's death on to him. Norma never questioned Will's behavior toward Jackie because she had too many mouths to feed, and she had become totally dependent on Will for the survival of her children.

Katherine was active in school and played clarinet in the school band, was a majorette, and played for the church's small ensemble. The school activities were her way of getting out of the strict home environment. She was respectful to Will, but their relationship was one of child and caretaker. She was not allowed to question her parent's decisions, and her opinions were not respected, which often leaving her feeling alone and invisible. She also suffered from severe headaches and extremely painful menstrual cramps, and when these occurred she stayed home from school, took pain medication and stayed in bed.

One evening when Katherine had come home from school with a blinding headache, Will came into her room to ask what was wrong. Katherine was in pain and just wanted to be left alone. Will left and came back wearing a black industrial glove on his hand. As he approached her, he suggested that she just needed him to help her relieve some stress. When Katherine pulled the cover up tight around her neck and screamed "No!", he finally left the room. Katherine never knew what Will had planned to do, but she thought her mother should know had what happened. When Katherine told Norma what Will had done, Norma did not say anything, but instead began to treat Katherine differently. *Had Norma not believed Katherine, or thought that she had provoked Will?* She would never know. An air of mistrust developed between Katherine and Norma, and the matter was never discussed again.

Katherine had no contact with her biological father. He never reached out to her. She saw him in passing whenever her family went near where he lived for family gatherings. He would see Katherine in the car and just wave at her. She always wondered why he never wanted to get to know her, or why he didn't treat her as his daughter. This lack of acknowledgment by her father only increased her feeling of loneliness and isolation. She desperately needed to feel that someone thought she was special, so it was no surprise that at age 15, she appreciated the advances of James, one of the boys in her school who lived in her neighborhood. He made her feel special, complimented her, and listened to her. How lucky she felt when she was with him. Because her parents were so strict, she was not allowed to date, so she and James had to see each other at school activities. He played football and she was a majorette—they were a perfect pair.

The relationship between James and Katherine became serious enough to make them think they were in love and would be together forever, so they decided to take the relationship to the next level involving sex. Katherine felt special and appreciated when she and James made love, and she also felt a little defiant, because she was breaking her parent's rules. When they were together at his house, they were the only two people in the world that mattered. Because they were both young and inexperienced, they knew nothing about using protection.

Katherine soon realized that she had not had her painful periods for a couple of months, and feared she was pregnant. When she told James, he had no answers, but only knew he was not prepared to be a father. Katherine knew she would have to face this situation on her own. She trembled at the thought of telling Norma, but knew she had to do something before she started to show. As expected, Norma was furious! As watchful as she had been of Katherine, she could not see how this could have happened, and was even more upset when she discovered Katherine was three month along in the pregnancy. Norma said, "Now it's too late to do anything about it!" Katherine did not understand at the time what "too late" meant.

For six months, Katherine felt Norma's wrath in the form of hurtful remarks and the occasional smack across the head. The school system would not let pregnant girls stay in school, so Katherine was expelled from school during her pregnancy. Will isolated her even further, and with James out of the picture, no one was there to support her through this ordeal. Katherine knew nothing about having babies, and her sister Cheryl made things worse by making rude comments and cruel remarks. Cheryl had never been one to hold her tongue, and this was a constant source of frustration to her parents and to Katherine.

Though Cheryl teased Katherine, she promised to help Katherine take care of the baby, and Katherine was grateful for any type of support. In those days there were no programs available to help Katherine complete her senior year courses, so she did not graduate with her class. Completing school would have to be put on hold.

She felt God was punishing her for her behavior with James.

When Katherine gave birth to her beautiful eight-pound baby girl, Jasmine, she was amazed at what her body had done. The delivery was difficult, but Jasmine was worth it. As soon as she saw Jasmine's innocent face, all of the pain of the last nine months faded away. Norma was present for the delivery, and she softened her coldness toward Katherine when she saw Jasmine. Norma put her pride aside for the sake of this next generation. After coming home with Jasmine, Katherine did her best to pull her load in the family by doing housework and whatever was asked of her, because she did not want to have any words with Will.

One evening, when Jasmine was just two months old, Will had been drinking and confronted Katherine in the kitchen. He called her a whore and said that nobody would want her now that she had a baby to feed. Katherine could only stand there hurt and confused. She could no longer take Will's insults, and began to tell him how she felt about his remarks. Will suddenly grabbed her by the throat and choked her! As the color left her face, and her lungs began to shut down, he let go. Norma saw the incident but did nothing to stop Will. When Katherine picked herself up off the floor, she went to the phone and called her grandmother (Norma's mother) Mami, and asked if she and Jasmine could come to live with her. Katherine quickly packed her and Jasmine's things, and left without looking back. Norma did nothing to stop her.

Katherine's grandparents, Mami and Pete, had always treated Katherine with kindness. Pete was especially fond of her, and he was very protective of his wife and grandchild. Even though they were strict, Katherine knew they loved her. Norma had taught Katherine how to cook, but Mami told her she did not have to find a job. She just wanted Katherine to concentrate on being a good mother. Even though she was not in school, Katherine still saw her classmates in the community. Many of the boys in her class were being drafted or were enlisting in the Vietnam War. One of the boys in her class named Al had enlisted, and Katherine was best friends with his sister, who was always trying to get the two of them together. Katherine had her hands full caring for Jasmine and was not interested in taking on another "project." After much persuasion, Katherine agreed to write to Al while he was in Vietnam. Many of the girls in the neighborhood wrote letters to the soldiers to help keep them encouraged, so she felt she was doing her part for the war effort.

Al was well known in the community, and Mami and Pete were impressed with him because he was dark, handsome, charming, witty, and a Marine. His family and Katherine's family thought that when Al came home from Vietnam, the two should get together. Katherine was still not impressed with him, but she considered what Al could offer her—security and freedom. After frequent exchanges of letters for over a year, Al sent Katherine an engagement ring in the mail, and she felt he was serious and worth considering. Because they were both underage, their parents would have to sign for them to get married, so when Al came home from his second tour in Vietnam, their parents signed and they went to the court house and got married. There were no frills or thrills, just married.

Seventeen-year-old Katherine felt that this was her opportunity to be free from the strict environment of her grandparents' home. Even if she did not have a lot of knowledge about life and being married, she was willing to learn, and Al had promised to teach her what he knew. Love would have to follow. What mattered most to

Katherine was that she was free and could make her own rules, in her own home.

After the courthouse wedding and the "I do's" were said, Katherine turned to Al, looked him sternly in the face, and said to him, "I have already been raised, and I will not tolerate you beating on me!" He was a bit shocked, but agreed to her terms. Al took Katherine to her grandparent's house to gather her and Jasmine's things, and the newlyweds headed for the Army base in Ft. Jackson, South Carolina, where Al was stationed. Katherine wanted to be a good wife and learn to love her husband. Through trial and error her cooking improved, and she kept their little base housing trailer neat and clean. Katherine felt like she had been freed from prison, but little did she know that she was headed for another type of prison.

The tours in Vietnam had left Al with unpredictable behavior and cruel words. He drank "white lightning" heavily on the weekends, and habitually smoked marijuana. The alcohol made him crazy and irrational. Katherine was inexperienced when it came to drugs. The first time she smelled marijuana, she thought someone was burning the grass!

Even though Al did not abuse Katherine physically, he did not hesitate to verbally and emotionally abuse her. He could be domineering, controlling, and have the cruelest words and continued putdowns by making fun of her body, and calling her stupid. Even though he treated Katherine badly, he loved Jasmine, and Jasmine was very attached to him. Katherine tolerated the putdowns as long as Jasmine was happy.

Katherine tried hard to make the marriage work because she felt that she had nothing to go back to in Houston. She decided to try to fit in with Al's lifestyle, and began smoking cigarettes and drinking alcohol. Her tolerance for hard liquor was poor, so she often settled for mixed drinks. No matter what she did, Al was still abusive with his putdowns. One day, after three years of the unpredictable, crazy marriage, Katherine thought in her heart, "This marriage will not work." She never told Al, but that thought stayed in the back of her mind. She was determined to keep trying to make her marriage work anyway.

Katherine and Al were expecting a child by this time, and Al felt confused and unprepared. He was uncomfortable with the idea of being a father to his own child. Katherine had hoped that news about the new baby would help Al settle down and act more responsibly; instead, he began drinking and smoking marijuana even more. When Katherine was seven month into her pregnancy, she developed stomach cramps and began bleeding, and she knew this was an emergency. Al panicked because they did not own a car, so he went to a neighbor who took them to the base hospital. Soon after they arrived, the baby boy was delivered stillborn. After months of anticipation of being a new mother, Katherine's arms felt empty and she felt lost. All she could do was cry for her dead son.

Al did not know how to handle the loss, and he left Katherine at the hospital alone. One of the nurses observed the situation and stayed with her all night to comfort her. *Katherine would always be grateful to that nurse for her care and concern.* Katherine called her mother and grandmother to tell them what had happened, and both of their responses were quiet and reserved and did not express any sympathy, or offer any words of comfort. Mami eventually sent her an encouragement card. Katherine felt trapped in a bad dream. *What had gone wrong? Was it her fault?* Al offered no support or comfort and began drinking even more, staying out late, and became more and more verbally abusive. Katherine had nowhere to go, no high school education, and no money of her own, but at least she had Jasmine.

Katherine sank into a deep depression with crying spells caused by postpartum depression, and because she was home sick. In addition, Al's drinking problem had become even more problematic. One evening, he and one of his black Marine friends had been drinking heavily and were driving around the base, and came across a white Marine on the walking path that had been drinking, and they offered him a ride. The white Marine they picked up began to shout racial slurs to Al and his friend. Together, Al and his friend almost beat the man to death. They were both sentenced to three years in the brig (military prison). During that same time, 19-year-old Katherine was pregnant again.

When Al went to jail, the military suspended his pay and his base housing allowance. Because of her history of a miscarriage, Katherine was very concerned about this pregnancy. As the pregnancy progressed, Katherine threatened to miscarry, and knew that she needed to go home to Houston. She needed her mother. She called Norma and told her what was happening, and Norma and Will sent bus tickets for her and Jasmine to come to Houston. Norma understood the feeling of being pregnant, alone, and needing help. Katherine and Jasmine stayed with Norma and Will, but often had to endure Will's unkind remarks regarding the sad condition of her marriage and being pregnant again.

Katherine noticed she was much larger with this baby than with her other pregnancies. Cheryl teased her about the baby being so big, but she also protected her from Norma's occasional unkind words.

As Katherine's pregnancy progressed, the doctor suspected and then confirmed that she was having twins! Her tummy was huge, and Katherine could not find a comfortable position to sleep. Because of the twins, the military released Al from the brig early so he could support his wife during the delivery of the twins. Instead of him coming directly to Houston to be with Katherine, Al went on a drinking binge and missed the birth of his twins, Carl *(8 pounds, 6 ounces)* and Caren *(7 pounds, 13 ounces)*. Katherine's family and neighbors were amazed at the twins' sizes, and they all helped her get what she needed for the babies.

Katherine, Jasmine, and the twins had to share a small, crowded room with Cheryl. The room had two twin beds, so Katherine slept with Jasmine in her bed, and Cheryl gave up her bed for the twins, and slept on the couch. Katherine had her hands full. If she had to go to the store, she had to take two baby carriers, diaper bags, and Jasmine hanging on her leg. Mami felt sorry for her and blessed her with a double stroller.

When the twins turned six weeks old, Al finally came to visit, but he was afraid to hold the twins, saying they were too small. Katherine had to put the babies on pillows so he would hold them. Soon after that visit, Al loaded up his growing family and took them back to South Carolina. With his base housing reestablished, and with more children, they were allotted a larger house (a small two-bedroom house). Al was still no help to Katherine caring for the children, because he kept his distance from them. One evening, while Katherine had a baby on each hip and one hanging on her leg while she was trying to cook dinner, Al came home and instead of offering to help, asked, "What's for dinner?" She broke down crying! Al could not see what the big deal was, because she was home all day and should have had time to fix his dinner. Katherine let all of her frustrations out about what her day looked like with three kids, housework, laundry, and cooking. Al was unmoved.

Al's lack of concern and his disrespect toward Katherine did not end with dinner. That night he flaunted of his girlfriends in her face. She was the wife of a married couple they had socialized with, and the couple had visited their house frequently. The wife would often visit without her husband when Al was home. Katherine suspected that there was something between her and Al when she noticed how they would sit and drink together, laughing and talking. Katherine pulled the woman aside and asked her to respect her home by not returning. Al denied the accusation, but did not allow the woman to come to the house anymore.

When Al's mother died, he went to Houston alone for the funeral because it was too cumbersome and too expensive for Katherine and three children to travel. Red Cross paid Al's expenses to go home for the funeral. Soon after the death of his mother, Al was discharged from the military and the family was again headed back to Houston. After being in North Carolina for three years, Katherine was right back where she had started, but this time she was ready to go home and be around her family. They moved into the house with Al's father, his sister and brother-in-law. The conditions were crowded, but it would have to do until they could find a place of their own. The house was in a constant state of chaos due to Al's sister and her husband fighting, and he frequently beating her. Al did nothing to stop his brother-in-law from hurting his sister.

Katherine could not tolerate how her sister-in-law was being treated and threatened to shoot her husband with a shotgun if he did not stop the abuse. The brother-in-law moved out of the house, but eventually Al's sister invited him to move back in. Soon after that he nearly beat her to death, leaving the woman scarred for life. Al would never come to his sister's rescue, and Katherine decided in her heart that she would never tolerate that type of abuse from Al or any other man.

During the time Katherine lived with her father-in-law, Katherine helped her sister-in-law clean out Al's mother's things, and found numerous pictures of Al and another woman that had been taken at Al's mother's funeral. When Katherine questioned Al about the pictures, he said she was a family friend. Later the woman in the pictures began stopping by the house under the pretense of coming to see Al's sister. She came so frequently that Katherine and Al's sister would say, "Well, I'll be damned!" whenever they saw her coming. Finally, Katherine confronted Al about "I'll be damned" and told him that the woman was never allowed to come to the house again. Then Katherine confronted the woman about her relationship with Al, and told her that she would not allow her and Al to disrespect her in front of her children. The woman never returned to the house, but Katherine found more pictures of Al and the woman that he had hidden in his mother's things. She knew she wanted out, but did not know how she would survive with three children in tow, no job, and no money.

After two years of living with Al's family, Katherine wanted out of the madness, so she spoke with her grandfather about her and Al renting a home he owned in Acres Homes. She also found out she was expecting another baby, and they needed more room. Al had not made any effort to get them their own home. The house in Acres Home was small and crowded, but at least they would only have their own demons to deal with.

Al did not bring other women home, but he often left for days at a time with no word and later returned home as if nothing had happen. He had problems holding down steady employment because of the PTSD *(Post Traumatic Stress Disorder)* he developed after his Vietnam tours. He would get frustrated and just walk off his jobs. PTSD also left Al with problems sleeping, restlessness, binge drinking, and constantly smoking marijuana, but he refused to get help for his issues and addictions.

Katherine kept the family going by working the evening shift as a custodian at the neighborhood elementary school from 3:00 p.m. to 11:00 p.m. because evenings paid 75 cents more per hour than the day shift. She also liked being home during the day to make sure the children had a good meal prepared when they got home from school. She expected Al to be home with the children in the evening, but he would often disappear, leaving the children home alone. Katherine tried to involve the children in positive activities to help cancel out all of the negativity they were exposed to by taking them to church every Sunday, reading to them, and taking them to the library. Once a month, if they behaved well, she would take them to McDonald's for a treat. She did not have much, but she wanted them to experience some joy in life.

When Katherine's fourth child, Amy, was born, Al was not there to support her, just like her had not been for the other births. Amy was a beautiful, sweet baby, and Katherine became even more committed to going back to school to complete her education. She wanted a better life for her and her children. She knew with a better education, a better job and more independence would come. She was stressed out and tired of the roller coaster life with Al.

The elementary school that she worked for offered GED classes, and Katherine started attending classes on weekends. The instructor allowed her children to sit in the back of the class if they were quiet, because the instructor saw that she was smart and that she wanted to learn. After studying for just a few months, she passed the GED test on the first try, and she thanked God for this break in the clouds.

Katherine planted a vegetable garden in her back yard because she loved the feeling of dirt between her fingers and making things grow, and she definitely had a green thumb. Al had different plans for their new location, such as fixing people's cars in the yard, but Katherine never saw any of the money from his work. She would do without new shoes and clothes so that her children would have decent things, and was grateful for the yearly supply of underwear and bras that her mother and grandmother bought her for Christmas.

After losing job after job, Al resorted to growing things in Katherine's garden—marijuana plants! He started selling marijuana out of the house, and he still smoked marijuana constantly. Al would have huge rolls of money hidden in his tool box and in drawers around the house, but he did not offer Katherine any money to help with bills. He would not give an explanation about what he did with his money. Katherine lived in constant fear that there would be a shooting, or that the police would raid their home and her children would be taken away because of Al's drug dealing. All she could do was pray. She could not understand how Al could sell drugs to children when he had children himself, and the children were getting old enough to know what was really going on.

When Jasmine was 11 years old, she became very ill and had to be rushed to the emergency room. She had a fever, abdominal pain and nausea, but the doctors could not give Katherine a diagnosis. Katherine felt that the stress of all they had been through had made Jasmine ill, because she had become withdrawn and clingy. Katherine also noticed a change in the other children. Caren would lash out and be very rebellious at the slightest incident, and targeted her outbursts at Al. Carl had also become angry and was mean to his sisters. Even sweet Amy was cranky and sullen.

Katherine decided that because the stress had finally affected her children, she needed to get them out of that stressful environment. Because Al would not pay the bills, their utilities were frequently turned off. If the lights were off, Al would go to the meter and turn them back on, so the city eventually removed the meter. The same thing would happen with the gas and water being turned off—Al would turn them back on, and the meters were eventually removed. Al was dealing drugs, but still would not use the money to help his family. They were suffering.

Katherine gave Jasmine permission to date in her junior year. Al did not like the fact that she was dating, and would look through Jasmine's purse and personal items to see who her boyfriend was. Jasmine would come to Katherine crying about Al's invasion of her privacy. Katherine reminded Al that she had approved of Jasmine dating, but he continued to harass her every week about having a boyfriend.

When Jasmine was 18, in her senior year, she became pregnant. Katherine was hurt because she did not want to see her daughter go through the same thing she had been through. She wanted a better life for her daughter. Al threw a fit when he found out Jasmine was pregnant and kept telling Katherine it was her fault because she wouldn't listen to him. Al pressed Jasmine to tell him who the father was, and she said that the father was her boyfriend. Jasmine apologized over and over to Katherine for disappointing her. Katherine was not going to degrade Jasmine like her mother had done to her, and told her she was there for her.

Al continued to make a scene about Katherine letting Jasmine date, and kept insisting that was the reason Jasmine was pregnant. Katherine had no time to focus on the past and began to make room in the tiny house for the new addition because, ready or not, grandmother-hood was coming. When Jasmine's baby girl, Tiffany, was born, Katherine questioned Jasmine again about who the father was, and she stuck with her story about her boyfriend, but the baby did not look like him at all. Al was not there for the birth of his granddaughter either. It did not matter to Katherine because she loved her new granddaughter, and she helped Jasmine bond with and care for Tiffany.

One evening, Katherine and the children were watching a PBS *(Public Broadcast Station)* documentary called "What Happened to Amelia?" The story was about a young girl who had been molested by her father, whose mother did not believe her. Katherine was moved by the story and said she could not see why the mother would not help the girl. She told her children it was important to tell the truth, and not to be afraid to speak up if something was wrong. She noticed that her children were extremely silent after watching the movie.

A week later, when Katherine had gotten off from work late one night and was checking the mail, she noticed a letter in the stack of bills marked "For Mama Only." Katherine thought it was one of the children asking for something for school and wondered how much it was going to cost her. When she opened the letter, she noticed it had been written by her 14-year-old daughter, Caren. In the letter, Caren wrote about how Al had been sexually molesting her, and that she could not take it anymore. She wrote that he was doing the same to Jasmine, but that Jasmine did not want to tell. She said she was speaking out because Al was planning to start doing the same thing to Amy, who was only 12 years old, and she did not want her to be hurt.

Katherine had a million reactions running through her head, and she almost fainted from the thought of Al harming her children. Her heart was racing and she broke out in a sweat as she kept thinking that she had to keep her head and think fast. She sat for a long while with her hands clenched and eyes closed. She cried and prayed as she had never done before as the flood of emotions raced through her mind. Her first primal impulse was to kill Al! Light bulbs started to go off in Katherine's mind as she thought about how Jasmine had been sick and clingy, how Caren had been rebellious and lashing out at Al, and how Carl had become distant and angry.

Katherine thought of how Al had been so upset about Jasmine dating, and then she has an even sicker thought—that she was sleeping with the man who was molesting her daughters. That thought caused a chill to come over her body and she almost threw up. Then, an even deeper thought occurred—her granddaughter was Al's baby! *How could this have gone on without her knowing about it?* Al had caused so much confusion with his drinking and smoking, and the financial strain, until Katherine had not noticed what was happening to her children. While she worked evenings, he had the opportunity to do as he pleased with the girls.

Caren's letter also said that Al had threatened the girls by saying that Katherine would go insane and be put in a mental institution if she ever found out about the molestation, and that they would never see their mother again. Caren's letter ended with her asking Katherine for forgiveness and hoping that this news would not cause her to lose her mind. All Katherine could think about was that she had to be calm around Al and not let him know she was aware of his actions. She knew Al was unstable, and if she confronted him with the anger and hatred she had in her heart at that moment, he would probably try to harm her and the children to keep them silent. She had to think fast.

Through a steady stream of tears, Katherine called a close friend and told her what had happened. She had to tell someone, or she would start screaming. Her friend told her that she and the children could come and stay with her if she needed a place to go where Al would not find them, and Katherine accepted her offer. She knew Al would come looking for her at her mother's or grandparents' homes, and she did not want to put them in harm's way. Al was too cunning and unpredictable.

Katherine placed the letter in the pocket of her work smock so it would be hidden from view. She went into the bathroom, dried her eyes, and practiced how to keep her face straight and not to show fear. The children had all gone to bed, so she made her usual rounds, kissing them goodnight. When she got to Caren, she whispered to her that she had gotten her letter, and reassured her that everything would be all right. Caren began to cry and told her mother thank you. Katherine thanked her for telling her what had happened, and kissed her forehead, telling her that she had done the right thing.

As she kissed each child goodnight, she told them to gather all of their books out of their lockers at school the next day and bring them home. They asked why, and she told them not to ask questions, just to bring the books home. That night, Katherine met Jasmine in the kitchen and confronted her about the letter. Jasmine's face went pale and she froze in her tracks. Jasmine was speechless, and Katherine thought the girl might pass out. Jasmine did not answer, but just stood there, pale and trembling. When she asked Jasmine if Al was Tiffany's father, she still could not answer, only cried. Jasmine had kept the secret for so long that the shock of it being exposed was overwhelming. Katherine reassured Jasmine that everything would be okay. Jasmine finally broke her silence and wanted to know what the plan was, but Katherine said she would let them know the following day. She told Jasmine to gather a few things for herself and the baby, and to put them in her backpack. She kissed her sweetly on her cheek and told her goodnight.

Katherine went to bed as usual and lay down next to Al as if nothing unusual had happened. That night would be the longest night of her life. As she lay there all night long, she did not sleep, and she constantly prayed, "Help me, Lord!" She needed God's help to give her strength to keep her composure, and to keep from killing Al in his sleep. She was so angry and hurt that it took all she had not to get the gun that was under the bed and blow Al away. She knew that if she harmed him, she would play into the devil's hands, and that her family would be destroyed if she went to jail for murder.

As Katherine lay there praying, she thought of all the mean things Al had done to her—how he had made fun of her body and her hair, and her clothes. He had not been there for the birth of the twins or Amy. Their family had suffered because Al could not hold a job and would not give her money to pay the bills. Her mind flashed back to the night Al had come home drunk and demanded that she have anal sex with him, and when she declined, he held her down and raped her. He was extremely strong and she couldn't fight him off, and all she could do was put her head in the pillow to keep from screaming. When he had finished, he told her that she was his to do with as he pleased, because he had paid $5 for her *(the cost of the marriage license)*. She almost screamed out loud when she thought of what her girls, her babies, had endured when Al had raped them. "Lord, help me, please!" was her plea.

When day finally broke, Katherine rose as she did every morning, fixed the children's breakfast and sent them off to school, reminding them to clean out their lockers. Al asked what did they need all of their books for, and Katherine told him she had some work she wanted them to help her with at her job and they would need their books to study when they finished. Al did not think that was unusual, because she occasionally took them to work with her to help her and keep them out of trouble. Al suspected nothing when she told him she had some errands to run.

Katherine went to a pay phone, called the counselor at the school where she worked and told him what had happened, and needed to know what to do next to get Al arrested and brought up on charges. The counselor had her come to his office, where he helped her contact the police, CPS (Child Protective Service) and other agencies that could assist them. By that evening, there was a warrant issued for Al's arrest and a restraining order to keep him from picking the children up from school.

When the children came home from school, they had brought all of their books with them. She loaded them up into the car, along with little Tiffany under her arm. They waved goodbye to Al as if all was well and headed down the road. When they were about two blocks down the street, Katherine had to pull over. Her muscles relaxed and she lost her grip on the steering wheel. She began to tremble from the tension and just started shouting over and over, "Thank you, Jesus! Thank you, Jesus!" Hot tears flowed down her face as she praised God for safely delivering her and her children out of their situation. She did not know what the next day would hold; she was just thankful for THAT day of deliverance! Katherine was determined that she and her children would never spend another night in that house with Al. After Katherine collected herself, she drove to her friend's house, where they would find safe shelter.

The next day Al realized that Katherine and the children had not returned home and called her family members and her friends, trying to see where she was. When Al heard there was a warrant for his arrest, he ran from the police for a week, until the police arrested him. When Al was taken into custody for questioning, he nonchalantly admitted that he had molested the children. The judge sentenced him to six years in prison and registered him as a sex offender. Because Al confessed, the girls did not have to testify in open court. They gave their statements to the judge behind closed doors. Katherine and the children stayed with a friend for three weeks, until she could get paid and rent her own place.

Katherine was too overwhelmed to ask the girls the details of the molestations, because she felt her heart could not bear another thing. She filed for and obtained her divorce from Al when he went to prison. A few weeks after Al was sent to prison, and Caren saw that they were safe from Al, she told Katherine some details of Al's abuse. She told about how Al had gotten Carl high on alcohol and marijuana to keep him from realizing what he was doing to the girls. Al had gotten little Amy drunk also to keep her unaware. Carl would never admit that Al had molested him, but Katherine suspected that Carl's later behavioral change of repeated drinking, smoking, and getting arrested was his way of dealing with what he felt was unmentionable. Jasmine would not discuss what Al had done to her, but seemed to be angry at Caren for telling Katherine about the molestation. It was as if she was protecting Al and missed him. Katherine was worried about the effect that the abuse had on her children, and took them to counseling as often as she could. Often times her car was broken down, or she would not have money for gas and could not get them there. She knew they all needed help, but often could not get them to the help they needed.

After Caren's revelations, Katherine's youngest daughter Amy came to Katherine and told her that she too had been raped by one of Al's nephews when she was nine, during the time they lived with Al's relatives.

Katherine's soul shut down. She now realized why Amy had reacted so viciously toward her cousin when he came to live with them briefly. Amy said the boy had threatened to harm to her if she told what he had done. Katherine began to see the generational spirits of abuse, incest, and rape that were present in Al's family.

When Katherine heard Amy's story, she could not deal with another thing emotionally, but she did contact the cousin's mother and told her she was to never bring her son to her house again—she did explain why. Katherine knew that she would eventually have to deal with Amy's situation and get justice for her too, but just not then. She always felt that Amy resented her for not taking her issue more seriously and bringing the cousin to justice at that time.

Al served only three of his eight-year sentence, and after his release, he suffered with heart problems that caused him to be frequently admitted to the hospital. Al did not try and contact Katherine after his release from prison, but Katherine heard through a family member that he was living with a woman who had young children. Katherine often wondered if Al was doing the same thing to those children as he had done to her children.

During one of Al's many hospital admissions, Katherine visited him. She had no particular explanation why she wanted to see him after so many years. Perhaps she wanted to see what had become of the monster that had brought so much pain into her life, and the lives of her children. When she walked into Al's hospital room, he froze in mid-motion as he was about to sit in a chair near his bedside. He looked frightened, as if he did not know what to expect from her. Katherine spoke to him and told him to have a seat. She sat in another chair across the room. Here Al was, frail, weak, and scared—he didn't look like a monster at all!

Katherine actually felt pity for him. They made polite conversation about him needing to do what the doctors asked him to do, but Al never acknowledged what he had done to the children, nor did he offer an apology for the suffering he had caused. When Katherine realized that Al had no remorse for what he had done, she stood and left the room as quietly as she had come. It was if a load had been lifted from her soul, so when she got to her car, she broke out laughing. She laughed so hard that she cried! God had revealed to her that she had nothing to fear ever again from Al. He was defeated. Before the day was over, she received the news that Al was dead. The children attended the funeral, but Katherine did not.

Katherine's family is still in the healing process from the abuse. They share with each other some of the things they endured together. Katherine began going for counseling, realizing it would take years for her to heal. She has seen how generational curses have affected her family, when later her granddaughters were molested by their stepfather. Katherine also championed getting justice for her granddaughters, and teaching them that the abuse curse ends with them.

Katherine understands that hiding the truth, and being silent about past hurts, only destroys the future. She tells her story in order to raise awareness about incest and rape that can occur in families, and how to recognize the signs. Katherine knows with prayer and faith, healing can and will take place. By raising awareness about family abuse in her own family, Katherine hopes to protect the future of her great-grandchildren.

After 10-plus years of studying, taking classes, and never giving up, Katherine completed her associates degree. She later enrolled in DeVry University in 2008 and received her bachelor's degree in 2011! She wanted to lead her family by example to never give up on your dreams. The next chapters of Katherine's life will be all about overcoming and the fulfilling of dreams for her family, with the help of an unfailing God.

Reflection on Katherine's Story

By Rev. Ella McCarroll, M. Div.

Katherine's story has the themes of abandonment, family dysfunction, and redemption intertwined throughout.

Abandonment: Katherine's story reflects the vulnerability that girls are subjected to when abandoned by their fathers. The father has been given a unique role and responsibility to provide for his children, and not provoke them to anger. He is to bring them up in the discipline and instruction of the Lord. *("...fathers, provoke not your children to wrath; but bring them up in the admonition of the Lord." Ephesians 6:4).* Some girls who lack growing up with a stable father figure seek love, and boys are more than willing to offer it, with the expectations of sex in return. The internal motivation for girls and boys, however, is quite different.

Girls are more vulnerable to giving of themselves and their bodies in the name of love, seeking to find the long-lost love of their father. Some boys, on the other hand, seek sexual gratification, exploitation, and experimentation to prove their masculinity. All the men who promised to love, protect, and provide for Katherine abandoned her. *"If the Lord had not been my help, my soul would soon have lived in the land of silence." (Psalm 94:17)*

Girls can often mistake controlling, domineering relationships as a sign of love, when in reality they are disguised as abuse 101: "Wolves in Sheep's Clothing." There is a secular and biblical illustration of this. One recorded in Aesop's Fables describes a wolf that put on a sheep skin so that he could disguise himself as a lamb. The biblical context of a wolf in sheep's clothing says, *"Beware of false prophets who come to you in sheep's clothing but inwardly are ravenous wolves." (Matthew 7:15).* The principle is that there are wolves in this world seeking to kill and destroy the mind, body, and spirit.

Second, Katherine's story reiterates the reality of predisposed generational curses that recreate family dysfunction. The emotional abuse Katherine experienced from her father and stepfather were not worked through before entering new relationships with men. One cannot begin a healthy new relationship until the previous relationship has been healed. Marriage is the stage for acting out unresolved issues stemming from the family of origin. Unresolved hurt, pain, and grief lead to confusion and blur one's ability to be fully present and aware of abuse, even when it is prevalent in your own household. Generational curses can continue only when there is no awareness of the emotional processes still at work, and the skills to respond differently. One of the characteristics of a dysfunctional family is the **conspiracy of silence**. It is the unconscious survival role children and adults play to survive.

Thirdly, Katherine's story is one of redemption. Forgiveness and healing are victory twins for moving beyond the past. Rick Warren of Saddle Back Church says, "God never wastes a hurt." *"God comforts us in all our troubles so that we can comfort others. When we are weighed down with troubles, it is for your comfort and salvation! For when we ourselves are comforted, we will certainly comfort you. Then you can patiently endure the same things." (2 Corinthians 1:4, 6 NLT); "For I know the plans I have for you," declares the* LORD, *"plans to prosper you and not to harm you, plans to give you hope and a future." Jeremiah 29:11 NIV*

"Sharonda"

By J. Harris

Reflection by Min. Leah Jordan, M. Div.

GOD HAS GIVEN EACH OF US SPECIAL GIFTS and talents to glorify God, make this world a better place, and be a source of love and encouragement, but Satan takes special effort to try and destroy those gifts. It is up to us to recognize those gifts, and to make every effort to protect them and bring them to fruition. These words came to mind when meeting Sharonda, a gifted and talented young woman. She is a walking, living testimony of how God can rescue misused talent and restore it to its intended purpose for His kingdom. Sharonda is gifted with a beautiful singing voice, and to hear her sing is a soul-stirring experience. And, to hear Sharonda's story of what God has brought her through, and the many times the enemy tried to take her gift, makes her singing all the more beautiful.

More often than not, living in poverty can be a vehicle that the enemy will try and use to destroy people's spirits. It is not always how we start out, but how God allows us to finish that matters. In the 1980s, Sharonda realized as a young girl living in the government housing developments of Dallas, Texas, that she had a tough beginning. Her mother, Judith, was fighting an uphill battle to raise five children on very little money. There never seemed to be enough money, food or anything good. Judith saw her children become overwhelmed and fall prey to a system that was supposedly intended to advance her family, but instead caused even greater setbacks.

Judith's story is not any different from countless other mothers who have found themselves in that same government-regulated environment. She was raising her children with her new husband, Travis, in an attempt to find a better way of life for themselves and their children. Sharonda's biological father was no longer in the picture because of his heroin addiction. He had taken from his family's scarce possessions to support his drug habit. He had been in and out of their lives, and his contribution to the family was more pain than gain. Judith made the decision to sever that relationship for the greater good of her family. When she met and married Travis, he willingly took the responsibility of heading the family.

A girl in this world needs her father to be her protector, not a hindrance. There are too many forces that can cause harm to a female child in the projects. Judith and Travis did their best to surround their family with love and protection by taking them to church and exposing them to Christ. They had to give their children something that would be a part of their lives to protect them when they were not there. Sharonda loved the church, and as a small child she discovered that she could sing. People applauded and praised her for her gift, and she loved the response. With two sisters and one brother at home, attention was sometimes difficult to come by. So, Sharonda appreciated the attention she received at church. Giving her life to Christ at six years old was easy for Sharonda, because life did not have any negative history, and her praise was innocent and pure. Christ was a good fit for her.

Sharonda excelled in school and was a fast learner, so school became an outlet and a change of scenery from the chaos of the projects. She also got praises at school too, and tried to stay in that arena as much and as often as possible. When Judith was not dealing with systems, such as housing authority, welfare, health care, racism, and the institute of marriage, she spread her attention on Sharonda. That extra attention from her mother kept Sharonda in constant conflict with her other two sisters. They felt that Judith paid more attention to and loved Sharonda more, causing frequent fist fights and arguments between the sisters. They envied the attention she received at church with her singing, and at school from the teachers, causing Judith to feel more like a referee than a mother. The closeness that one sister should feel for another was not in their home, so Sharonda and her little brother Mark were the best of friends. With him she found acceptance, peace and protection, and Mark did his best to protect Sharonda from her sisters.

Sharonda enjoyed spending time with her girl cousins, often spending the weekends at each other's houses like one big slumber party. She would much rather hang out with her cousins than with her sisters, because there were no arguments or knock-down, drag-out fights, just quality girl time. Of course, there was the occasional dispute over dolls, clothes, or toys, but not the wrath due to envy and jealousy from her sisters. Sharonda's 15-year-old boy cousin, Tyree, was often displaced out of his room and off his favorite sports channel when the sleepovers occurred. He would yell at the girls to get out of his life, but he was outnumbered by the nine- and ten-year-old girls. He was a cousin by association, meaning he was the child of a close friend of Sharonda's aunt, and she had taken him in because his own family was broken and could not care for him. Thus, Tyree became family through association. One weekend, the sleepover at her cousins' house would not be like the others for Sharonda. This good thing was about to come to an end.

Nine years of age for Sharonda would always be a landmark in her life, because the innocence of childhood was about to be shortened, and life would become much too complicated for a little girl trying to find her way in this world. At one typical weekend sleepover at her cousin's house, Sharonda was awakened by Tyree in the dead of night. Toys were strewn about the room, and everyone was sound asleep. Tyree came to where she was sleeping and quietly slipped his hand over her mouth. He had a look in his eyes that she had never seen before, a look of sheer evil. Sharonda almost did not recognize him because of the look on his face. He was out of place in the girls' room late at night.

Sharonda was startled, and almost screamed. *Had he come to deliver some bad news? Had something happened to her mother or her family?* He whispered, "Come with me," as he took her by the hand, led her to his room, and began to push her around. She was amazed at how strong he was! *Why was he treating her like this? Had she done something to make him mad?* He threatened to kill her if she screamed out, and the look in his eyes showed that he meant it. Tyree pushed her down on his bed and began to pull her panties off, tearing them a little. Sharonda struggled and tried pleading with him to stop. She cried, saying, "We are cousins! This is not right!" He told her to shut up. His heavy body pressed her small frame down, and he forced her legs apart with his leg. She cried tears of disappointment and shame as he forced himself into her, and pain shot all through her innocent body. Sharonda cried out to God, but there was only pain. *Where was God when she needed Him most?* She had sung so beautifully to Him, but he was not here in this dark place to help her. A million thoughts rushed through her mind, and none of them made sense.

Sharonda needed protection from someone, anyone! A father with addiction problems could not protect her. A stepfather with his hands full raising a ready-made family could not help, and neither could her baby brother. All of her male protectors were not around. Sharonda could not go to her mother, because she may think she was lying to get attention. After all, this was family that was hurting her, and she couldn't break up the family. Tyree moaned and groaned as he moved in and out of her body. For Sharonda, the pain was unbearable! He kept his hand over her mouth to keep her from screaming or crying out. She felt helpless and used.

When Tyree was done, he lifted his heavy, sweaty body off hers as if nothing had happened, and she now recognized his face. He leaned down and whispered to her, "If you ever tell anyone what happened, I will kill you!" Sharonda believed his threat as she lay there paralyzed from fear and pain. She envisioned what her dead body would look like, and no one would know the cause. Something died in her at that moment, along with her innocence. Blood was everywhere, and Tyree brought her a towel to clean her private parts. When Sharonda saw the blood, she thought he really had tried to kill her. Through her tears she cleaned up as best she could, then put her torn panties on. As she tried to find the will to walk out of that room, Tyree shoved her out the door as if she had offended him. He warned her again, "If you tell, I WILL kill you!" It would be their secret.

Sharonda limped back to the room where her girl cousins were sleeping and laid quietly sobbing in her pillow, trying to process everything that has just happened to her. To her it seemed as if the rape had lasted for hours, but had only been a few minutes.

Sharonda's world had forever been changed, and no one was applauding or cheering at this major event. Instead, this was a place of shame, fear, pain, darkness, guilt, and loneliness. Sharonda had no knowledge of sex before this happened, other than when she had overheard her sisters talk about boys and "getting some." She had no idea sex was like this. If only she could tell her sisters what had happened, maybe they would treat her better. Her oldest sister had her own hell to deal with, being trapped in an addiction to crack cocaine.

Sharonda felt she could not tell her mother what happened, feeling her mother would be so disappointed in her, and would have to bear the expense of burying a dead daughter. That thought was too much for Sharonda, so she slowly withdrew from the world and its reality, because the reality was too painful. The weekend sleepovers with her cousins were no longer something that Sharonda looked forward to. She began to encourage her girl cousins to come to her house, and would make excuses for not wanting to go to their house. Her cousins wanted to know why she no longer wanted to visit them, so to avoid more questions and spilling the truth, she gave in to going to their house. Each time Sharonda visited her cousin's house for their weekend sleepovers, Tyree was there. He would wait until everyone was asleep, crawl into the girls' room, kneel beside her bed, and make Sharonda come to his room, where he would repeat the rape. She would beg him not to do it, telling him that it was wrong because they were family, but he continued with the threat of taking her life if she told. Sharonda was miserable and felt no one could help her. The rapes continued each time she would visit her cousins, and each time she felt dirty and ashamed.

Sharonda enjoyed her girl cousins whenever they came to her house, because Tyree was not there and she could relax and enjoy their fun and games. When she was 11 years old, she came home from school and found Tyree and his bags at her house! Sharonda's aunt had fallen on hard times, so Judith had agreed to help out by taking Tyree off her hands. He had no other family that wanted him, so Judith took him in. Sharonda was shocked. *How could this happen?* She had enough to deal with fighting with her sisters. Now Tyree would have easy and frequent access to her. God had left the building!

Tyree lived up to her expectations and continued to come for her in the night. Sharonda tried everything she could think of to throw him off track by pretending she was in deep sleep, or ignoring him when he would crawl beside her bed. She even tried staying up late watching TV and sleeping on the couch, but he would still come for her. Sharonda was beginning to show signs of stress by being cranky, rebellious, talking back to her mother and stepfather, and finding interests outside the home. The streets seemed safer than the nightmare that was going on at home. Her grades began to fall, going from an A-B student to Cs and Ds. Sharonda stopped singing at church because she felt God had abandoned her, because a loving God would not have allowed Tyree to use and abuse her body as he was doing. She had no song in her heart for God, and decided to give the world a try.

By age 12, because of the stress at home, Sharonda began drinking alcohol and smoking weed. In the housing projects, if you show yourself friendly enough, you can get anything you want. Sex was her way to get what she wanted and needed, and to make her forget her pain. Sharonda no longer believed in love. It was now strictly about business and survival. She decided that if Tyree was going to continue to live at her house, she needed to find a new home. She wanted to have her own place, where she decided who came and went. Even though she was smart, school was taking her too slowly to success, especially when she saw the nice things the drug dealers had acquired from their profits. Even though her sister was a drug user, Sharonda found that the drug dealing business paid well. Neither Judith nor her stepfather could protect her from Tyree and provide her with a safe place to sleep, so Sharonda did what she felt would get her some money and a place of her own the fastest way—dealing drugs.

Judith was constantly required to come to the school to meet with Sharonda's teachers and principals because she was out of control. Judith tried punishing her by making her stay home, but Sharonda would find a way to slip off. Staying home was not a place she wanted to be with Tyree waiting there for her—the streets were safer. Sharonda continued to try and find that feeling of being appreciated before the rape, so she sought satisfaction by having sex with her many boyfriends. With each boyfriend, the relationship was always the same: short and uncommitted. It was hard for her to concentrate in school when she was hung over from drinking and smoking late nights. Her goal was to be drunk and high enough to be numb when Tyree took her body.

When Sharonda was 16 years old, she got a job at a local friend's chicken restaurant, because she did not want Judith to know about her drug dealing. She needed a real job to cover for all of the extra money she had. She used her money to support her drinking and smoking habit, while she saved money for her own place. Because she was underage, no one would rent an apartment to her. One evening at work, Sharonda was burned severely on her foot with some hot oil and had to be off work from the injury. The people she hung out with told her she had a good "case" and encouraged her to file suit for her injuries. Sharonda took their advice, obtained a lawyer, and won her case: $10,000!It was Christmas in July! *(Sharonda still carries the burn scar.)* She had never seen that much money at once in her life, not even with drug dealing, so she saw the money as her ticket to getting out on her own and away from Tyree. Judith begged her to put the money up for college, but Sharonda only wanted out on her own.

Finishing high school was no longer a priority for Sharonda. She only wanted to stay high and have enough sex to be numb. Sharonda had spent most of her nights with her new boyfriend to avoid going home, and in her search for love and acceptance, she was about to face a new reality: motherhood. Sharonda noticed that her body did not feel the same, but blamed it on too many sleepless nights. When the nausea and weight gain came, she had a suspicion that she might be pregnant. The relationship with her boyfriend was not working out, and Sharonda knew that a baby in the picture would not help the situation. She had to figure out on her own what to do and decided not to inform her boyfriend about the baby. Sharonda went to the free neighborhood clinic, and the doctor confirmed that she was pregnant.

Sharonda told Judith about the pregnancy with the hope that she would get some motherly support. Instead, Judith felt hurt, and gave Sharonda the "I told you so" speech. Judith said she had predicted that something like this would happen if Sharonda's life continued to be out of control. Now there was another life in the middle of the whirlwind. Sharonda knew that her lifestyle had to change for the baby's sake—no more drugs and alcohol. She continued to go to school, but concentrating was especially hard with no drugs in her system to help her get though the day. Sharonda had missed so many days from school that she decided to stay home until the baby was born, and go back the next year.

Tyree did not let Sharonda's pregnancy stop him from trying to approach her, but this time Sharonda fought back. One evening they got into a huge argument when she refused to go along with his sex acts, so she picked up a flower vase and hit him across the head! Judith had to break up the fight, and asked what started it. Neither of them told the reason, only giving Sharonda's pregnancy as the reason for her change in temperament. Judith contacted Tyree's relatives and suggested that they come and get him for a while. A week after the fight, Tyree's relatives came and got him, and Sharonda was relieved that he was gone. She wondered why she had not fought him like that sooner.

Sharonda felt free for the first time in years, and each week her tummy grew larger she stayed sober. She felt she had something special to live for and wanted to give her baby a better life than she had. She vowed to protect her child from predators like Tyree, and give her baby a safe, happy home. Sharonda's church members embraced her while she was pregnant because they saw a new life on the way, and a new opportunity to make a difference. Judith was there for Sharonda during the pregnancy by making sure she ate right and went to her doctor's appointments. When it came time for Sharonda to deliver the baby, Judith was there for her. Sharonda's 17-year-old body had been through a lot, and delivering a baby was not easy. She was rewarded for her pain and struggle with a beautiful, healthy baby girl named Ebony. She had finally done something right, and decided to break her silence with God by thanking Him for her beautiful baby. Ebony looked so much like her boyfriend, and once again Sharonda debated if she should let him know he had a daughter. Ultimately, she decided not to inform him because she was afraid he would try to take Ebony from her. She knew she could not bear losing her baby.

Just when Sharonda had settled into motherhood, the news came that Tyree was moving back to her house! All she could think of was how peaceful her life had been while he was gone, but this time she would not stick around to go back through that hell. She made up in her mind that if Tyree approached her, she would kill him. Sharonda took the money she had saved from her settlement and had one of her older friends pay the deposit to get her an apartment. Judith was upset and worried when Sharonda told her she and one-month-old Ebony were moving out. Sharonda told her that she used what was left from her settlement money to cover her apartment deposit, and in addition would get a job. She could not tell Judith that her real motivation for moving was to get away from Tyree. Sharonda was also counting on her drug dealing friends to set her up in business again in order to pay her rent.

Not very many 17-year-olds have their own apartment and their own car, but Sharonda was an exception to the rule. She managed to have her own place, be a mother, and go to school, but it was tough. She enjoyed doing whatever she wanted with no parental supervision. She eventually resumed her lifestyle of drugs and drinking, because the pain of abuse continued to creep into her mind as she replayed the scenes. Sharonda felt she needed something to dull the pain, so sex and drugs worked for her.

Sharonda returned to school to complete her senior year, and Judith and her sisters babysat little Ebony. On one occasion the school had a blood drive, and Sharonda and her friend decided to participate to get the free T-shirt giveaways. As part of the blood collection process, each donor's blood was tested for HIV/AIDS and other diseases. A few days after the blood drive, Sharonda was notified by the blood bank that they could not use her blood, and she was asked to contact the health department. Sharonda did not want to hear the news, because she had her suspicions that they had found some type of disease. She remembered her cousin Gary, who was dying from AIDS he had contracted from a girlfriend. She would often go and help care for him, and knew the suffering AIDS would bring. Gary had stabbed his girlfriend when he found out she had given him HIV. He still lived with that bitterness, especially since he was now in full-blown AIDS.

Sharonda let a week go by before she decided to follow up on her test results with the health department counselor. The counselor confirmed her fear—she was HIV positive. The shock from the news sent her mind racing out of control. *Who, when, how?* She had no answers because she had covered a lot of territory with different partners, and had not always used protection. The counselor explained to her that if she did not start treatment soon, she could develop AIDS. She knew she had to start treatment, but was not ready yet.

Her emotions came in waves, with her first reaction being a flood of tears, then anger, then shame. She felt dead inside. Sharonda cried all the way home and locked herself in her room for three days. She did not want to talk to anyone. She took care of Ebony, but that was all. School was no longer a priority, even with graduation a few months away. She no longer had a desire to finish school, because she felt her life was finished. Her poor lifestyle choices had come to haunt her, and she didn't know if she could face the music. Sharonda had just wanted to get away from Tyree, and now had run into more trouble. *How would she tell her mother? Would her family forsake her?*

She finally decided it was time to tell Judith, and with tears flowing, she laid her head on her mother's lap and told her of the diagnosis. Judith fell apart and went into hysterics! Sharonda needed Judith's strength, but it was not there. She had to find her own strength and go back to where the real source was—God. Hidden in her heart was the feeling that God had deserted her long ago. Without Sharonda's knowledge, Judith shared Sharonda's diagnosis with her grandmother, aunts, uncles and sisters. The news sent the whole family into a panic.

Sharonda's meeting with Judith had left her depressed and alone. So, she and Ebony went to the New Year's Eve church service to seek God's favor in her circumstances. When she arrived at church, she found out Judith and her sisters had told the entire congregation about her diagnosis! People came to Sharonda asking if they could pray for her, and telling her how sorry they were about her diagnosis. Sharonda was so embarrassed and thought, *"How could my family do that to me?"* She was angry, and left Ebony at the church with her mother to go to her brother's house. She and Mark had always has a good relationship; surely he would understand.

Sharonda arrived at Mark's house in tears and broke the news to him about her diagnosis, and how Judith and her sisters had told everyone at church. Mark's reaction to her news came as a total surprise when he began telling her how hurt he was, and started yelling at her, "How could you let this happen?" Sharonda could not believe what she heard! She and Mark had always been able to talk and not judge each other. She reacted to his cruel remarks with more cruel remarks, and they came to blows, rearranging the whole house. *(Mark later apologized to her, and told her he was reacting out of fear and love. He said he loved his sister so much, and could not bear that this had happened to her.)*

Sharonda ran from Mark's house in tears because she felt her family was acting as if she was already dead. *Where were the words of encouragement and hope that she needed?* She began to combine her own fear with the fear she had seen in her mother's eyes as she jumped into her car. Sharonda decided that life was not worth living, and she would end it all. She found herself driving down the freeway, going over 100 mph. She made the decision to cross over the freeway and run head-on into the first 18-wheeler that came along, ending it all.

Through blinding tears, Sharonda recalled the sadness she had experienced in her young life that started with the rape by Tyree, and that horrible secret she had held in her heart. She thought of her reckless lifestyle, the HIV diagnosis, the fight with Mark, and little Ebony. When she thought of Ebony she had a moment of clarity, and could see her daughter's innocent, beautiful face. *What would happen to Ebony if she died?* At that very moment God spoke to her heart, **"This is not the end!"** Sharonda suddenly felt herself taking her foot off of the gas and easing on the brake. She slowed down, pulled over to the side of the freeway and stopped, crying uncontrollably. Sharonda finally realized that it was no longer about her, but knew she had to fight for her life, to be there for Ebony.

Sharonda made her way back to church to pick up Ebony, and when she saw Ebony's smiling face, her heart melted. She felt so undeserving of such a sweet child. *Did the smiling face looking back at her know that her mother had received a death sentence?* Sharonda's depression deepened as the voices from the dark convinced her she was too damaged to be saved. No one, not even Jesus himself, could save her from her fate. She thought money, drugs, alcohol, and sex had been the answer to all her problems, only to find those things had led to her destruction.

As Sharonda sat in the back of the church, Judith sensed how depressed she was and felt she should not be alone. Judith convinced her to come home with her. After Sharonda kissed Ebony and put her to bed, she watched her fall asleep and decided that Ebony would be better off without her. Surely there was a way to end this quietly, so Sharonda searched her mother's medicine cabinet and found a full bottle of prescription pain pills. Sharonda decided to take the pills and sleep from this life to the next, holding Ebony in her arms. Judith must have sensed that something was not right and came into the room. Sharonda was sitting on the edge of the bed with the pill bottle in her hand, contemplating life over death. Judith did not panic, but quietly sat beside her and took the pills from her hands. Judith spoke to Sharonda softly and said, "God is the author and finisher of your life, and He has not said that your life is over. There is a wonderful life ahead of you. Find a way to live it!" Sharonda broke down crying, laying her head in her mother's lap. She could not stop herself from crying, and Judith did not try to stop her.

As Judith stroked Sharonda's face, she spoke life into her child who wanted to die. She told her about how the Bible promised that if she held onto her faith, that she would "live and not die." Judith affirmed her love to Sharonda and apologized for sharing her diagnosis with the family and the church, but she was afraid, and would not be able to bear losing her. Judith reminded Sharonda that her life was not just about her. Ebony needed her mother. No one could love, raise, and fight for her child like she could. Then, Judith prayed over her as she had never prayed before, asking God to remove the spirit of depression and despair from Sharonda and replace it with joy, and a will to live. Suddenly, Sharonda stopped crying, and a sense of peace came over her. She wanted to live! The Lord spoke to her heart, telling her to open up her mouth and praise God through song and testimony. He affirmed to her that her willingness to speak about HIV would help to save other young people and adults from making devastating choices. Sharonda was still not able to tell Judith about the rape, because she still had a fear that Tyree would make good on his promise and find a way to kill her, or Ebony.

Sharonda, Ebony and Judith attended church together for New Year's morning service, and at the end of the service, Sharonda asked the pastor for the opportunity to speak. When she was given the mic, she told the congregation of her HIV diagnosis, and how she struggled with thoughts of suicide. She told them how God spoke to her and said her life was not over, and that she now wanted to live! She than sang with all of her heart, and the presence of God seemed to fill the congregation. People came to the altar for prayer and rededication of their lives to Christ, and many of the members surrounded her and prayed for her and Ebony. It was a moment that would forever change her life, because she wanted to live and not die.

Sharonda renewed her life in Christ and placed her situation in God's hands. She started going back to church, but was not ready to sing in the choir. She found treatment for HIV and started taking her medications faithfully. Initially the numerous pills with the side effects of nausea, weakness, and stomach upset were disheartening, but she was determined to do what she needed to do to stay alive and raise her child. She soon found a job at a local hospital clinic office and gave up dealing drugs. Sharonda and Ebony still had their own little apartment, but Judith insisted on babysitting her granddaughter. *(Tyree had been shipped off to relatives in California and would no longer be around Judith's house.)*

Different churches and organizations invited Sharonda speak and educate them about HIV/AIDS and to tell her story. Occasionally she would sing at her speaking engagements, where it brought healing to the listeners and to her. She no longer needed or wanted drugs to make her feel better; she just wanted to do what God was calling her to do. At one of the events, a tall, handsome young man named Von came to her and told her how her testimony affected him, because he too had been diagnosed with HIV as a result of his drug use. He had served in the military and often suffered from PTSD *(Post Traumatic Stress Disorder),* but because of his relationship with God, he was able to deal with the stress instead of seeking drugs. He poured his heart out to her about the isolation he'd endured from his family and friends since his diagnosis. Von said he had not found the courage to speak out about his condition as she had. Sharonda felt his pain and wanted to reach out to help him through his struggle, so they agreed to meet for lunch the following week.

During their meeting time, Sharonda found Von genuine and conversational. It had been a long time since she had a civil conversation with a man that did not involve drugs, alcohol or sex. She found herself attracted to him, and appreciated talking to someone openly who could truly identify with her diagnosis. Von told her that he had contracted HIV through sharing contaminated needles during his heroin and crack cocaine use. He said he had been clean from drugs for two years, had a good job with the city, and lived with his mother.

Von's testimony drew Sharonda closer to him, and him to her. They began to see each other often, and the relationship blossomed into mutual love. After a few months of dating, Sharonda allowed him to meet Ebony. She was very protective of who she allowed around Ebony, because she did not want anyone to hurt her child as Tyree had hurt her. Little Ebony bonded well with Von, and the two became fast friends. After six months of dating, Von asked Sharonda to marry him, and she accepted. He had previously married and divorced very young, and had one daughter that he saw on a regular basis, but he was now ready to settle down and have a family. Sharonda and Von went to counseling at the HIV clinic regarding having a family when both parents were HIV positive. They were told that they could have children who would be HIV-free if Sharonda was given certain drugs during and prior to delivery.

Judith had her reservations about Von, because he was older and had a history of drug use, but her even greater fear was that Sharonda would die young. Judith wanted Sharonda to be happy with the time she had left. Von and Sharonda had a simple Friday evening ceremony performed by the pastor at Sharonda's home church, with family and a few friends gathered. Whatever reservation those present had about the relationship, they kept to themselves, because they all knew the issues the couple was dealing with. The couple decided to live in Sharonda's small apartment until they could save and get a larger place.

Their honeymoon night, Von left "to run an errand" and did not come home for two days. Sharonda was afraid that something had happened to him and called Von's mother and relatives, but they had not heard from him. She called the nearby hospitals to see if he had been to their emergency rooms, but he was not there. Sharonda was worried that he may have become ill and not been able to reach her. Von had gotten paid that Friday, and she was worried that he may have been robbed. Late that Sunday night, Von came home with eyes red, unbathed, and broke. Sharonda immediately began to question him about where he had been, and where was his money. Von looked at her through glazed eyes and told her it was none of her business, and to leave him alone. Sharonda was totally confused by his comments and demanded to know what was going on. Instead of explaining where he had been for the last two days, he fell asleep on the couch and slept through Monday, and missed work. Sharonda had been around enough drug addicts to know one when she saw one—she just had not planned to marry one. She felt in her soul that this marriage was built on lies and would not work, but she would do her best to be a good wife. Maybe Von would get help for his addiction problem.

Sharonda would find out that this was not Von's first time going on crack cocaine binges and missing work. Von's supervisor called him that Monday and fired him because he had missed so many days. What a way to start a marriage! Sharonda felt she had married a man like her father—drug addicted, irresponsible and harmful to the family. She was determined to make her marriage work, even with Von being out of work. As the months passed and Von looked for work, Sharonda found out she was pregnant, and that they would need a larger apartment. Von was excited about the new baby, and worked hard at staying clean and finding another job.

They went to church together as a family, and Von loved to hear her sing. Worship seemed to focus him and keep him away from desiring drugs. Perhaps with the move to a larger place, Von would be motivated to work harder to give their family a chance. The doctor reassured them that Sharonda should have a normal pregnancy and delivery if she continued to take her HIV medications. Two months before Sharonda was to deliver, Von found a job at a warehouse, and the extra money was really needed for the larger apartment they moved to. Life was finally turning around with Von staying clean. Paydays were always the test as to whether Von would relapse or not.

The weekend before Sharonda was to deliver the baby, Von disappeared for four days. This time she did not call family or hospitals to look for him—she knew where he was, and she feared the supervisor would call to fire him. She was unable to compete with his crack addiction, and she did not know how to help him. When he finally came home, his attitude had changed toward her, and his language was harsh and critical. Arguing with him was useless, because he was in his own world where he felt he was right. All Sharonda could do was pray for his deliverance. Surely God knew what she was dealing with. She just wanted peace in her marriage. Perhaps the new baby would settle Von down, and he would seek help for his addiction.

Von managed to be present and sober when Sharonda went into labor. She was glad he was there, and prayed that the baby would be HIV-free. The delivery went without complications and Von Jr. arrived healthy and sound. Von was thrilled to see his new son and promised Sharonda that he would be a better husband and a good father. Sharonda heard his sincerity, but knew his history. When they brought Von Jr. home, Ebony fell in love with her little brother and took her role as big sister seriously by wanting to help with her brother's care. For about three months, Von stayed on his job and did not miss days, and for that Sharonda was thankful. Sharonda had her hands full with a toddler, a newborn, and a husband who was unreliable.

Sharonda could tell when Von was getting ready to "disappear" because he would become restless, start useless arguments, and call her names. He would demean her body, criticize her cooking, and complain about the house. The verbal and emotional abuse was almost too much to bear, but she let Von know in no uncertain terms that she would not tolerate him hitting her. Her days on the streets taught her how to fight and protect herself, and she was not going to allow him to beat on her. Von would make threats to hit Sharonda, but he was reluctant to follow through on them. Over the next ten years, Von continued to go on his drug binges, and would continue to lose jobs due to missed days. On one instance he stole his employer's company car to go on one of his drug binges, and of course they fired him. Sharonda always struggled to keep the rent paid, the children fed, and her car running. Often Von would take her car on his binges and leave her with no way to get to work.

Between the breakups, the drug binges, verbal abuse and Von's unemployment, they had another son, Mike, who was also born healthy and HIV negative. Sharonda kept her promise to God to never stop worshiping or singing, no matter what she was going through. The children were often the silent witnesses to Von causing their mother to cry when he would curse her out and belittle her in their presence. At one point they broke up and went through with the divorce, but within months they remarried. Their relationship was dying, and it was as if they did not know how to put it to rest.

The ups and downs of Von's drug binges and constant unemployment kept the family in financial distress and frequent moves due to evictions. After 12 years of marriage, and yet another bad breakup, Von called Sharonda constantly on her job and at home, begging her not to give up on their marriage. He continued to promise her he would do better. One day when contemplating Von's words, and that she should give him another chance, Sharonda mentioned to Ebony that she was thinking about giving her marriage another try. Ebony, then 13 years old, spoke with tears in her eyes and pleaded with her mother, "Are we going to do this to us again? He keeps stealing from us, and we never have enough money for rent, or enough food to eat. Why? Mama, please don't do this to us again!" Sharonda was shocked and embarrassed when she heard her daughter speak truth to the situation. She had not realized how much her quest for keeping a dead marriage alive was affecting her children. She suddenly had a moment of clarity and gathered Ebony and the boys together. Sharonda asked her children what they thought about their dad coming back to live with them again. They did not hesitate to tell her that they did not want to go through the arguments and not ever having what they needed again. They told her they loved her, and didn't want to see her cry anymore.

Sharonda went to her room and thought long and hard about the words of her children, and reflected back on all they had been through. She thought of all of the excuses she had had to make at church for Von's behavior if he came to church high. How many times she had to ask the church, family, and friends for help with their bills and rent when Von had smoked up his paycheck. The many nights she had sat and waited for him to come home with the car after being out all weekend and leaving her to catch rides to get the children to school, and her to work. How he, without regard to her or his children, selfishly took money that was needed for their food or rent and binged on drugs instead. She thought of how many jobs Von had lost because of his drug use.

For the last 12 years, Sharonda had carried the weight of the family with very little help from Von. He had belittled her by telling her no one wanted her but him because she had HIV. When she added it all up, she had to agree with Ebony. "Why would she to do this to them again?" She would have to practice what she sang about, leaning and depending on God to sustain her and her children. Von was not the answer, God was!

255

Sharonda had been worshiping and obeying Von instead of God. God was calling in the markers on her faith. Would she continue to serve man, or choose to serve the Lord?

Sharonda got up, went into the closet and collected all of Von's clothes. She folded them, put them in trash bags, and placed them in the garage. When she called Von, he thought she was calling to say she was taking him back. Instead she told him to come and pick his things up from the garage. She told Von that he didn't even need to bother coming in the house, just pick his things up and go. Von came to the house shouting and cursing at Sharonda, calling her insulting names as the children stood with their mother in solidarity. His parting words to her were that she would never be anything without him, and no one else would ever want her. Sharonda felt she had not achieved anything with him, so she had nothing to lose. Von had worn her spirit down to the point of not caring what he called her; she just wanted him out of her life. After Von sped off with his trash bags, Sharonda and the children gathered in the living room and cried, thanking God for freedom. They each shared reasons why they were proud that she did not take Von back. They had gone without so much for so long, they were tired too.

Sharonda went to Legal Aid the next week and filed for divorce with a renewed spirit that everything would be all right. Twelve years was more than enough time to dedicate to a marriage that was doomed from the start. Von could not afford an attorney to fight her for custody of the boys, and did not have any place for them to live even if he won the fight. He had given all of his money to the drug dealers. Ebony had become a rebellious teen and needed Sharonda's undivided attention, so she had to change her focus to her children and their recovery.

For the next two years, Sharonda focused on keeping Ebony on track and the boys in activities. She continued to minister to others through song and her testimony, and each time she shared her story, she grew closer to God. The Lord spoke to her heart and let her know he needed to "detox" her spirit. She had been under the influence of Von and his drama for so long that she had gotten contaminated with Von's "spirit." God wanted to give her a fresh anointing and a new song to sing. Sharonda felt stronger and more in touch with God day by day. Each day she began to set aside a time for prayer and meditation to refocus her worship. Von still tried to get Sharonda to come back to him, but he no longer had the power over her he once had. She had lost her "taste" for him. She now tasted the goodness of the Lord, and it tasted wonderful!

Sharonda completed her medical coding classes and was able to get a better paying job. During the years with Von and his drug habit, she had fallen behind financially. She needed to catch up because her growing children needed to be fed, housed and clothed. With every move she made to better herself, God seemed to open doors that led to her increase, and not her destruction. She was lonely, but did not feel she was ready for a new relationship. She still needed to heal and find out who she was.

With two years of life without Von, Sharonda matured emotionally and spiritually. She often ministered to young people in schools and churches, sharing her testimony. Her children knew her story about her HIV diagnosis, and were proud of her willingness to help other people. Ebony had become very rebellious and would often run away, but Sharonda was determined not to give up on her child. If she could put up with Von's issues, she could help Ebony through her struggles. Sharonda knew all too well what it was like to be a teen who felt lost and alone.

Sharonda and Judith joined in prayer for Ebony, and Judith reminded Sharonda of how she had been rebellious as a teen, and how heartbroken she had felt. Sharonda had grown out of her fear of what Tyree would do to her and decided it was time to share with Judith about the rape. Judith was shocked and hurt, saying over and over, "I didn't know, I didn't know! Why didn't you tell me?" Sharonda explained how Tyree had threatened to kill her, and explained that her need to escape Tyree became rebellion and running away from home. She told Judith that when Tyree returned to live with them, she could not tolerate him anymore, and that was when she began hanging in the streets. Judith cried as she apologized to Sharonda for not being more aware of how Tyree's presence had affected her. The two of them cried together and agreed to not let the past ruin their relationship. That moment of truth seemed to bring them closer together. Judith called the relatives in California who were housing Tyree and warned them about Tyree's behavior. It was too late for Sharonda to file charges, but perhaps in California, justice would be served if Tyree tried to harm anyone else. As sad as it was, Tyree seemed to have fallen into misconduct due to his abandonment and passed on his pain to others.

Sharonda was often approached by men who wanted to date her, but after she would pray about the relationships, she felt they were not right for her. She no longer settled for having someone in her life just because she was lonely. One evening she found a new online dating website for HIV positive people. When she saw the profile for Lance, God spoke to her heart and said, "This is the one for you!" Out of blind faith, she contacted Lance and they began corresponding online for a few months. He seemed nice enough, but Sharonda was not making any decisions on relationships without prayer and doing her homework. She did not want anyone with drug addiction problems or any kind of violent past, and they had to have steady employment. After four months of communication online and on the phone, they agreed to meet for Mardi Gras in New Orleans, where his family lived. Sharonda told Judith about Lance and how they met. She asked her to pray for her to be able to walk away from this relationship if it was not what God wanted for her. Judith agreed to pray with and for her, and watched the children while she was away.

Sharonda told Lance her story, and about her stormy marriage with Von. She made it clear that she would not tolerate any abuse, nor did she have time for games. Lance shared his story and was looking for someone he could share the rest of his life with in peace. They were the same age, both were HIV positive, he was a faithful Christian, and he was in the military stationed on the East Coast. He was originally from Louisiana and had three children by a previous marriage. When they met in New Orleans, it was an instant connection. This was Sharonda's knight in shining armor! Lance was kind, a gentleman, and treated her like a queen. He took Sharonda to meet his family, and they instantly loved her, and she them.

Over the next four months they would travel back and forth to meet, or would meet halfway between Texas and the East Coast. Sharonda and Lance were in love! Von would occasionally call and try to convince her that he was the only man she could ever love, but for Sharonda, Von's magic was gone, and so was her dysfunctional attraction to him. With God's help she had "detoxed" her spirit of Vons' influence, and was now under the influence of God, and Christ her Savior. God had sent her someone who knew how to love her and treat her with respect. Eventually Sharonda's children and Lance's children met to get to know each other, and they were one big family. Their children helped the couple make up their minds by giving their approval for the relationship.

After a year of traveling and corresponding long distance, Lance proposed to Sharonda, and pledged his love to her and her children. They were married in an intimate ceremony on the East Coast, and their children later joined them. God made good on His promise by making Sharonda's latter greater than her past, and had restored joy to her life because she had put Him first.

Sharonda and Lance worship and pray together, and she shares her beautiful voice with her new East Coast congregation. After a few years of rebellion and running away, Ebony returned home to settle down and complete high school. Ebony has a beautiful singing voice as well as Von Jr. and Mike, and they often sing as a family at church with Sharonda. Once Sharonda put God first in her life, God added all that she needed. She has kept her promise to always keep God first in all that she does, and gives thanks for deliverance and restoration, choosing to live and not die.

Sharonda's message to other women in abusive situations is, "Hold on to God's hand, even in the storm. God will always be there, just don't give up. The rainbow will appear if you just hold fast."

Reflection on Sharonda's Story

Reflection by Minister Leah B. Jordan, M. Div.

"...and lo I am with you always, even until the end of the earth." Matt 28:20

Out of all the ways that that the Gospel of Matthew could have ended, it ends with one of my favorite promises in the Bible: "I am with you always." Life can be awful sometimes, even when we don't want to admit it. And when things around us are awful, we sometimes become very angry with God, and nobody ever wants to admit that. Whether we acknowledge it or not, the real reason that we become angry with God is because we have forgotten exactly what was promised to us.

As bad as life can get, we go on to poison ourselves with the question, *why*? Why am I here? Why am I *not* somewhere else? Why can't I have what I want? Why can't I have it right now? Why would God allow such things to happen to *me*? This line of questioning, though it may seem logical, is only a weapon against us that the enemy wants to use. These questions all center on the things that we don't have, and the things that we are not happy with, and take our attention away from God. Anything that will take our attention away from God surely will steal our joy.

So what *do* we have in the midst of all we see around us? Again, we have God's promises. The first promise we have (literally the first) is that we would have free will. God tells us early that what we say will be so, and that we can eat what we want, and quite simply, all of that boils down to choice. Unfortunately, those who hurt us have been promised all the same things too. They can choose to rape us, to leave us, to hate us, or even take our lives. Those are horrible choices, but they have been promised. God also said that vengeance is his, and that's a promise too.

The first promise from God, even though it can truly be a gift, really gives other people the power to hurt us, and certainly gives us the power to destroy our own lives. But it is the last promise that I love so much, which comes in the very last verse of the New Testament. It is that the grace of the Lord Jesus Christ will be with us:*"The grace of the Lord will be with God's people. Amen"* Rev. 22:21

That's it! As difficult as it may be for us to wrap our minds around, we are not promised companionship or health. We are not promised an easy childhood, or a wealthy future, just that the grace of Jesus Christ will be with us—and truly, it is sufficient.

My prayer is: God, no matter how I or the people around me misuse your first promise of free will, your last one is my peace and protection, and I know that you are with me. If I choose to stop singing to you, it is because I have forgotten that you are with me. If someone else chooses to take something from me that you gave me, they can never take your presence out of my life. You are with me and I am with you, forever. Amen.

"Annie"

By J. Harris

Reflection by Min. Thelma Osai, M. Div. , Chaplain

WHEN YOU HAVE THE OPPORTUNITY to look into the wise eyes of an older woman, you may see so many expressions: happiness, pain, sorrow, pleasure, shame, guilt, joy... just to name a few. Don't be afraid to ask what her life has been like, and then cling to every word for nuggets of wisdom to live by. Annie is such a soul. She is a youthful 90 years young, on fire for the Lord. She has a restless energy, always looking for opportunities to learn, travel, and serve. She has a magnetic twinkle in her eyes and a ready smile. When asked why she wanted to openly share her story, she simply said, "Maybe I can help some young woman to find her way." Listen to her heart through her experiences of living in the 1930s, 1940s, 1950s...into present day. Listen to how the value systems of those times compare to those today, and how it affected her decisions in life. It seems that the more things change, the more they stay the same.

Annie was born in Pittsburgh, Pennsylvania, in 1933 to a stable lower-income, African-American family in a community called "The Hill." They lived in a duplex that had a basement, first and second floors, and an attic on the third floor. She was one of five children, three girls and two boys, and her mother, Callie, was a housewife. Her father, Dan, was a hardworking man who worked as a janitor at night, a bus boy by day, and in between drove a jitney *(bootleg cab)* for extra money. He did not want Callie to work, so he took on all the extra work he could find to support his family. Options were few for blacks in Pittsburgh, and with little education, Dan's options were even fewer. He could not afford top of the line food, clothes and shoes for his children, but everyone had something to wear, something on their feet, and something in their bellies. Dan made sure that his family went to church every Sunday at the Church of God in Christ.

Dan was a good man who was not without his faults. He was known to have an occasional drink on the weekends after dealing with the strain of providing for a large family, and facing the day-to-day prejudices that black men had to tolerate. Although the children in the house never saw Dan and Callie argue, they could tell if Dan had too much to drink and got out of hand. Callie would go downstairs in the basement and hide until he left the house.

In those days, neighbors looked after each other and shared what they had with others. The neighborhood store would extend Callie a line of credit to buy groceries between Dan's paydays, and she had to manage every penny carefully to make sure her children had what they needed. Education was valued, and Annie and her siblings were encouraged to attend school and get an education. Dan and Callie knew education was their children's way out of poverty and hard labor. Annie recalled Callie taking her across the street and watching her walk to the school on the corner. All of the schools in the neighborhood were segregated. Every summer, Annie, her sisters and brothers would start school one week later than the other children. Callie's cousin had a summer resort in Monroe, New York, and would allow Callie and her family to come to the resort for a week after all of her summer guests had left. The children would swim, ride horses, feed the farm animals, and eat from the garden. They looked forward to their yearly vacation at the end of the summer, and then would start the school year.

When Annie started high school, she convinced her parents to let her attend the integrated Deerfield Trade School for Girls on the other side of town instead of the all-black high school in the neighborhood. Annie felt she would have a better chance of getting a good job and being able to support herself if she graduated from the trade school. At the trade school, Annie learned to sew and cook, but also learned of the prejudices between whites and blacks. All of her teachers were white, and they were quick to praise the white students' work, but not the black students.

The trade school's cooking program prepared the food for their school and the nearby junior high school. Whenever they had to prepare potato salad, Annie noticed they did not teach them to add onion and a little vinegar, like her mother did. Being headstrong, Annie would add her special ingredients without her instructors knowing, and all of the teachers would ask for seconds on the potato salad. Her instructor did not know what Annie was doing to the salad, but always insisted that she be in charge of the potato salad.

When 16-year-old Annie reached the tenth grade, she was able to get a part-time job at a restaurant in her neighborhood as a waitress and cook. She was proud to have the job and her own money. Callie was not able to give them allowances, so Annie was glad to have money to buy the little things she wanted. At the restaurant, she noticed a young man with a nice brown hat who would walk by each day as he went from his house to the bar next door. He would do things to catch her eye, and occasionally come in to eat. He introduced himself to her as Grady, and would sit at her table and leave her a big tip of 15 to 25 cent. Grady was five years older than Annie, and was a man of the world. Annie was young, naive, and curious—just what Grady was looking for.

Annie had grown tired of school and the day-to-day prejudices, especially when one of the white students accused Annie of stealing her Rosary beads. Annie had no idea what Rosary beads were or looked like. Annie had never been one to hold her opinions, and she did not have a problem letting the teachers know that she felt she was treated unfairly and lied on. Callie came to Annie's defense and got them to drop the allegations. That was the last straw for Annie. She did not tell Callie, but she decided not to go back to school.

Grady's frequent visits to the restaurant to sit at Annie's table progressed to talk of the wonderful things he could provide for her. He worked construction by day, gambled by night, and always had money in his pockets. Grady swept Annie off her feet with his big promises, and she took him to meet her family. Her parents took note of how much older he was than Annie, but Annie hoped they saw in Grady what she saw in him. Annie's older brother knew Grady from the streets as being a hustler and a heavy drinker. Everyone was polite to Grady at the visit, but when he left, everyone gave Annie their opinions. Her brother told her about Grady's rough reputation, and that she should break it off with him because he thought Grady was bad news. Her parents told her he was too old and experienced for her, and that they felt he was not the right type of man she should date. Annie was in love and did not care what her brother or her parents said about Grady. He was who she wanted, and he wanted her.

The next day when Grady came by the restaurant, Annie took him up on his offer to spend some time with him. She was not going to let her family ruin her chance at happiness, so when she got off work that evening, Grady came by and took her to a nearby motel, where they spent the night. Annie was a virgin and had never had sex explained to her, and did not know what to expect. She trusted Grady and felt safe with him. He took his time and was very gentle with her, savoring her innocence. Annie yielded to his touch and felt special as he made her a woman. After that evening, Annie did not go back home or back to school. Annie's parents came by her job and tried to convince her to come home and return to school, but Annie was determined to be with Grady. (Annie would later find out that she became pregnant that first evening with Grady.)

Grady's big talk of he and Annie's wonderful life never materialized, and Annie always found herself living in one rundown, one-room rooming house after another. These dingy places were nothing like her parents' nicely lit, roomy home. She tried to make the shabby places warm and inviting, but the slums didn't seem to get as much sun as the better neighborhoods. The only thing that took her mind off the grimy little rooms was looking forward to the new baby, and Grady coming home from work. In the rooming houses, the couple had to share the bathroom and kitchen with other tenants. Annie loved cooking Grady's meals and having them ready for him when he came home from work. He seemed to appreciate her cooking, and rewarded her with hugs and kisses.

The couple was happy in their dreary conditions, until Grady would go out drinking with his brothers and come home drunk with another personality. When he was drunk he would call Annie names, criticize her acne problem, and make fun of her pregnant figure. He seemed to wait until he was drunk to tell Annie that she thought she was better that he was, because he had been raised in the slums. Annie tried to convince him that his upbringing did not matter to her, but Grady was scary and unpredictable when he was drunk, and Annie kept her distance. She would visit her mother occasionally and pretend that everything was fine. Annie dared not tell her parents about Grady's drinking and how he made her feel, because she did not want to hear, "I told you so."

One Saturday evening, Grady came home from drinking and started his usual arguments and criticizing, but took things further. He threatened to hit Annie. She was seven months pregnant and did not want to risk him hurting the baby. She made her way to the door, ran out of the house, and did not stop until she got to her parents' house. Callie did not fuss or complain about Annie's condition, she just moved the furniture around in the dining room and put a small bed in there for her. Callie told Annie that she was welcome to stay, but Grady could not stay because they were not married.

Annie was not concerned about living arrangements for Grady at that time. Her concern was for her baby. The doctor had informed Annie that she would have to have a C-section, and if she had any labor pains, she was to come to the hospital immediately. Because of all the excitement and irritation from Grady, Annie went into labor early. When Callie and Dan took her to the hospital, they sent word to Grady, and he came to be with her. At the hospital, Grady was all apologies and begged for her forgiveness. Annie was glad that he was sorry and prayed that he would not drink again. As she lay there being prepared for surgery, Annie thought of how she was living, and prayed that God would forgive her for her sins. She knew that she and Grady's living together was not pleasing to God, and she had not been to church because she did not want to face the criticism. She missed the singing and preaching at church, and pleaded to God to bring her baby safely into the world, promising she would do better.

When Annie awoke from surgery, she found she was the mother of a beautiful baby girl, and was amazed at how tiny and perfect she was. Now she understood how much her mother loved her, because she had that same love for her daughter. After seeing her beautiful baby, Annie even forgave Grady, and they decided to name the baby Jill. Grady beamed with pride at being a new father. When all was quiet and everyone was gone, Annie took Jill and prayed over her, promising God to protect and care for her with all that she had.

Because of the C-section, Annie was not well enough to go back to work or the rooming house, so Callie took her and Jill home to care for them. Callie was patient with Annie and taught her how to care for the baby, and care for herself. Annie missed Grady, but knew Callie would not allow him to stay in her house. He could only visit, and he had to leave at bedtime. When Jill was three months, old Grady decided it was time for him and Annie to get married because he did not like living alone, and Annie's parents' home was much nicer than the rooming house. Annie eagerly accepted his proposal, and they went to the Justice of the Peace and got married. Callie and her sister attended the ceremony, but there were no flowers or celebration. Annie's tummy was still swollen from the C-section, so she wore her green and white checkered maternity dress for the ceremony. Life had not turned out like Annie had wanted, and she wished she had listened to her brother and parents when they objected to her dating Grady. It was too late now, so she had to try and make the best of the situation, and pray that it would get better.

After they were married, Callie allowed Grady to move into the house, and fixed a room for the little family on the second floor. Annie hoped that with the change in living environment and the new baby, she and Grady would get along better. Instead, Grady grew more resentful of Annie's upbringing when he would compare Annie's parents' home to the shack he was raised in. Grady continued to argue that Annie thought she was better than he was. Even though Annie tried to reassure him that she did not feel that way, Grady continued to be jealous. He wanted Annie to drink with him, but she did not like drinking, especially after she saw how it made him act. The couple decided to move out in an effort to try and give their marriage a fresh start. Against Callie's wishes, because Annie had not completely healed from the C-section, Annie and Grady moved in with Grady's sister, her husband, and children.

Initially the couple seemed to get along better, until one weekend Grady and his brothers were out drinking. This time Grady's brother told Grady that Annie and Grady's brother-in-law were possibly having an affair. Grady came home that evening drunk and crazy with jealousy! Annie could not convince Grady that it was not the truth. Fortunately, Jill was staying with Callie for the weekend to give Annie some rest. Grady threatened to beat her for cheating, and started coming after her. Annie ran to the door, and ran down the street, screaming all the way home. Grady then took all of Annie and Jill's clothes, threw them out of the window, and set them on fire!

That day, Annie moved back in with her parents, feeling helpless and afraid that Grady would try to kill her. All Annie wanted was a normal family environment for Jill, but here she was back at her parents' home with a new baby, an unhealed incision, and all of their clothes burned. As always, Grady came to visit Annie, telling her how sorry he was and promising to change his behavior. He told Annie he found out that the rumor about she and his brother-in-law was a lie. Grady's peace offering was new clothes for Annie and Jill that he bought with his gambling winnings.

Annie gave in to Grady's request to come and visit her and Jill, but in her heart she was growing tired of his abuse and unpredictable behavior. Annie and Grady agreed to separate, but stay in touch for Jill's sake. One evening Grady had been out drinking and came to visit, and started in again about how Annie looked down on him and his family. That day Annie was tired from caring for the baby all day, and told him she did not feel like arguing. Grady was determined to make her listen to him, and shoved her through the window of her parents' second-floor room! If it had not been for the porch outside the window, she would have fallen two stories.

This time Dan put his foot down and threw Grady out of the house, and told him to never come to his house again. Callie could see how miserable Annie was, and tried to comfort her as much as she could. For an 18-year-old, Annie was a tired, injured soul. Annie was not injured physically by the fall, but emotionally she would have scars for life. Annie knew then that she had to get away from Grady before he killed her and left Jill motherless. When Grady left the house, he threatened to kill Annie, so the next day Annie and Callie went to court and got a peace bond issued against Grady. Because Grady had moved to another rooming house nearby, Annie always felt he was watching her and looking for an opportunity to catch her alone to kill her.

One evening Annie went to the movies while Callie watched Jill. She needed a break from the stress of caring for Jill and worrying about Grady. As Annie watched the movie, Grady suddenly appeared and sat next to her. She was paralyzed with fear, but would not let him know she was afraid of him. Annie calmly got up, went to the bathroom, and informed the maid attending the restroom that a man was bothering her, and asked her to call the police. When the police came, Annie pointed Grady out, and they took him to jail.

Annie quit her job at the restaurant and went to work as a live-in maid and babysitter for a wealthy white family. Only Callie and her sister knew where Annie was. Callie kept Jill on the weekends, and Annie kept her through the week as she babysat her employer's baby. One weekend, Annie went skating at the local rink *(the tradition then was to skate with a partner),* where a young man who she grew up with agreed to be her skating partner. Annie felt good to be out with young people her own age, even though she was a mother and wife. Annie was only 18 and still had a teenager's heart. As she walked down the steps from the skating rink, Grady was there, and ran toward her before she could think what to do. He grabbed her, beat her up on the steps, and left before the police got there. Annie felt so humiliated and embarrassed in front of her friends, and her skate partner did not know how to protect her, so he walked her home. Annie never saw him again.

The next week Annie got a second job at a dry cleaner near her home. She needed to work extra in order to ensure that Jill had food and clothes, and she had money to give her parents for their room. Annie worked hard every day with the goal of saving enough money to get a divorce from Grady, but no matter where she went, Grady would find her. One day Grady came to her job at the cleaner, grabbed her as she was going in to work, and threw her into a cab. He locked the doors and kept her in the cab as he begged her to come back to him.

Annie began to feel that it was her fault her marriage had not worked out, and she needed to try harder. She agreed to go back to Grady, but told him she would not tolerate any more violence, and he agreed. She went to her parents' home and picked up her and Jill's things, and told them that she was moving back with Grady to try and make the marriage work. Callie told Annie that the door was always open if she needed help. Annie loved her mother for her patience and unfailing love.

Soon after moving back with Grady, Annie became pregnant with her second baby. Jill was two years old, and Annie would have her hands full. Because she'd had a C-section with Jill, she would have to do the same with this baby. She worked at the cleaner until she was about seven months pregnant and the doctor stopped her from working. Grady was still going out with his brothers and getting drunk, and Annie was growing tired of the cycle of drinking and abuse. One evening Grady came home drunk and passed out. Annie saw this as her chance to get out of this mess once and for all. Jill was spending the weekend with Callie.

The boarding house had three rooms, and she and Grady occupied the front room. In the middle room was an elderly woman tenant, and next room was the kitchen that they all shared. Annie turned the gas furnace in their room up high, blew out the flames, locked the door, and went to the movies. She had become desperate and, nothing was too extreme. When she returned from the movies, she had hoped to find the rooming house blown to bits with Grady in it! Instead, she found out that the elderly woman had smelled the gas and woke Grady up in time to cut it off. Annie acted very concerned and shocked, but Grady never knew that the gas was meant for him. Annie begged God for forgiveness, because she had not realized that she would have killed the elderly tenant in the explosion. She had to question if she was going crazy!

The next few months seemed to turn things around for the couple when Grady hit the numbers and it paid off big, and he moved his little family to the new projects. He bought all new furniture for their two-bedroom apartment. They had their own kitchen and bathroom and no longer had to share with other tenants. Annie was grateful for the changes. After their son Dillon was born, Annie stayed with her parents for a few weeks, then went back to her new apartment. She had decorated Jill and Dillon's room with bright, cheerful colors. Annie felt like the extra money was what they needed to relieve some of the tension, and perhaps Grady would not feel the need to drink.

One evening while Annie was still off from work and recovering from the C-section, she decided to go to the local barbershop to get her hair trimmed while Callie was watching the children. She ran into an old friend from the neighborhood at the shop, and he and Annie talked a while about family and neighborhood news. After getting her hair cut, Annie went by Callie's, picked up the children, and went home. Grady had passed by the barber shop and saw Annie talking to the man, and waited for her to get home. When Annie arrived home, Grady confronted her about talking to the man and accused her of cheating. Annie tried to explain what had happen, but Grady was beyond reasoning. He took some laundry that had been folded, threw it on the floor, tore Dillon from her arms, and threw him on top of the clothes! Annie screamed and begged him not to hurt the baby, but before she could move, Grady took his forearm and slammed it across her stomach, hitting her in her incision. The pain from the blow caused Annie to almost pass out. Grady stormed out of the apartment, leaving her crying in pain, and their son on the floor.

Annie took Dillon in her arms and thanked God that he was not injured. Fortunately her incision was not reopened, but she knew then that things had gone too far. When Grady returned home, he acted as if nothing had happened. The blow to her incision left Annie extremely sore for weeks after, but she returned to work in spite of the pain. When she returned to work, she found out that the owners of the cleaner were refusing to pay her the back pay she was owed. They told her she had not worked the hours that were on her time card. Truth was, the cleaner was in financial trouble and was trying to not pay the workers in order to save money. Annie desperately needed the money to get away from Grady, so she told Callie about her check being held. Callie took Annie to a lawyer to file suit on the owners of the cleaner, and the cleaners terminated Annie. She was able to find work at another cleaner because she specialized in pressing wool, and was good at her job.

At her new job, Annie befriended a woman who worked there and also lived in the same apartment complex she lived in. The woman confided in Annie about the violence she was experiencing with her husband, and Annie shared with her about Grady's drunken, violent rages. As was normally the rule in the projects, everyone minded their own business, but the two women agreed that if they ever heard one another's cry for help, they would call the police. Annie felt relieved to have someone to call on, because she could not discuss with her mother all of the things that she tolerated from Grady.

Meeting this neighbor was a blessing from God for Annie when one evening, Grady came home drunk from a night of drinking and started to beat her. She did something she had never done before—she yelled for help. Her co-worker heard her cry and called the police as they had agreed. When Grady heard the police coming, he jumped out of the front window! Annie now had a glimpse of hope that God had heard her prayers. Grady returned after a few days as if nothing had happened, but Annie was not the same woman. Annie had grown wiser for her 20 years, and was totally tired of the drinking and the abuse, and was ready to get out at whatever the cost. Once upon a time, the thought of having a nice apartment with all new furniture was an ideal life for Annie, but it had cost her too much in wear and tear on her body and soul. She was ready to leave it all behind in order to gain her freedom. She would have to go someplace Grady could not find her.

The next week after the yelling for help incident, Callie called Annie and told her that her lawsuit had been settled with the cleaners. Annie had been awarded all of the back pay they owed her. The check totaled about $300! Annie and Callie agreed not to tell any of the family about the check, and the two of them took a jitney to the other side of town to cash it. Annie didn't trust anyone, so she took the money, divided it out, wrapped it in handkerchiefs, and pinned the small packages to the inside of her bra and under clothes.

Grady was working construction, and if it rained, he did not work. Annie waited until it was a bright, sunny day, and put her escape plan in action. After he went to work, she packed her and the children's clothes to leave. Suddenly it started to rain, and she quickly unpacked the clothes and put them back. Then the sun came out again, and she packed again. This time she went to her parents' home and told Callie and Dan she was leaving for Cleveland, Ohio, to live with her older sister, Jen. Callie was glad to see her prayers answered, and told Annie to leave the children with her until she got settled in Ohio.

Annie caught the street car to the bus station and bought a one-way ticket to Cleveland, Ohio. Her heart was racing from fear, and she thought she would pass out! While she waited for the bus Annie went to the upper balcony, where her back would be to the wall. She wanted to be able to see all of the entrances to the station, in the event Grady showed up. She took time and prayed to God, saying that if he really was her God, he would let her travel safely to Cleveland.

On the bus headed to Cleveland, Annie reflected on all the things she had considered to be symbols of her living a good life—the new apartment, new furniture, and new clothes. None of those things mattered now, she was free! As the bus headed toward Ohio, she finally had a chance to relax and let go. She took a handkerchief, covered her face, and cried. She cried for her disobedience and not heeding the warnings of her brother and mother about Grady. She cried for the times she returned again and again to Grady, only to end the same miserable way. She cried for the years of her youth that she had missed by putting energy into a worthless marriage. Most of all, she cried for her sweet babies that she had left behind, and how her arms ached to hold them. She knew she had to get settled soon and get them a decent place to stay. As she rode toward Cleveland, Annie sank into a deep sleep, something she had not had for years.

When Annie arrived in Cleveland, Jen picked her up from the bus station. Jen lived in a house with their cousin, but Annie could tell from their attitudes that she was not wanted there. Annie knew she had not done anything to deserve the cold shoulders she received, but could not let that distract her from getting adjusted to her new surroundings. She immediately found a job at a cleaner as a wool presser. Even though she was miles away from Pittsburgh, she still looked over her shoulder, fearing she would see Grady come out of nowhere. When Annie called home, Callie told her that Grady had come and gotten Jill to live with him, but did not take Dillon because he was too young. Callie did not argue with him about keeping Jill because she did not want any trouble out of him. Annie was helpless—she was running for her life, and her children were scattered. Even though she was free, fear still held her captive.

Annie tolerated the cold shoulders from her sister and cousin long enough to find her a room at a rooming house. She still had her "bank" safely pinned in her clothes at all times, even when she slept. She never felt comfortable at the rooming house because the room was poorly lit and dingy, and her cousin's house had been sunny and fresh. She just couldn't make the adjustment to the small, dark room, perhaps because it reminded her of some of the slum shacks she and Grady had lived in. Annie became homesick, and after a few weeks she decided to leave and go to Pittsburgh to visit her children and mother.

Her father, Dan, met her at the bus station and took her home. Annie did not go out anywhere for fear Grady would find her, so she stayed hidden the entire time she was there. Grady did not live far from her parents, so Annie was able to see Jill walk to school. It hurt her heart that she could not put her arms around her daughter, but she was able to hold and love on Dillon. She just needed to feel her children close to her, because they were all she had, and all she was living for. Dan took her back to the bus station after her weekend stay and asked her if she needed anything. Annie said no, and was just appreciative of her dad for staying and watching after her at the station.

When Annie got back to Cleveland, she found a room at a large, roomy boarding house run by an older gentleman named Mr. Williams. Annie immediately liked the room because it was sunny and bright, and would be enough room for her and the children. Mr. Williams took notice of Annie and her youthfulness, and made her an offer that she did not have to pay rent if she would agree to "spend time" with him. Annie had enough of men's bargains, and politely told him "no thanks" and paid her rent on time each week. Annie had been tied to a jealous, drunk maniac for the last four years, so she was ready to see what life was all about living on her own terms. She went to parties and hung out with other young people her age. She worked hard, but she played even harder. She was young, petite and beautiful, and she wanted the world to notice.

At one of the parties, Annie met a young man that she liked, and he liked her. Annie was so starved for love until she sought love in the arms of this stranger. She did not care what his name was, and she did not want him to know anything about her life. She wanted to keep it simple—companionship for one night. Annie had not been with another man other than Grady, and she was curious to see what she was missing. It was refreshing being with a man who was not drunk and seemed to appreciate her, even if for just that brief moment. Annie never ran into the young man again after their encounter. The next month, Annie discovered she had missed her period and suspected she may be pregnant. Her head reeled with the possibility of bringing another child into this world alone. She just couldn't do it!

Annie went to work as usual, but was in a daze. What was she to do about a baby she did not plan? She confided in her cousin, and her cousin gave her the name and address of a doctor who discretely did abortions. Annie was desperate, and took the local transit to the address, and climbed the long set of dark stairs to the doctor's office. The office was clean but impersonal, and the doctor asked her for the $50 fee upfront. He escorted her to a small exam room, and told her to take all of her clothes off and replace them with the gown he provided. Annie looked at the surroundings and did not know if she would wind up losing her life. She suddenly put her clothes back on and left before the doctor came back to the room. Something in her spirit would not let her go through with the procedure. Annie was alone, and she had no one to help guide her in this situation.

Annie was undecided, and time was running out for abortion choices the longer she waited. One evening she went across the street to the beauty shop to get her hair done, and the beautician's uncle, Calvin, came by the shop to visit. He immediately noticed Annie. He was recently divorced and had moved with his niece until he found a place to stay. Calvin was about 12 years older than Annie, short and light brown skinned. He had all the features Annie did not like in a man. She preferred her men tall, dark, and young. Calvin worked as a pharmacy assistant and made a nice salary, so even though he was not her style, she considered talking to him. There was just one problem—the baby she was carrying for another man. Annie knew she needed help to get settled and get on her feet, and Calvin seemed to be the answer to her prayers.

Annie began to spend time with Calvin, and she told him about the pregnancy and how it came about. She shared with him about Grady and her children in Pittsburgh, and about how she had come to Cleveland running for her life. He did not judge her or turn her away, but supported her in her decision to have the baby. He brought her all of the things she wanted when she had weird cravings, and allowed her to cry on his shoulders. Even though he did not meet her ideal physical preference, Calvin was just what her heart needed. When Calvin got his own place, he invited Annie to move in with him, and she continued to work and get public aid to pay for the baby's delivery.

Calvin had a nice car and drove Annie to see her parents, because she wanted to bring Dillon back with her. Annie confided in Callie about the pregnancy, but did not want her father and sisters to know she was pregnant. At dinner, Callie positioned Annie at the table where it would hide her stomach. Calvin took to Dillon immediately, and he treated him like he was his own son. Callie confided in Annie that she really liked Calvin because he was a family man, and she could see that he really cared for her. Calvin wanted her to be his wife, but Annie continued to put him off. Annie was not ready for another committed relationship. She was still struggling with Calvin's physical appearance and was overlooking his character.

Right before Annie was ready to deliver, Callie came to Cleveland and took Dillon back with her. When Annie went into labor, Calvin took her to the hospital for her C-section. After the baby boy was delivered, Annie did not bond well with him. She carried him home after the hospital stay, kept him dry, fed him, but that was all. Calvin helped with the baby and tried to get Annie to bond with him, but Annie could not handle the additional strain. One Sunday when the baby was only a few days old, Annie bathed him, wrapped him in a new yellow blanket, and went to a church in the community. She sat at the back of the church to make sure everyone saw that she had a baby, and before church let out, she got up and went to the entry foyer, and left the baby on a table. Annie walked away with no regrets. For her own sanity, she could not have any attachment or emotion about her decision.

The next day, there was a write-up in the paper about a baby being abandoned at the church, and the church had contacted the police to get a social worker involved. It took only a few days to match the baby's footprints to Annie. The social worker paid a visit to Annie, who admitted being the baby's mother. Annie explained to the woman what her life had been like in Pittsburgh and how she had made her way to Cleveland in fear of her life. She told her she just couldn't take on another child, and out of sympathy the social worker said she would do what she could to bring some resolution to the problem.

A few days later, the social worker contacted Annie and arranged for them to meet. The social worker brought the baby boy to the meeting place, along with an African-American couple and an old woman on oxygen. The social worker explained to Annie that the old woman was standing in as Annie's mother, saying that it was all right for her grandson to be given up for adoption. Annie was numb to the formalities; she just wanted the whole thing behind her. After the old woman spoke, the young couple took the baby and left. The young couple said they were from down south and were on their way back. Annie did not remember signing any papers, and she never saw the couple who took the baby, the old lady, the social worker, or the baby boy again. Annie explained to Calvin about the adoption and he did not judge her, but supported her as she struggled with her decision.

Annie and Calvin lived together as he spoiled her by giving her whatever she wanted. She still did not want to marry him, because she was still working through the emotions of her last marriage and the heartache it brought. She appreciated Calvin for supporting her and loving Dillon as his own, but she was not ready to be his wife. Annie still had unfinished business in Pittsburgh to get Jill away from Grady. She decided to create a well-designed plan to get her and Jill out of Pittsburgh safely. Due to an emergency, Calvin had to go to the Dallas, Texas area to see about his father and stepmother, who had been injured in a serious farming accident. (The couple had been picking cotton, and a water barrel had fallen on his father, who later died as a result of the accident.) Calvin had to travel between Cleveland and Dallas to manage his father's estate, so Annie and Dillon would occasionally ride the train to Texas to be with

Calvin. Annie heard that Grady had gotten as far as Akron, Ohio, looking for her, but did not know she was in Cleveland.

On one visit to Dallas, Calvin met her with a warm embrace and told her how much he missed her presence. He surprised her with the news that he had found them a nice two-bedroom apartment in the Dallas projects and he had bought all new furniture. Calvin had gotten a job in a Dallas hospital in the pharmacy. He went to Ohio and moved all of their things to Dallas. Annie was able to get a job at the hospital also. Once again, Calvin asked Annie to marry him, and again she said not yet because she still felt scattered. She wanted Jill with her. She thanked God for protecting her from harm, and even began to be thankful for Calvin being in her life. She knew he really was a good man and exactly what she needed. Once they got settled in their new apartment, Annie told Calvin that he was going to be a father, and he was ecstatic! He was thrilled to have a baby with the woman he loved, and life could not get any better. Annie made their apartment warm and comfortable, and began making a nursery for the new baby.

No one could have anticipated the massive tornado that would hit Dallas in 1957 that tore the town apart. In the path of the tornado was Calvin and Annie's apartment, and Annie knew nothing about tornadoes because they didn't have those in Pittsburgh. Annie was at home with Dillon and Calvin was at work when the storm occurred. The storm happened suddenly, and Annie heard what sounded like a train coming through the apartment that seemed to be shaking apart. The sound was deafening! Out of instinct, Annie picked Dillon up from the bed and ran into the hallway. Suddenly a large piece of glass fell on the bed, on the very spot Dillon had been. Annie was seven months pregnant and afraid they would not live, so she went into prayer as she covered Dillon with her body to protect him from flying glass. As suddenly as the storm came, it was over, and the hallway was all that was left of the apartment! Annie and Calvin lost everything except for the clothes on their backs. (Annie later found out a little boy next door had been killed.)

After the storm was over, the Red Cross was able to help Calvin get to Annie as they provided aid to the affected families. Annie told the rescue team she was pregnant and would have to deliver by C-section, so they helped her get to the hospital. The excitement of the storm started Annie in early labor, and at 32 weeks she delivered Madison, a healthy baby girl. Calvin and Dillon were at the hospital with Annie when the baby was born, and Calvin gathered his little family and thanked God for protecting them through the storm, the safe delivery of his daughter, and his Annie coming through the operation successfully. He loved his little family, but there was only one thing missing—he wanted Annie to be his wife. Coming through the tornado and the safe delivery made Annie appreciate her blessings and realize that Calvin was a good provider. She knew how much he loved her, so she decided to file for divorce from Grady. Grady did not fight the divorce because he realized that he had lost his family, but he still had Jill, and that was enough for him.

The Red Cross relocated Annie and Calvin to another apartment and helped get them some used furniture and clothing. After the wait period for divorce, Annie and Calvin got their marriage license. The couple was married in the pastor's office of their church, and Annie wore a purple and white suit the Red Cross had given her, because all of her clothes had been damaged. What should have been a joyous experience was clouded for Annie because she did not have Jill in her life. She developed a plan to safely get Jill to Dallas, but told no one, not even Calvin.

Annie called Callie to tell her she was coming for Jill's fifth birthday, and asked her to get Grady to bring Jill to her parents' house for birthday cake. Grady would allow Callie celebrate Jill's birthdays with her, but did not allow her any other contact with the family. After the long train ride to Pittsburgh, Annie came to Callie's house and brought new clothes for Jill. Annie and Jill were so excited to see each other, and Jill was excited about her party and new clothes. Annie told Jill that they were going on a train ride, and they would finish the party on the train. Dan and Callie drove Annie and Jill to the train station, not knowing this was the last time their daughter would come to Pittsburgh. Annie hugged and kissed her parents goodbye, and she and Jill boarded the train bound for Texas. Annie had kidnapped her own daughter! A bright and curious Jill asked for the ice cream that went with the cake Callie had made for her. Annie did some quick thinking and purchased an ice cream cone on the train to complete the birthday celebration. Annie felt complete, she had her daughter back. *(In her heart, Annie had convinced herself that her son had been adopted by a loving and caring family).*

When Annie arrived in Dallas, Calvin was surprised to see Jill with her, so Annie shared with him about the kidnapping. He did not judge her decision, because he knew how Annie's heart had ached for her daughter. Jill was so happy to see Dillon and meet her new little sister. Callie called Annie and told her when Grady came to pick up Jill, he was furious. He said he felt deceived, but knew he had no money to fight for custody. Annie finally felt free and whole, because Grady no longer had reign over her life.

Calvin would spend his life spoiling Annie and his children. He affectionately called her "his baby," and

Annie loved being his baby. Annie loved Calvin with a sense of appreciation and devotion, but could not bring herself to have the deep, passionate love that some couples experienced, that she had felt with Grady. Those emotions had been destroyed by the years of abuse she had experienced. Calvin accepted and appreciated their marriage for what it was and loved Annie and the children with all that he had. For Annie, this love became enough, because it gave her everything she needed and she felt so valued and appreciated by her husband. They recovered from the tornado and built a new home in Dallas, and Annie was a good wife who provided a safe, clean, and loving home for her family. The family began attending service at a new church, started in the pastor's home, that would eventually become New Believers Tabernacle in West Dallas. Calvin became one of the head deacons, while Annie worked with the youth department. Annie got a job with a major airline while Calvin continued to work at the hospital pharmacy.

They had been married for 45 years when one evening after work, Calvin suffered a massive stoke while sitting in his recliner at home. He was rushed to the hospital and lived for one week before he died with Annie at his side. Annie's faith sustained her through the ordeal, and she was able to accept Calvin's death as the natural order of things. She has never grieved Calvin's death, because she knew he was a man of faith who was ready to meet God in good standing. She has faith that she will one day join him in heaven.

After being a member at True Believers Tabernacle for 54 years, Annie is still active in church and continues to help with the youth department. Annie knew that there would never be another man who would love her like Calvin did, and has accepted God as her partner for the rest of her life. She feels her mission is to minister to and help other women who have suffered abuse to overcome, and live a life of freedom and redemption.

Reflection of Annie's Story

By Minister Thelma Osai, M. Div., Certified Chaplain

Annie's story is one that resonates with God's grace and mercy in action. Her life choices were partially shaped by black cultural norms in a biased society, with the limitations that the larger system placed on poor black family life. Annie had a desire to have a better life with better choices, but instead found hard lessons and broken dreams. The reality was that through the struggles and hard decisions, Annie had to make she understands the preciousness of the gift of life. She also understands the mercy of God that makes up for human imperfections.

Exodus 2:23-25 says, *"During that long period, the king of Egypt died. The Israelites groaned in their slavery and cried out, and their cry for help because of their slavery went up to God. God heard their groaning and he remembered his covenant with Abraham, with Isaac and with Jacob. So God looked on the Israelites and was concerned about them."* This passage reminds me of Annie's journey of being trapped in repeated violent acts toward her by her first husband. Having been a witness to family dysfunctions, I stand with Annie as she too experienced a groan in the spirit that occurs when you feel helpless and vulnerable.

Like the Israelite slaves, Annie recalled the promise of God she had learned as a child, that God would deliver her in times of trouble. As she made her escape for freedom from oppression for herself and her children, God showed mercy and made a way out of no way. God showed up in the presence of supportive parents, a godly man to love and care for her and her children, and a caring pastor and church family. The lessons Annie learned from the past have placed a desire in her heart to help other women by sharing her experiences about a God of grace. It is Annie's hope they too will seek that same God, and that same grace.

"Candy"

Story by J. Harris and reflection by J. Harris

GOD IS NOT DEAD! He's yet alive, and I know that He's still working miracles in our lives. Candy's story is a testament to a God that is yet alive. We can become angry with God, and that's okay, because God is big enough and great enough to take our small fists shaking in the air, questioning his wisdom. He loves us anyway, and makes it known to us by and by what His purpose is for us. Candy, like the rest of us, had no voice in how her life would start out, who would be her parents, and the circumstances under which she would be born. That was God's design, but she learned to make a choice in how the rest of her life would be lived—by committing her life to God.

The red dirt of the Oklahoma plains was by no means the glamorous, thriving metropolis that many dream to live in, but this was Candy's humble beginning. Her family put the "D" in dysfunctional. Her father, Albert, was 37 years old when he married Candy's 19-year-old mother, Flo. Albert was retired military, and Flo was a pretty, naïve southern girl. Albert had a history of having an unnatural desire for young girls, and therefore his decision to marry Flo, who was much younger, seemed right for him.

To the community, Albert was the model of an upstanding, faithful, devoted Baptist church member.

He and Flo and their two daughters, Mary and Candy, were at the church whenever the doors were open. Albert led prayer and served the congregation in whatever capacity he could. He and Flo disciplined their children strictly at church for any misconduct. Candy had been so disciplined to the will of Albert and God that she gave her heart to Christ at seven years of age. She prayed for God to make her life at home better, because Candy understood that God was good, and good things came from Him. But she had not been taught that there was a devil, or of evil, and that sin was born from the devil. She would soon come to know Satan and his helpers firsthand.

From the outside, Candy's family was as normal as any of the other poor white families in the neighborhood. Candy could recall picking cotton with her family in the cotton fields when she was two, and bathing outside on the front porch in a #2 washtub because there was no running water in the house. Candy did not get her first pair of shoes until she was seven years of age. Her family was among the poorest of the poor.

Albert not only demanded discipline in public, but at home as well, because when he spoke, everyone listened. Flo was young and would rebel against the strict lifestyle demanded by her husband. She would work during the days and spend the evenings partying with her friends. Candy and her sister would look forward to the weekends, when Flo would come home and spend precious quality time with them. The times that Flo spent away from her children gave Albert opportunities to do his deeds. Around the age of nine when Candy would get home from school, Albert would ask her, "Have you been a good girl?" When she would answer, "Yes, I've been a good girl," he would take her to his room and force her to have sex with him. She tried saying that she had been bad, but it yielded the same result. Candy learned to understand that sex was something bad, and that it happened to you because you had been bad. She would later find out that he was doing the same thing to her sister Mary.

After Candy had been with Albert, she always felt filthy and ashamed no matter how many times she bathed. She could not seem to wash his smell off her. She had learned in church that it was wrong for men and women who were married to have sex with someone outside of their marriage. It was difficult for her to understand why Albert had chosen to have sex outside of his marriage with her and her sister. Candy tried several times to tell her mother, but Albert's threats caused Candy to be afraid of what he would do to her.

When Candy was 12 years old, Flo went to work one day and never returned home. Flo would write letters to Albert from different locations around the United States, and send the kids her love, but did not want to come back home to him. Flo moved around so much that Albert got a large map of the U.S., put it on the wall, and whenever he would get a letter from her, the girls would put a pushpin in the location where their mother had written them from. After being gone for a year, Flo came home for one day to see her girls, but not Albert. Whenever Candy would miss her mother, she would close her eyes and recall the dress Flo wore and the smell of her hair as she hugged her before she left. She needed to feel the safety of her mother's arms, but Flo left as quickly as she came. From that point on, the girls would only hear from Flo through the mail, and they were left to be Albert's "good girls."

Candy and Mary had girl friends who would come over to spend the night. Albert would talk the visiting girls into going to another part of the house alone with him, where he would molest them also. Eventually Candy and Mary had no friends who would come to visit them. Their friends never told anyone about the rapes, or brought a formal complaint against Albert. For as long as Candy could recall, Albert had forced his way into her body. To survive the torment, Candy's mind would repress Albert's abuse by forming the acts into dreams. Candy had dreams that her daddy would come into her room, hold her close to him to the point of feeling pressure, and afterward there would be blood running down her leg. She would then put her finger in the blood and write on the wall, "Help Me God." Candy could not tell if this was a dream or reality, but as time went on, she realized all too well that it was real. She recalled feeling like she had the flu after she had been with Albert, because her body ached all over. Years later, when Candy had opportunity as an adult to share the "dreams" with her mother, Flo said that she would not argue that it was probably the truth, but would not discuss the incident with her any further. Flo acted as if she wanted to erase the whole matter from her mind as well.

When Candy turned 13 years old, she could no longer stand the visits from Albert and decided to run away from home, but Mary chose to stay there with Albert until she got old enough to marry. Mary had become trapped in the role as Albert's daughter and "wife" after their mother was gone. (*When Mary was 16, she became pregnant by the mayor's son, so Albert made her go to a home for pregnant teens where she gave her daughter up for adoption.*) Candy ran away to a friend's house, who hid her under her bed for a week. Albert went all over the neighborhood asking if anyone had seen her. After a week in hiding, Candy snuck home to get some clothes during a time she thought Albert was gone. She was planning to hop a train and go wherever it took her. Just as Candy had gathered all of her things, Albert came home unexpectedly. Candy was terrified!

She didn't know what he would do, so she dropped all of her clothes and ran out of the house, into the woods behind the house. Albert ran after her, but for Candy each step she ran meant freedom if she could only reach the railroad tracks. Albert kept calling her name, begging her to stop running so that he could talk to her. The years of discipline and obedience to her father caused Candy to stop and listen to what he had to say. Albert pretended to be concerned about her, and questioned her about why she was running away. Candy would find out that he was simply stalling until the police arrived.

Candy was transported to a juvenile detention center, where she shared with the counselor why she was trying to run away. She told the counselor that she could no longer tolerate her father violating her body. After hearing her story, the counselor explained to Candy that she would not be allowed to ever return home. Candy was relieved when she was sent to the Methodist Children's Home in Little Rock, Arkansas. She felt the new home was a much nicer and safer place to live. Even though she felt safe, she was filled with anger toward God. *How could He have let her face so many horrible experiences if He loved her? Why did her mother desert her? Why did her father molest her and her sister? Where was God when these things were happening?* Because of all her anger, Candy found herself in the office of the minister who ran the home, because she had discipline problems. The minister would counsel her about her behavior, and then would sexually molest her after the sessions! Again Candy was being molested after she had been "bad." She lived at the home for 18 months, and the minister molested her for the entire time she lived there. She felt powerless because she had no one to confide in to report the abuse. *Who would believe her?* It would be the word of a juvenile delinquent against the word of a minister.

Candy attended public school while living in the home and made new friends, but none she could trust with her awful secret of the minister's "counseling" sessions. At school she met a breath of fresh air named Gerald, and she loved everything about him. He was the first male she had encountered who did not want her for a sex object, just for the wonderful person he told her she was. They were both 17 and felt their love was real. Gerald would come to call on her at the home like a gentleman should, but the staff did not like him because he looked much older than his age. Gerald wanted Candy in his life so desperately that he decided to join the Air Force to give himself some sense of stability, and wanted to be allowed to continue to see Candy. Gerald's joining the military only made matters worse, because the school staff viewed him as an adult. Gerald was stationed at a base in North Carolina, and wrote to Candy daily, begging her to join him there. The home started to intercept their letters and would not allow her to receive letters from Gerald. He then sent letters through his friend who lived in Little Rock and was coming to visit another girl at the home. Gerald and Candy began to plan her escape from the home.

Candy's chores at the home included taking the trash out at 5:00 a.m., so she and Gerald arranged for Gerald's friend to come by one morning and pick up Candy's suitcase when she went to empty the trash. The next morning when Candy took out the trash, the friend picked her up and took her to the airport, where Gerald had her ticket waiting. On this occasion they got to the airport too late and Candy missed her flight. She stored her suitcase in a storage locker at the airport, and the friend took her back to the home with plans to pick her up the next morning. The next morning the friend picked Candy up as scheduled, and got her to the airport on time.

Candy was on her way! She had made her great escape, and would soon see Gerald, and would not have to submit to any more "counseling" sessions. She arrived in North Carolina on a Friday, and Gerald had reserved a motel room for their romantic weekend. Saturday, while Gerald was out getting food, there was a knock on the motel door. It was the authorities there to arrest Candy. The children's home had tracked her through Gerald, and when he left the hotel, the police approached him regarding Candy. The authorities told Gerald he could be charged with statutory rape and dishonorably discharged from the Air Force if he did not tell them where Candy was. He was left with no choice but to reveal where she was. Candy was taken back to Arkansas and spent four days in jail on the charges of being a runaway.

Because Candy and Gerald were minors, they could not marry without permission from their parents. Candy could not be released from jail to her father, and her mother's whereabouts were unknown. She could not be released to Gerald either, so Candy was released when Gerald's mother in Oklahoma agreed to declare herself as Candy's guardian. Gerald's mother signed for him and Candy to get married. Gerald flew to Oklahoma, and he and Candy went to the courthouse and were married by the Justice of the Peace. They were then free to go back to South Carolina and start their new lives. The past has a way of leaving scars that get in the way of the future.

Gerald had his own issues because he was still grieving the loss of his brother, who had been tragically killed by a gravel grater on a construction project. (The gravel grater's chain gave way with his brother underneath, and the blade fell, splitting his brother in half.) Gerald was never the same after that loss and suppressed his grief and pain. Gerald had been raised in a home where he was not taught to be affectionate, and love and tenderness were not something his family showed toward each other. This affected how he showed affection toward Candy. She had ghosts of her own as she struggled with sex being associated with her being a "bad girl." Gerald was not always patient and understanding with his new bride, but the sex drive of a healthy 19-year-old male is naturally impatient. Candy wanted to make her husband happy, so she learned to put her anxieties about sex aside.

Candy became pregnant with her first child, Darla, at the age of 19. She was excited about being a mother, and declared she would never abandon her baby as she had been abandoned by her mother. Candy was so fascinated with her new baby girl, and treated her like she was a baby doll. She had no skills going into parenthood. Before she was discharged from the hospital, the nurse would bring Darla to her for feedings, and Candy would just hold Darla and stare at her. She could not believe that this tiny, precious being came from her body. The nurses had to teach her how to change diapers and feed her newborn, while Gerald was even less prepared to be a parent than she was. He could not understand why he and Candy could no longer go partying on the weekends, and why he could not hang out every day with his friends. Candy eventually settled into being a mother, but after Darla's birth she refused to have sex with Gerald for three years. Gerald finally got Candy to consent to be with him when he expressed that he wanted another baby. She consented for that purpose only, and their second child, Eric, was born.

With her limited parenting skills, Candy often made some unwise parenting decisions. Once when Darla was age two, Gerald had gone out drinking with his friends. Candy had insisted that he stay home for some family time with her and the children. Darla, being a typical two-year-old, demanded her mother's attention. Out of Candy's frustration with Gerald, and her life in general, she beat Darla severely. She could not stop herself from hitting the baby! All of the rage and pain that Candy had been through poured out from her onto poor Darla. Candy beat the baby unconscious. She had no idea where that rage had come from, or why she had snapped like that. Perhaps it was the sickness her father had deposited in her body; or the minister that had forced himself on her; or the helplessness she felt when pondering the cards life had dealt her. Whatever it was, that rage had landed on poor, innocent Darla. The incident frightened Candy to the core, so she lay by Darla's bed for two days, crying and praying that God would forgive her. She promised God that she would be a better mother. Darla eventually recovered without complications, and Candy never again spanked Darla or Eric after that incident, because she was afraid that the monster would return. Gerald had stayed out all that weekend and never realized what had happened, and Candy was too ashamed to tell him.

After three years in the Air Force, Gerald wanted out. He had only joined to get Candy to marry him, and he was beginning to feel that decision was a mistake. He still wanted his freedom to hang with his friends, but he had the responsibility of a family and the military on his shoulders. Gerald decided to rid himself of one of his burdens, so he went AWOL (Absent Without Leave) from the Air Force for 29 days. He then checked in on the 30th day to avoid court marshal and a dishonorable discharge. The Air Force agreed to release him with a conditional honorable discharge.

After the AWOL incident, Gerald and Candy decided to work out their problems and move to Oklahoma to live with Gerald's mother until they got settled. Candy felt that without the pressure of the military, Gerald would feel less pressure to hang out with friends, and focus more on becoming a father. In Oklahoma they both found good jobs at a warehouse where Candy did stocking, and Gerald drove trucks and frequently had to make out-of-town runs. Their marriage still had its problems, but their boss was kind enough to counsel with them at work, and recommended that they get their own place. They bought a house in hopes that their own home would help resolve some of their problems.

Gerald had to make more and more road trips further away from home, and this only drove them further apart. Finally, while traveling, Gerald decided to leave his little family. He called Candy while she was at work, and told her that after five years, he was calling it quits. Candy was stunned and went into hysterics! *How was she going to raise two children alone?* Her boss saw how upset she was, and offered to take her to lunch at a nearby hamburger stand to calm down. They drove there in his new convertible Corvette, and while she sat there pouring out her heart about her broken marriage, her boss and counselor asked her, "Will you have an affair with me today, right now! I've wanted to sleep with you since I first saw you." Candy was speechless! In all of the counseling sessions she and Gerald had had with him, they had disclosed very intimate information about their sex life.

Her boss confessed to Candy how those counseling sessions had only fueled his desire for her. He admitted to intentionally scheduling the long road trips for Gerald as a part of his plan to get Gerald out of the way, so that he could be with her. Candy felt so betrayed, and her opinion of men in general was destroyed. She let her boss know how angry she was with him for playing games with her life, and refused to go to bed with him. With her refusal to sleep with him, her boss fired her right there in the parking lot of the hamburger stand. All in one day, she had lost her husband and her job. In the middle of the madness, Candy realized something important had happened—she had refused to let someone use her body as they pleased, and felt strong for standing up for herself. Candy went home, packed her and her children's belongings, and moved to Louisiana where her mother was living. Her mother had a new husband and a son that Candy had not met.

Candy just wanted her mother's love and comfort, and rest from the wild ride life had given her. Flo welcomed Candy and the kids, and saw a chance to be a mother to Candy and grandmother to her grandchildren. Flo didn't want Candy to work, just to stay home and be a good mother. When Candy filed for divorce from Gerald, she informed him of the game their boss had played with their relationship. Gerald was outraged, but felt their marriage was finished long before that occurred.

During the time Candy lived with Flo, Candy's cousin went to jail, and they wrote to each other trying to catch up on each other's lives. His cellmate wanted a pen pal, so he asked Candy if she would write to him occasionally as well. She figured it was pretty safe because there was distance and bars between them. Candy corresponded with her pen pal occasionally, until he was moved to another prison and she lost track of him. Later, she began receiving letters from her pen pal's new cellmate, Robert, who had stolen her address from his cellmate. Despite the theft of her address, Candy thought Robert seemed to be a nice guy who had gotten a bad break by being with the wrong people at the wrong time. Candy felt sorry for him and continued to write to him for the next four months.

During the time Candy was writing Robert, Flo introduced her to Hank, a friend of Flo and her stepfather who was a truck driver. Hank stayed at Flo's whenever he came through town. He was a friendly guy that everyone liked, but something about the way he looked at her made Candy uncomfortable. Hank started small talk with her about her relationships, and Candy explained that she was just trying to get her life together and wasn't interested in any new relationships. Candy had seen Hank occasionally when she went to church with Flo and remembered him having a beautiful singing voice that would bring the audience to tears. Whenever there was a church picnic or outing, Hank was a hit on the playground playing with the kids. All of the women would comment that someday he would make a wonderful father.

Candy had gotten a part-time job at a local department store, and one evening Hank came to pick her up from work. Flo or her stepfather usually picked her up from work, but Hank told her that Flo had sent him. He told Candy that the two of them were to meet Flo and her stepfather at a local hangout to have a beer. Candy reluctantly went with him, but could not understand why her mother had not arranged it with her earlier that day. She and Hank went to the bar and waited for almost an hour, but Flo did not show up.

Hank had bought Candy a mixed drink to sip on while they waited. Finally, Candy went to a pay phone and called her mother to see why she had not shown up. Flo informed Candy that she had cooked dinner and was waiting for her to come home, but she had not arranged for Hank to pick her up. Candy could tell by Flo's voice that she knew what was going on, and this was her way of trying to get her and Hank together. Hank had won Flo over. Candy told Hank what Flo said, and she wanted him to take her home. He admitted that he just wanted to get to know her better, and encouraged her to finish her drink while they talked. After a while Candy became sleepy and asked Hank to take her home. She wanted to discuss this little arrangement with her mother when she got home.

While riding in the car, Candy began to feel dizzy and had a blinding headache. The next thing Candy remembered, she was in a motel room with Hank, and he had removed all of her clothes. He had put something in her drink at the bar that had caused her body to be paralyzed and unable to speak. All Candy could do was cry, because she was too helpless to fight him off. Immobile and defenseless, she could only watch him as he had sex with her limp body over and over for hours. She could only feel pain and pressure. *Had she been bad again?* As she lay there being violated, all Candy could think was how she had no control when her father had raped her, and how she had no control when the counselor raped her. Candy could only cry and pray to God for this madness to stop, and to gain control of her body and her life. When Hank finished, he cleaned her up, dressed her limp body, and carried her to the car. When Hank brought her home, he told Flo that Candy had had too much to drink. He put her to bed, covered her up, and left as if nothing had happen.

For Candy the night was long, vague, and filled with tears. As the night turned to day, Candy gradually regained movement and speech. The following morning she was able to walk, and went to inspect the damage Hank had done to her aching body. She had bruises and scratches all over her body, especially her vaginal area. Hank was an inhumane beast! At breakfast that morning, Candy tried to explain to her mother what Hank had done to her, but Flo did not believe her. Flo reminded Candy that Hank was a good man, and that he would never do a thing like that, so Candy gave up trying to convince her. Hank called Candy almost daily, but she refused to answer.

A few weeks following Candy's rape when she was at work, Hank came to Flo's house to visit. Later that evening, Flo caught Hank trying to molest Candy's younger brother in the bathroom. Flo threatened to kill Hank if he ever showed his face in her home again. When Flo told Candy what Hank had done, Candy asked her to reconsider believing her story about Hank's date rape, but Flo still refused to believer her. When it came to Hank, Flo had a blind spot—even after witnessing him doing wrong. (Years later Candy's brother would be in and out of jail and never seem to get his life on track.) Candy would never be able to understand Flo's infatuation with Hank, and at this point it did not matter. Hank was out of their lives.

Candy focused on taking care of her children, going to church, praying, and getting control of her life. A few months after Hank was gone, Candy's pen pal, Robert, got out of prison and came straight to Candy. Robert sat on the end of Candy's bed and declared his love for her. In her letters she had told him of some of the abuse she had been through with her father and Hank, and how she wanted a better life. She had expressed to him that above all, she wanted to be loved and respected. Robert promised her he would be good to her, and treat her with the respect she deserved. Candy was lonely, so she and Robert spent a pleasant, romantic weekend together, where he treated her like a queen. Candy appreciated being treated and spoken to decently, so she decided she had finally gotten it right.

Candy was excited about her relationship with Robert, and shared her excitement with Flo. Instead of being happy for her, Flo was furious that Candy had decided to date Robert instead of Hank. She asked Candy and the kids to leave her house! Candy was so hurt to lose the closeness her and her mother had developed after all the years they had been separated.

She would do anything to win her mother's approval, but sacrificing a chance at happiness with Robert was something she could not do. Even with Candy telling Flo about Hank's cruelty, Flo still wanted to see her and Hank together. It didn't make sense!

Candy gathered her and the children's things and left the house with Robert. He had found a job driving trucks, and took her to his small apartment. Robert's apartment had been a hangout for some of his friends who did different types of drugs, but he told them they could no longer come around because Candy and the children were moving in. Candy felt life had taken a new and better turn with a man who understood her and treated her with respect. She and Robert got married the next week, because Candy did not believe in living together without being married.

They did not have much materially and were struggling financially, but they were happy. Candy decided that it would be better for Darla and Eric if they went to live with their father until she could provide for them better. She contacted Gerald and proposed for him to take the children for a short time until she got settled. He seemed to understand her dilemma and was willing to help out, but wanted to have her sign custody of the children over to him temporarily in order to put them on his insurance. She stressed to Gerald that she still wanted to be able to see the children and visit them. Gerald agreed to her terms and came to pick up the children. Candy hugged and kissed Darla and Eric while telling them that she loved them, and promised to come visit them often. She explained to the children that as soon as she had better living arrangements, she would come and get them. Candy was determined that she would not abandon her children like Flo had done to her and her sister. The kids hugged Candy's neck hard and cried before leaving with their dad.

The following months, Candy visited with Darla and Eric as often as she could, and each time she left them, she left a piece of her heart with them. Two years later, Candy found out that she was pregnant with her third child. She was glad that she had made the decision to let Darla and Eric live with Gerald, because they were well cared for. Robert's jobs were not always reliable, and he had difficulty getting work because of his prison record. When Candy gave birth to Lilly, she felt she had gained some parenting skills—at least enough to know what not to do.

When Lilly was only two weeks old, the water and gas had gotten turned off in their apartment because they had gotten so far behind. Robert did not want Candy to work while she was pregnant, which meant the money they needed to survive was not there. The technician from the light company came out to turn the lights off and saw the tiny newborn on the sofa. He told Candy that he would take a chance on getting fired, because he could not in good conscious turn off their lights with a new baby in the house. Candy thanked him over and over again for that blessing. When Robert came home, he had made enough money picking up odd jobs to pay the bill and keep the lights on. The couple was struggling financially and emotionally due to the constant lack of finances, and this caused numerous disagreements. When there is never enough to eat, and utilities are constantly being turned off, young love does not seem so sweet. A year after Lilly was born, Candy gave birth to Robert Jr. This only added to the already strained finances of their family and marriage.

Candy's visits to Darla and Eric became less frequent, because she did not always have money to spare for bus fare. She missed them, but their father seemed to be taking much better care of them than she could. When Gerald informed Candy that he wanted permanent custody of the children, Candy felt Gerald was taking advantage of her vulnerable circumstance. She begged him not to permanently separate her from her children. She had never said an unkind word to Darla and Eric about their father because she didn't want to get them into the middle of their conflicts. With Gerald's new request, Candy noticed that when she visited the children, they acted distant. Gerald had begun to turn them against her. Candy was angry that Gerald had turned on her, especially when he knew her situation. Gerald knew Candy did not have money to hire an attorney and fight for her children, so Candy had to consent to his wishes. The loss of her children left Candy feeling helpless and defeated.

The promise Candy had made Darla and Eric to always be there for them, and never to leave them, had been broken. She had done to her children what Flo had done to her, and she knew the empty hole that abandonment could leave in a child's heart when your mother leaves you. She cried at the thought of Darla and Eric having those sad, lonely feelings. Candy decided being with Robert had cost her too much—her children. The lovely life Robert had promised her had turned out to be nothing but a series of broken promises and missed meals.

Candy had a hard decision to make. She would have to divorce Robert and move back in with Flo. With two children in tow, and nowhere else to go, she returned to Flo's door step. When Flo saw the condition of Candy and the babies, she let them back in, and the two women talked for hours as Candy told of all the struggles she had been through with Robert. All was forgiven after a long "I told you so" lecture from Flo. When you don't have anywhere else to go, you have to put up with some things you can do without. Robert did not contest the divorce because he had no money to fight it.

The last four to five years of Candy's life had not worked out like she had planned, and she was too angry to consult God on how things should be. Candy felt God had abandoned her long ago. Harboring anger can destroy hope, and Candy found this to be her position in life. Again Flo did not want Candy to work, but just take care of her children. Candy wanted so desperately to have her mother's approval, even when her mother asked her to consider Hank as a husband. Hank had been forgiven by Flo and her stepfather, and the incident with her brother had been viewed as a misunderstanding. Flo was enchanted by Hank's charming personality and wonderful singing voice. To her those things outweighed his flaws, and for some reason she wanted him in her family.

Daily lectures of how wonderful Hank was finally convinced Candy that Hank was about the best she would be able to do, considering her present status—four kids and two divorces. Flo's advice and rationale for Candy being with Hank was, "You could do worse." Candy wanted so much to please Flo that she agreed to date Hank whenever he came to town. When Candy encountered Hank, she immediately reminded him that she knew what he had done to her the last time they met, and she was not going to tolerate any of his slick tricks this time. He admitted that he had put a date rape drug in her drink that evening, and sincerely apologized for his actions. He said he wanted her so bad, but he did the wrong thing to have her. Hank vowed that he was a changed man and would never do anything again to hurt her. He pledged that he would take care of her, and love her children as his own. The children liked Hank because he would shower them with toys and treats, and they had gone so long with nothing. Candy needed help with the growing children, and needed some things in her life as well. Hank seemed to be the only thing coming to help.

After a few months of dating, and Hank being respectful, Candy took Flo's advice and decided to marry Hank. They had a nice ceremony at Flo's house, and of course he sang to her. Flo kept the children while Hank took her in his shiny new big rig truck to New England for their honeymoon. They went to an area near the Canadian border, where the countryside was beautiful, but their first night as man and wife was a nightmare. Hank had not changed his ways at all—he was still a beast! The sex was violent as he totally dominated Candy's body. Hank proved to be a sex maniac, and brutally violated her body over and over again until she went unconscious. Candy's body would never be the same after that night. The more she begged and cried for him to be gentle, the more violent he became, slapping and choking her. As she cried during the violent sex, she asked herself, "What have I gotten myself into this time?" Again she had no control over what was happening to her, and felt even more hopeless. She tried to fight him off, but the fighting seemed to turn him on even more. She was a long way from home with no one to help her, and she missed her children desperately. She even missed her mother.

Hank contacted his job and convinced them to transfer his ship-out point to Maine. He would not agree to take her home until she agreed to move her and the children to Maine. She was in a bad situation with no money and no control. Candy was trying to be a good wife and not disappoint Flo. She felt she had no choice but to do what Hank wanted. *Candy would not realize until later that it had been Hank's plan all along to move her away from her family.* Distancing Candy from her family would allow him to be able to totally control Candy and her children. She tried to convince him that she needed to stay near her family to have help with the children, but he sternly informed her that she was now his wife—his "property"—and that her place was with him. Anytime Candy would argue with him, Hank would slap her around enough to let her know who was in charge. His temper was as large as his intimidating 6'3," 250-pound frame. He was strong and did not mind showing his strength against Candy's small frame. His temper was unpredictable, explosive, and violent.

After the "honeymoon from hell," Hank brought Candy back to Louisiana and informed her family that they loved Maine and Canada so much that they were moving there. Candy played the part of the happy bride, and Flo proudly told Candy that she knew Hank was the right choice for her. Flo went on and on about what a wonderful opportunity it would be for Candy and the children to get a fresh start in Maine. Candy was still seeking her mother's acceptance, and found herself agreeing that maybe this was best for her. Candy reluctantly gathered their belongings, and she and the children returned with Hank to Maine. She left behind anyone that could possibly help her if she needed help. Candy was at Hank's mercy. She felt God had abandoned her long ago, so she could not even call on Him. Lilly and Jr. were excited to move to a new place, and had no problem kissing their grandmother goodbye. Candy was afraid of what the future would hold, or if she would ever return to her family alive. She did not get an opportunity to say goodbye to Darla and Eric, and this really made the trip hard. Candy's family thought she was crying tears of joy, but had no idea of the sorrow and fear that was in her heart.

Upon returning to Maine, Hank picked up where he left off with his wild and violent sexual behavior. These violent sex acts caused Candy to develop severe vaginal hemorrhaging each month. She became pale and weak from the loss of blood, and eventually became bedridden most of the time because of her anemia. Hank would allow the children to come in briefly each day and visit her, then order them out by saying their mother did not feel well. Hank did not care about Candy's medical condition, only his needs. Whether she felt like having sex or not, she was his "property" to do with as he pleased. Candy was so sick and weak that she did not notice the change in Lilly and Jr. as they became afraid of Hank. They would often want to sleep together. Candy did not see this as unusual because they were so close in age, and there was a deep bond between them.

Candy went to different doctors to try to get the bleeding to stop, only to be told that it was a common problem for women. Finally a woman Candy had befriended in the neighborhood informed her of a doctor who could possibly help her. Candy gathered herself up for yet another one of those exams, in hope that she could get the help she needed. This particular doctor would prove to be different, and had Candy explain the intimate details of her sex life with Hank. After the doctor's examination, he knew immediately what to do for her. She was diagnosed with cancer of the cervix. The doctor explained to Candy that Hank had a sexual disorder and needed professional help. Because of the damage Hank had imposed on her body, she would have to have a hysterectomy immediately, or she'd eventually bleed to death. Candy did not care what needed to be done, she just wanted to feel better.

When Candy told Hank about her condition, he was frustrated that Candy had to have surgery, because this interrupted her tending to his sexual needs. Despite his protest, a week later Candy had her surgery. Even though she was weak from the blood loss, Candy began to feel better with each passing day. Hank gave her a six-week break after the surgery, but insisted that as soon as she was healed, she needed to start back taking care of his needs. Candy was not well enough yet to take care of the children, so she begged Hank to take her home to Louisiana in order for Flo to help take care of her and the children. He finally agreed, and got his ship-out site transferred to Louisiana. Hank had not allowed her to go to church, and Candy looked forward to going to church with her mother. After eight years in Maine, Candy was finally coming home.

Candy was so happy to see her mother that she put aside her anger toward her for suggesting that she marry Hank. She just wanted to be near someone who could care for her. After they returned to Louisiana, Hank found them a nice apartment, but his temper did not cease. He would hit and slap Candy for no reason, then threaten her not to tell her family about the unexplained injuries to her face he'd caused. It was not uncommon for her to have bruises and black eyes. Candy felt that their marriage had been one long nightmare she could not wake up from. When Candy started feeling better, she began to spend more time with Lilly and Jr. One day when Hank was not there, Lilly came to Candy sobbing and trembling, saying she had something to tell her. Lilly managed to tell her mother through tears that Hank had been forcing her to have sex with him for years, and that he had done the same thing to Jr. Candy was stunned, and her heart sank like a brick! History was repeating itself. *Was God punishing her for not praying or going to church? Was she still a bad girl?*

What had been done to Candy had now happened to her children. Hank had taken advantage of her illness and molested her children. Candy's father had done the same thing to her and her sister while her mother was away. During her illness, Candy did not have a clue what was happening to her children because she had been so focused on Hank's madness. Candy didn't want to believe it, but in her heart she knew it was true. She knew personally how brutal he could be, and of his violent sex drive. Just the thought of Hank forcing himself on her babies was too much for her to bear. She called Jr. in and questioned him about what Hank had done to him, and he told her Hank would molest him, then threaten to snap his neck like a twig if he told his mother. Hank told Jr. that he would snap his neck, lay him out on the steps, and tell everyone that he had fallen and broken his neck. To a small boy, that threat could be very real.

Candy's head was reeling from anger and shock. She knew that this was no time to lose her mind, but to do what she needed to save her children. Her first consideration was murder, but she knew that would leave her children alone in this world. Her first priority was to get her and the children to safety immediately, because she knew firsthand how violent Hank could be. She was also afraid that Hank would track her down to kill them wherever they went. Candy took a chance and went to Flo about what the children had told her. Flo's response was, "You can't always believe everything kids say." Candy was outraged! How could Flo be so casual about something this serious? Candy told her that she wasn't going to sit around and let Hank hurt her children anymore.

Flo got on the phone and called the rest of the family about Candy's decision to leave Hank. All of them came to the house to try and convince Candy not to leave Hank, but instead stay and work things out. Candy had to literally pull her children away from family members to get them to the car! They were like an angry mob, yelling at her that she was wrong to leave Hank. *What was Hank's hold on her family?* Flo told Candy that she was wrong for walking out on Hank, because it may not even be true what the kids were saying. Flo called

Candy selfish and ungrateful because Hank had put food on the table, clothes on their backs, a roof over their heads, and money in the bank. Candy told her those things didn't matter. Her children's safety was more important than material things.

Candy and the children sped off from Flo's house as she went to the bank to cash Hank's paycheck, but they wouldn't let her cash it. Candy then went through the house packing their things, while she looked for anything she could pawn for gas money. Hank had just bought a new computer, so she took the computer and pawned it for gas money. Candy and the children started down the road and never looked back. She was taking control. The thirst for freedom was much greater than the fear for her life.

Candy and the children had not even gotten three blocks away from the house when the kids started screaming and crying, because they were finally free from Hank. Candy was crying so hard that she had to pull over on the side of the road for about 30 minutes for all of them to finish screaming and crying. For the first time in years, she threw her head back and thanked God for releasing her. She and the children hugged and kissed each other as if they had been separated for years, and told each other how much they loved each other. How sweet and precious freedom was! Candy cried for the things that had been done to her by her father in the name of love; for the violations of her body by men with power; for the suffering of her children; and for God hearing her cries and delivering them from bondage. Candy had thought God had forsaken her, but in that moment she knew He was her deliverer.

Candy called Robert and told him what had happened to the children, and that they were headed to Oklahoma. Robert was outraged and was ready to find Hank and kill him for hurting his children. Candy convinced him that at this time, they needed to work together to give the children a safe place to stay. She drove straight through to Oklahoma, and they arrived safely on Robert's doorstep hours later. All Candy wanted was to be left alone with her babies. Discussion around she and Robert's relationship would have to wait. The following day she went to Legal Aid and filed for divorce from Hank to put closure to that nightmare. Her next step would be to get justice for her children.

She went to the district attorney's office in Oklahoma City to file charges against Hank and was told that the charges would have to be filed in Louisiana. That was unexpected, but was not a deterrent for Candy. She was willing to walk to Louisiana barefoot on cut glass to get justice for her children For once she wanted to fight back, and win. Robert, Candy, and the children went to Louisiana to meet with the district attorney. They were informed that since the children were no longer living with Hank and were out of the environment, they would not pursue charges because they were out of immediate danger. Even if they had proceeded with the charges, Lilly and Jr. were too terrified of Hank to testify on the stand. The thought of seeing him again frightened them to the point of hysterics.

Candy did not give up, and a year later tried again to get the Louisiana DA to file charges. That time she was told that since there was not any physical evidence, the case wouldn't even make it to court. Candy had to be satisfied that Hank may have escaped man's justice, but would not escape God's justice. (*Hank to this date is still driving trucks all over the country, and possibly still hurting women and children.*)

Hank did not fight the divorce, and when her divorce was final, Candy and Robert worked out their differences and remarried in Oklahoma City at the court house. Robert found a job with an apartment complex as the maintenance man, and they hired Candy as the manager. They received salaries and free rent. The apartments were located in a rough neighborhood of Oklahoma City, where there was heavy drug use and traffic. In the apartment complex were at least six apartment units that drugs were sold out of. The police were well aware of the drug activity, but seemed to look the other way as long as the activity did not get out of control. The police would only intervene if there was a shooting or stabbing incident.

Candy and Robert made friends with a couple in the complex who smoked crack cocaine, and they would occasionally invite Robert and Candy over for cookouts and beer. At the gatherings before the evening was over, the "crack" couple would start arguing over drugs. Candy could not understand what the fascination was with the foul-smelling addictive rocks, and she and Robert would not smoke with them when they offered to share their drugs. They saw what crack was doing to people in the apartment complex, and wanted no part of it. They had enough problems.

One evening during one of their visits to the "crack" couple's apartment, the usual fight over drugs began. To settle the argument, the couple decided to offer Candy the "push." *(The push was the built-up drug residue in the handle of the glass crack pipe.)* This residue had three times more potency than the rocks had when initially smoked. Candy thought there would be no harm in taking the "push" that one time, and she didn't want to insult her host. The host prepared the push by using a small, broken piece of metal scouring pad to push the crack residue to the end of the pipe, and lit it with the lighter. Candy took a big puff of the drug and immediately felt totally at peace! As she closed her eyes, she no longer felt the emotional pain from the rapes, beatings, and abuses she had endured. She did not have a care in the world. She told Robert about this peaceful feeling and encouraged him to experience what she was feeling, and he did. They were hooked!

Robert and Candy had easy access to more drugs because of the numerous drug dealers in their apartment complex. They both had jobs that paid good salaries weekly. They would get paid on Friday, and by Saturday they were flat broke. Because they did not have to pay rent or bills, they had money for their drugs, but that left no money for food for the children. Candy enjoyed the peaceful feeling she felt from the drug. Her soul needed a break. The drug would call her to the peace, and she willingly went. She and Robert would swear each day that they were going to stop smoking by breaking their crack pipes in the yard each evening, only to start over again the next day.

They smoked heavily every day for three and a half months, until one day Candy had enough clarity to realize that she had been sending her children to bed hungry night after night. She had been too high to realize that this was going on, and her children were suffering. Candy took Lilly and Jr. in her arms and cried when she saw how thin and ragged they had become. She promised to never hurt them again. Candy and Robert both stopped smoking that day and never went back to it. The price was too high, and they had been through too much to go out like this.

Robert had gotten in deep debt financially with some drug dealers at the apartment complex and had been receiving some threats. Candy and Robert decided that they had to get themselves and their children out of that drug-infested environment before they were harmed. They quit their jobs, gave up their apartment, and took their last paychecks and moved to a small house in the suburbs of Oklahoma City. It was away from the pressures of the city and the temptation to find false peace. They were truly trying to change their ways, but the past still followed them with threats from the drug dealers. Candy tried to make their lives as normal as possible by letting the children enjoy playing outside in the yard.

One evening Lilly came to Candy in tears, complaining that her arm was hurting so bad that she could not sleep. Candy couldn't see anything wrong with it, but thought it warranted going to the emergency room to have it looked at. Junior was asleep and Candy suggested to Robert that they leave him asleep until they got back. He was 12 and would be safe by himself, but Robert said they should take him with them. The four of them headed to the hospital, where it was discovered that Lilly's arm had been dislocated. Lilly finally told Candy and the doctor that it was an old injury she had received when Hank had twisted her arm during one of the times he forced her to have sex with him.

Candy felt terrible that she had not realized the child was hurt. She had gotten so caught up in the escape, the relocation, and then the drugs that she had not noticed how Lilly had been hurting, both emotionally and physically. Lilly said she had not bothered to tell Candy about her arm because she knew they did not even have money for food. It was a time of suffering for everyone. The hospital social workers got involved because of Lilly's confession. Candy informed them of the abuse and the charges that had been filed on Hank. The case was still pending, so they filled out the necessary paperwork at the hospital, got medication for Lilly, and headed home. The ride was long and silent. When they arrived home, they found the fire department putting out a fire that had burned their house to the ground! Just like that, they had lost everything. *When and where would the insanity end?* The fire chief told them that they suspected it was arson. Robert told Candy that he was almost certain this was done by the drug dealers he owed, but they couldn't tell the authorities their suspicions. Candy was just thankful that Jr. had not been in the house asleep when the fire occurred.

After the fire department left, Candy looked through the rubble of the fire to see if there was anything that could be salvaged. All they had were the clothes on their backs. In the ashes, she noticed what looked like the hardcover of her Women's Study Bible. It was black and appeared to be destroyed, but when she picked it up, she noticed that it was only soot on the cover. None of the pages of the Bible had been touched by the heat or the fire. It was perfect, just like God's word. She picked up the Bible, clung to it, and accepted it as her reassurance from God that He had not forsaken her. Candy vowed from that point on to never let go of God or His word again. (*To this date, Candy still has her Bible.*)

The Red Cross workers came to the fire scene and offered them food, drinks, and clothes. Because it was the Christmas season, they brought toys for the children. They also helped Robert and Candy look for better jobs and another place to live. Candy was so grateful for her new start in life, and saw how God seemed to always show His love toward her just when she needed it. After a month in the hotel, the agency had not found an apartment yet, so Candy and the children were placed in a shelter for women and children while Robert stayed with friends.

The shelter's conditions were crowded, and mothers were stressed because it was Christmas time and they were not stable. Candy was still harboring some anger in her heart toward God about the direction her life seemed to be headed...nowhere. Lilly and Jr. were constantly getting into fights with other kids in the shelter, and Candy felt out of control. The director of the shelter threatened to put them out if the disturbances did not stop. The director invited Candy to the Christmas concert a local church choir was giving for the shelter residents. Candy was reluctant to attend, but agreed to go to keep them from getting put out. During the concert Candy sat at the back of the room, her arms folded and her heart closed. As the choir continued to sing about a Savior, it ministered to her broken heart. She suddenly became overwhelmed and ran as fast as she could down the hall, crying and screaming at the top of her voice, releasing years of pain, bitterness and anger.

The director followed her outside and caught her in her arms as Candy cried uncontrollably. Candy told her of all the things she had been through since childhood— her family, her marriages, her children, the abuse—and all her pain seemed to flow up and out of her soul, and into God's ear. The woman encouraged her to release the pain to God and be truly free. Candy felt free, forgiven, and restored, knowing that God had brought her to the shelter for a reason—to speak to her heart and let her know that He loved her. The shelter allowed Candy and the children to stay longer, until she could find a job.

The Red Cross helped the family get an apartment, and helped Candy get a job at a local church as a receptionist, where she and the children started going to church. Candy had decided she could no longer depend on the men in her life for happiness and to sustain her. She could hardly concentrate on her work because of Robert's unstable work history, and she had to keep taking what little money they had to rescue him from the trouble he seemed to find himself in. Their relationship was deteriorating, and they argued constantly. The final straw came when Robert was arrested for assaulting a man during a fight and was taken to jail for violating his probation. The judge told Robert that since he had been a repeat offender and violated his probation, he was going to have to serve at least 20 years without parole.

Candy went to court to testify on Robert's behalf, and rounded up the few friends they had to testify also, but many of them had criminal records and their testimonies were useless. When Robert was sentenced to 20 years, Candy felt it was a good time to put an end to their flawed relationship. She filed for divorce when Robert went to the penitentiary. The children were upset at her divorce decision, but she explained to them that she had gone as far as she could go with their father. It was time for them to move on with their lives. Lilly and Jr. struggled with their own demons because of the rapes, while Candy sought out professional counseling for them.

Candy worked at the church for several years, got her confidence back, and moved on to a better job. She has since met and married a wonderful man who loves and respects her. She has been able to renew her relationship with Darla and Eric. The process for renewal is slow, but hopeful. Lilly and Robert Jr. continue to work through their problems, and Candy has been dedicated to helping them through those hurdles. God has brought Candy to a point of peace and joy in her life, and she actively ministers to other women who have been abuse victims. She realizes that God brought her through those tough times to be able to identify with other abused women and minister to them. Candy has given God control over her life, and He in return has given her freedom.

Reflection of Candy's Story

by Min. J. Harris

"I will put my spirit within you, and you shall live, and I will place you on your own soil; then you shall know that I, the Lord, have spoken and will act, says the Lord." **Ezekiel 37:14**

This chapter in Ezekiel tells of the restoration of Israel from destruction. The Lord shows Ezekiel a valley of dry bones that represents the destroyed house of Israel. The Lord challenges Ezekiel with a question of whether he thinks the dry bones can live again, and Ezekiel replies, "Oh Lord God, only you know." Candy's life had rendered her a valley of dry bones—broken family, broken heart and broken promises. Since childhood, her life had been riddled with abuse and disappointment.

Candy knew of God but had not truly experienced God, but an encounter with God does not return void. Each time Candy's story got off track and she could not deal with her pain, God continued to protect her. There is always the seeking of earthly comfort instead of God's power that can leave us in some dead, dry, unfruitful situations. This is where Candy had found herself when she had sought stability in the men in her life.

It was not until Candy's life "burned to the ground" with the loss of her home and all material things, that she embraced the indestructible word of God. As she picked up her Bible from the ashes, she realized that God was real and active in her life. She saw the word of God as giving life, not death, and hope springs eternal without disappointment. Candy realized that God did love and care for her, even in the midst of some dead situations. Once she found her strength in the Lord, not in man, did the dry bones take on flesh and live, because true freedom and restoration can only be found in God. When Candy allowed God to reign supreme in her life, she found true freedom from her past hurts, and God was able to breathe life into her soul. As Candy continues to grow in her faith, God will continue to restore all that she had lost. "Oh Lord, only you know!"

By J. Harris

Reflection by Dr. Esther Mombo

THE ELEMENT OF OVERCOMING AND RESILIENCE can be the key to survival and growth. Many people have stories of continual valley moments and defeat after defeat, never having a mountaintop experience. Often times these defeats are not due to lack of options, but not being willing to suffer to get what God has for you. Success cannot be achieved by someone else wanting it for you— you have to want it for yourself. They cannot want more for you than you want for yourself.

The cost to have mountaintop experiences is prayer, grit, and sheer "I won't give up, I won't give in!" It may not be easy, but it is not impossible. Are you willing to pay the cost of discomfort, sweat, tears, doing without, loneliness, brokenness and uncertainty to obtain a mountaintop view orchestrated by God? That is the question J had to answer and be willing to surrender to. It was not about her, but the generations that were to follow her. She made the decision to partner with God to help make a way out of no way, to pave a way that seemed too overwhelming. God would not give her what she was not willing to work for; they are partners. The message of not settling for less is in her story, and the story she wants her children and grands to follow: "Never settle for less than what God has for you."

West Texas life in the '50s, '60s and '70s was a place where families had plenty of room to grow. Except for an occasional dust storm, or the smell of feed lots, an individual could thrive and make a good life for themselves. J grew up in as a close-knit African-American community, where everyone knew everyone and everyone's business. Children played outside without fear, and were watched closely by adults who had permission to discipline any child that they felt was out of line. The schools were in the neighborhood where the teachers lived. There were churches on almost every corner, and everyone in the community went to one of them on Sundays, except for a few stragglers. The people of the community were all connected in one way or the other—through kinship, school, work, business or church. You felt safe and cared for, and if anyone in the community was ill or fell on hard times, there was always someone who would look in on you and help out. People didn't have a lot, but what they had, they shared. The homes were modest and wood framed, and garages were a sign of some prosperity.

J's grandmother, Claudia, had a garage and was usually the person who made sure everyone else in the community was cared for. She was one of the community matriarchs that set the social tone. She worked as a beautician on Saturdays in a shop she and her sister owned, and throughout the week as a maid and cook for some of the wealthiest white families in town. J would get her work ethic from Claudia, who often said, *"Never be afraid of hard work. Don't wait for them to tell you what to do, you see what needs to be done and do it the best you can. If a job is not immoral or illegal, it is a good job."* Claudia was not afraid of work, and insisted that no one in her family had that fear either. Claudia had two daughters, Jan and Bell, and Bell was J's mother. J's Aunt Jan had two children, Don and Donna, who lived one street over from J—same house number, different street. The house Jan lived in was owned by Claudia, and J and Bell lived in the other half of Claudia's duplex, so both of Claudia's daughters rented from her.

Bell had smooth, deep dark chocolate brown skin, a shapely figure, soft spoken, a quick wit and a sweet spirit. It served her well in her profession as a barber in the neighborhood barbershop, where three of the four barbers in the shop were women. Bell left J's father soon after J was born, but J visited him each summer on his farm in South Texas and looked forward to seeing him and helping take care of the animals. She adored her father and always wished her parents would one day get back together, but that would never be.

Bell and J lived very modestly on the barber's salary, with Bell working long, hard hours and often taking a second job cleaning offices or working at the Bar-B-Q store for extra money. She was a wonderful seamstress and made all of her and J's clothes, which often got her compliments from her teachers and the women at church, and envious looks from friends. From three weeks old, J was introduced to church by Claudia, who insisted that she take all of her grandchildren and great grandchildren to the Baptist church at age three weeks *(with the mothers staying at home for another two weeks)* to introduce them to God and society. Church was the one place J would always feel comfortable.

J was enlightened by a speaker who spoke to her sixth-grade class of her experiences as a social worker with the Peace Corp and was impressed with an African-American woman going to New York to help disadvantaged children. J had never heard of social work, and definitely wanted to get to New York, so she put the two together and decided she wanted to be a social worker . She had a heart for helping people and was always defending the kids in the neighborhood or at school who were bullied because they had poor clothing or were disabled. This social work thing fit her well, so she asked the speaker how long it would take to become a social worker and was told it would take four years and hard work. J decided four years of college it would be.

J was popular in school, head cheerleader in junior high, and in her senior year submitted her paperwork to attend the University of Texas in Austin. Bell had encouraged her to go to school away from home, and have new experiences and make new friends. Bell had not been able to afford college, so she attended Barber College. They had not planned for high school crushes and teen pregnancy. J's cousin Donna was three years older and had also become pregnant her senior year, and the family was still reeling from that and the birth of Donna's daughter, Shari. Claudia was trying to figure how to save face in the community, so she paid for Donna to take correspondence courses to complete her high school requirements, because public school would not let pregnant girls attend regular school. For the boys who got the girls pregnant, there was no penalty. Claudia stressed that abortion was not ever an option— the family would just live through it, and she would take the baby to church at three weeks old and keep it going. Life was too precious to be destroyed.

In junior high, J began talking to Travis, who was on the football team and was a grade ahead of her. She had seen him at youth meetings when her church's youth groups fellowshipped with other churches. He was loud, popular, and had a great sense of humor. Travis's father was a preacher who was well known in the community, so Bell agreed to let them talk on the phone, but no dating until high school, and that would be supervised. J and Travis were a couple from junior high through high school, and decided that they would wait until they finished college to get married. Their families watched them to make sure they courted properly, but when bad breakups and passionate makeups come into play, no one can watch you that close.

Falling in love had been easy, but falling out was devastating for a teenage girl, and good judgment can often go out the window. When J discovered she was pregnant, she was frightened and felt ashamed, so she confided in her cousin Donna, who had just been through that ordeal. They were as close as any sisters could be and called themselves "sister-cousins." Donna was a straight-A student and was attending college locally, and encouraged J to do the same after having the baby. J wondered about her University of Texas plan and how disappointed Bell would be, not to even mention Claudia. Since being baptized at age ten, the church had trusted her with leadership of the youth department, and now this. There would be no discussion of abortion, but the enemy did send thoughts of suicide because she felt she was such a disappointment to everyone, especially God.

Bell knew something was wrong with J, and had heard rumors through her friends that J was pregnant. When Bell confronted J about the pregnancy, J broke down and told her mother the truth. Bell went into hysterics—you would have thought someone had died! All of the dreams Bell had for J died, and in some ways it felt like she was mourning an actual person, and not just the bright future she had planned for J. Bell told Claudia, who immediately went into collateral damage control mode. She had experience with Donna's situation, so it was easier this time. Claudia had no time for tears—it was time for planning. Publicly, Claudia played the part of the shocked and wounded matriarch, and she subtly reminded a few of the community's other leading ladies that some of their children and grandchildren had also "fallen." J was dismissed from school by the school counselor with advice that she was not college material, and was advised that attending a trade school, such as cosmetology school, would be more fitting for a girl in her "situation." J was more determined than ever to prove everyone wrong. She would attend and complete college, even if it took her last breath. She owed her mother that much.

The pregnancy was long, isolated and shameful. Travis got a job and brought money to Bell every week to put on J's hospital bill, and would take J to the store each week to let her pick out the food she was craving, and get things for the baby. J bought a pair of tiny pink baby shoes to wish on, because she wanted a girl. She found herself growing more and more resentful of Travis and hated the fact that no one could look at him and tell she was pregnant. He was making plans to attend college on a football scholarship and would be able to have his college experience, while she would be at home changing diapers. This was not fair, they were both guilty!

Every week that Travis came over, J's bitterness grew towards him. He wanted to marry her, but she could not see herself with a baby, a husband, cooking and cleaning and no future. She would never make it to New York that way. J told Bell of Travis' marriage proposal, and Bell assured her that she would not force her to get married if she didn't want to. Bell told J they would work together to help her get through college, but J would have to attend college locally. Bell was firm about not assuming care of the baby while J went off to college out of town. The goal was for J to get an education.

After a very difficult labor and delivery, baby Ava arrived. A little battered, but she was strong and healthy. J thanked God for Ava and for blessing her with a girl, and the pink shoes fit perfectly. All the months of isolation at the school for pregnant girls, not being able to march with her high school graduating class, and being looked at down the noses of the church ladies did not matter when she looked at Ava's beautiful brown face. Oh, how beautiful she was! She would now change status from pregnant teen to a woman and a mother. *She had the stretch marks to prove it.*

J did not know it was possible to love another human being as much as she loved Ava, and was willing to lay down her life for her. At that moment she understood Bell's love for her, and why Claudia protected her clan as she did. This motherly love was amazing. Travis was proud of Ava also, and he took her to visit his family often. J did not mind Travis seeing the baby, but she did not want him in her life anymore. She felt it was time to close that chapter and move on. Claudia took Ava to church when she was three weeks old and showed off her new great-granddaughter, just as she had done with Donna's daughter, Shari. With Claudia, family was everything.

Ava was born in June and classes started in September. It would be a push, but J felt she would do whatever it took to get her life back on track. She regretted blowing her chance to attend UT, but knew more than ever that in order to give Ava a better life, she needed a college education, so local university it would be. J needed acceptance and a new beginning, so she did what she had been taught all her life—pray to God for forgiveness, and to order her steps. J wrote Travis while he was in college, calling the relationship off as part of her new beginning plan. She would not cut him off from Ava, but he definitely would be cut off from her.

College was exciting and a real challenge for J, because being an honor student in an all-black high school did not mean squat in a major university. J was so far behind her white college classmates who had attended all-white schools and college prep classes, but Bell was right there cheering her on. Bell and J put their money together and saved for each semesters expenses to keep J from incurring tuition dept. Claudia volunteered to keep Shari and Ava whenever Donna and J had to work or study, or just needed a break. Claudia prided herself in showing the other great-grandmothers how smart her linage was. J got a job at the college library, cleaned hotel rooms three nights a week with Claudia, and worked full time at the State School to pay her tuition and support Ava.

At 18 years old, J decided to move from home into a furnished rent house, because she felt she was an adult who needed to live like an adult—independent. Bell felt J was stretching herself too far, but could not convince her to stay home. Between a full school schedule, tutoring, and three jobs, she only had four hours a day to sleep, because no sacrifice was too great for Ava's future. With work and taking care of a baby, it would take her seven years instead of four to complete her social work degree.

During those seven years, a whole lot of living took place. Donna would make J shut down on the weekends to rest, and go out and have fun. Donna had gotten married and was like big sister, and J would mind her like one. Those were the days of the great music of the '70s, afros, hip-huggers, disco dancing, platform shoes, tie dye shirts, Dashikis, the Black Panthers, black power, album parties, bra burning and women's liberation. J made time to attend church and sing in the choir as often as possible, but time was not on her side. Claudia and Bell made sure Shari and Ava went to church every Sunday, even if their mothers were sleeping in. J made friends fast and dated a few guys, but had decided not to settle down for a while, because she wanted the right man in her life for her and Ava and knew she was too young to be a good wife to anyone. Her goal was finishing school, and she did not have time for the normal college experiences.

Bell's health began to fail due to diabetes and she had to undergo major surgery, so J and Ava moved back home to care for her. J made sure that she did not unpack all of her things, because she planned to move back out on her own when Bell was better. Bell was in and out of the hospital and J continued her grueling work and school schedule, adding caring for her mother to the list, but she did not mind.

When Donna finished her degree and moved to North Texas, J was lonely and Ava missed her cousin, so they visited Donna and her husband Alvin often. One time when J and Ava visited Donna, Alvin's cousin Mel was visiting while passing through on business. He was a very nice-looking guy, very polite, and seemed to really like J. Donna arranged for a sitter and planned for the four of them to go to a local restaurant and hang out together. Mel offered to take J to shoot pool, meet some of his friends, and meet Donna and Alvin for dinner later. Donna was comfortable with him, so J accepted his invitation.

On the way to the pool room, Mel told J that he needed to stop by his hotel room and get some extra money and invited J in, saying he would be just a minute. Once in the room, he slammed the door, locked it and began pushing her toward the bed. J was shocked at his sudden change of behavior and began to fight with him, asking what this was all about. She had never been hit or pushed by a man. Mel became an animal and told her that he was not letting her out of the room until he got what he needed from her. J started to scream and fight back, but no one seemed to care about a woman screaming for help in a motel at night. He was too heavy and strong, and eventually pinned her to the bed with his body. She pleaded with him not to do this, and kept asking how Alvin would feel about what he was doing. He said he didn't care what anyone thought, and threatened to kill her if she dared to tell what happened.

Mel proceeded to snatch her pants and underwear off, and forced his way into her body. He covered her mouth and told her to shut up, or he would snap her neck! J could only lay there and cry, wondering what she had done to deserve this. *Had she sent a sign that she was easy? What was it about her that caused him to act this way? Where was God when she needed him?* Maybe God was punishing her for getting pregnant with Ava. Mel was rough and uncaring, and it felt like he was tearing her body apart. She hated the smell of him. She just wanted this nightmare to be over. Mel was angry that she did not respond to him and hit her across the face, almost knocking her out.

After what seemed like hours, he had released himself inside her and rolled over in exhaustion. J could only lay there in pain and disbelief. *Who would believe her if she told, and would he really kill her?* She jumped up and ran to the bathroom, locking the door behind her, and put her clothes on. She felt dirty and demanded that he take her home. He grabbed her by the shoulders and slammed her into the wall, reminding her that he would kill her if she told. He pushed her toward the door and made her get in the car. As she cried, he told her to shut up and pull herself together.

When they got to the pool room, he grabbed her by the arm and held her hand as if they were a loving couple, escorting her into the parlor as if nothing had happen. People who knew him were greeting him, and he was slapping hands and laughing with his friends, and introduced J as his new lady friend. *Could these people not look at her red, swollen face and eyes and see that something was wrong?* J excused herself from him to go to the restroom, noticed a pay phone near the restroom, and called Donna. All she could say through tears was, "Come get me!" She stayed in the bathroom until she thought Donna had arrived.

When J came out of the restroom, she saw Donna and Alvin coming in the door, and when Donna saw J crying, she took her by the hand and they walked out of the building. Alvin had cornered Mel and was questioning him about what had happened. Once outside, Donna pressed J to tell her what was going on. As they walked to the parking lot, J told her what Mel had done and the threat he had made on her life. Donna was outraged and started yelling, "If there is going to be any killing, it's going to be me doing it!"

Donna took J by the hand and, almost dragging her, went back into the pool room to tell Alvin what J had said. Mel, of course, denied everything. Alvin was so ashamed, and apologized over and over to J and to Donna about what happened, saying he did not know Mel was like that. They all went to Alvin's car, where he got his gun out of the glove compartment. J begged him not to hurt anyone, but Donna was all for Mel getting shot. Alvin said he would use it to make a point. Donna was still mad, so she got her keys and invited J to a "car keying" party on Mel's brand new car. Donna and J took pleasure in keying the car! Donna urged J to press charges, but all J wanted to do was to put the whole thing behind her, because she could not imagine herself sitting in a courtroom reliving this mess. She could hear them asking, "Didn't you know better than to go to a strange man's hotel room at night? What did you expect would happen, stupid?" J had always been around family who respected and looked out for one another, and she has assumed that Mel would represent himself like family.

Alvin and Mel came out of the pool room walking side by side, very slowly, with Alvin's gun in Mel's side. They walked to where J and Donna were, and Alvin made him apologize to J for what he had done, but J was not ready to receive a forced apology and could look into Mel's eyes and tell that he did not regret what he had done. Alvin was so mad that he was crying, and he made Mel get into his new, scratched-up car, and Alvin got in on the passenger's side He told Donna and J to follow them. They all drove to the Texas-Oklahoma border and pulled over as they crossed the border. Alvin got out of Mel's car, cursed him out, pistol-whipped him, and told him that he never wanted to see his face again. Alvin told Mel that he was going to tell the rest of their family what he had done to make everyone aware of what he was capable of. Mel stayed silent and never denied what he had done to J. Mel's new, scratched-up car drove off into the night, and Alvin, Donna and J drove back home in silence.

J took a long, hot bath when she got to the house, then looked in on Ava, because she did not want the smell of rape on her when she held her child. Ava was sound asleep, and J held her sleepy baby in her arms all night and cried. She prayed to God to never let anything like that to happen to Ava, and promised to make sure Ava would know how to be careful and take care of herself. That night would change J's life forever because she felt a little less than human, a little less respected as a woman, and a lot less trustful of men. She felt her human value had decreased.

When J returned home, she dove back into her world of school, work, caretaker and motherhood with a different view of how the world really was. She did not tell Bell what happened, because Bell had enough to worry about. J went to a local free women's clinic for a check-up and explained to the doctor what had happen to her that weekend. The doctor examined her to make sure she had not contracted any diseases, and she was given the morning-after pill. The doctor wanted to know if she wanted to press charges also, but J still refused; what was done was done. J waited anxiously for the next couple of months to make sure she was not pregnant, and thought what she would do if she was. *Would she be able to love and raise a child produced by rape?* Thankfully, she did not have to make that decision.

Nearing the end of her junior year at college, J was growing tired and losing interest in going to school. The long hours of working, school, and taking care of Bell were taking their toll. Ava and Bell were more like best friends than grandmother and granddaughter. They were joined at the hip, constantly talking and laughing. Ava called Bell "Snoopy," and Bell called Ava "Scooby Doo." Bell made Ava beautiful clothes with matching clothes for her dolls. J was glad she had moved back home, because Ava seemed to give her mother a reason to live.

Donna and J still had their monthly outings, and one evening at the club, J ran into Rick, an old classmate from elementary school. He was all grown up and looking good. He had moved away and was back to help his dad out with the family business, and they hit it off immediately. J and Rick started seeing a lot of each other, and Bell knew his family and approved of him. Rick was a hard worker and often went to church with J and Ava, and Ava eventually warmed up to him. Ava was always cautious of anyone she shared her mother's time with, and J was cautious about who she let into their lives. No one was beyond suspicion. It felt wonderful being in love, and being loved back. She had to move past the incident with Mel, and get her life and body back, but there were occasions that the tape of that awful evening would replay in her mind.

Rick's family embraced J and Ava, and was always commenting on what a great couple they made. After about six months, Rick proposed marriage. J had always wanted her and Ava to be a real family like the ones on the "Leave it to Beaver" TV show—father, mother, children, and house with a white picket fence. J shared the proposal news with Bell, and she thought it was a good match. Bell was excited and wanted to make J's wedding dress, but her health had begun to really decline. J and Rick put their wedding plans off until Bell would be able to be a part of the celebration, but Bell's health was not improving.

In a three-month period, Bell had three major surgeries to save her legs from being amputated. With the third surgery, Bell suffered a severe heart attack and was placed on a ventilator in ICU *(Intensive Care Unit)*. With Bell on the ventilator, J and Claudia were faced with making the decision to take her off the machine, because there was no brain wave activity. For the first time J and Claudia were allies and had to lean on each other. They prayed together and stayed at the hospital for three days and nights as Bell fought for life. At the stroke of midnight on the third day in ICU, Bell's heart stopped on its own, and they did not have to make that decision. J was so overcome with grief that she had to be sedated when she saw the hearse drive away from the hospital with her mother's body. At the age of 22, J was motherless.

Bell's death would leave an empty feeling in J that no one could ever fill. Rick tried to console her, but J sank further into depression as she felt alone and abandoned. She became angry with God's choice of taking her mother, because Bell had been the one person in her life that she could depend on. What now? Poor four-year-old Ava was so lost and alone without her

"Snoopy," so she and J would cry themselves to sleep at night for weeks.

Claudia took Bell's death really hard because she had not planned to bury a child, and she never seemed to recover from the grief, losing the zeal she had for life. Bell had so many friends in the community, and because she was Ms. Claudia's daughter, the church was packed for the funeral. Several times a month, J and Ava would go the cemetery and put flowers on Bell's grave, crying and trying to remember every sweet moment they had together. It would take J several years to come to accept that her mother was gone, never to return. For an only child, that is a haunting thought.

Rick was patient and gave J space to mourn. One of the women at J's church, Sandy, who was a nurse, befriended J and helped her through those moments when she felt she would not be able to stand missing her mother. Sandy was older and had lost her mother when she was young also, so she understood J's grief and was able to speak to her issues. Sandy was one of those people everyone liked and felt honored to be in her circle, because of her kindness. J felt God had given her someone to stand in Bell's place, and they would become friends for life. Sandy had two sons and had always wanted a daughter, so she felt J was the daughter she never had. Their relationship was that of mother-daughter, friends and sisters in Christ. Sandy would teach J how to be a woman of character. God had not left J motherless and Ava grandmother-less.

Rick tried to help J move on after Bell's death by focusing on the wedding plans, so a year after Bell's death, they had a small wedding at their church, with Ava as the flower girl. Sandy and the church members were really supportive and helped the wedding to be really special, hoping it would help make up for J's mother not being there. Neither J nor Rick knew much about being married, but they were in love and would give it their best try. They begin to have problems because J was still dealing with Bell's death while trying to be a wife and mother, working and going to school. It was overwhelming.

Marriage has to be lived in the couple's own reality, not the reality of someone else's marriage. J and Rick struggled with communication and how to be respectful of each other's opinions and individuality. J had been raised by some strong-willed, independent women, so this caused constant arguments when J felt Rick was exerting his authority and being demanding. Rick began to leave home angry on the weekends and not return until Mondays to get ready for work, often missing church. This would only incite new arguments. Rick came home one Monday after being out all weekend and J questioned him on where he had been, and he casually told her that he had been with an old girlfriend who had come to town. J was furious because Rick was acting as if he were still single. This time J left the house with Ava in tow, and vowed she did not want anything else to do with him. She was sick of it all. They were barely one year into marriage, and it was falling apart already. The Leave it to Beaver family never had these issues.

J went to Claudia's house for refuge, crying and pouring out her heart. Claudia did not seem surprised and said, "That's what men do! Similar to dogs, they can't stay in their own yard. You can make a loving home, serve good food, and give them all the love they need, but they will still feel the need to wander into other yards and lay down." J decided that this marriage was not going to work, and she and Rick would have to call it quits. She loved him so much, but did not want to be miserable and raise Ava in a home filled with unhappiness. Life was too short. She asked Rick for a divorce, but Rick swore he would do better and apologized to J for cheating. She had never told him of the incident with Mel and her scars regarding trusting men. Maybe she had been unfair, so she kept those thoughts in the back of her mind as she agreed to give their marriage another try. Trying is easier said than done. They had periods of great times fishing, traveling, and just hanging out as a family. They also had periods of recalling past mistakes, past hurts, and playing the blame game. The past would not go away, and some things would not be forgiven. They unofficially went to their pastor for advice, but never sat down intentionally to receive professional counseling.

J ran into an old classmate, Marvin, at the store, and they talked of old times. He said he could see the sadness in her eyes. J smiled it off as nothing, and the conversation continued with the focus on him. Marvin smelled so good, and his voice was so soothing. Marvin invited her to call him if she needed "someone to talk to." J took the number, thanked him, and appreciated watching him walk away. The moment was brief, unexpected, and powerful.

One summer weekend following a big, heated argument with Rick, J had all she could stand of the constant arguing and mistrust. She packed a few things, and she and Ava headed for the farm to see her dad. She had Marvin's number in a safe place but opted not to use it...yet. She knew her dad was not known for showing his affection, and she did not ask for any. She just needed to breathe the fresh country air and think of where her life was headed. Marvin's cologne and kind words were still in her memory. When she arrived on the farm unannounced, her dad was glad to see her, and asked why she was there. J told him, "I just need some peace and quiet." He respected her answer. They talked occasionally, J cooked for him, she cried occasionally, and he did not interfere. Ava loved the farm and riding on the tractor with her grandfather. She thought they were on vacation, but her mother was in turmoil. Rick had called several times while she was at the farm, wanting to know if she was leaving him. He begged her to come back home because he missed her.

After a week, J returned home, and Rick was there waiting with roses in hand. He had cleaned the house, done the laundry, and seemed sincerely glad to see her and Ava. Their evening was one of passion and love, and they connected on a level they never had before. J thought that this may just work after all, because Rick was fascinated with her again. Rick wanted to know what brought on the new attitude, and J explained that she was trying to forgive him and move on with their lives. She then told him she did not want to do to him what he had done to her by going to someone else. Rick's whole expression changed when she mentioned going to someone else. *Who had she been with? What happened last week? Was she with someone at her dad's house?* The questions went on and on.

J could not believe he was accusing her, after what he had admitted to. The nerve! She told him about meeting Marvin and how he had recognized how unhappy she was. J thought telling him this would make him appreciate her more, but instead he took the emotions in another direction and threw a fit. They had just finished making love, and now were in an all-out fight. All she could think of was to never feel close enough to any man to share her deepest feelings with him, and definitely not to include another man in the conversation. There seemed to be a double standard for infidelity—men were to be forgiven, women were to be damned. J could not see the reason for him to be upset over a conversation with an old classmate. Rick saw it as outright cheating! She tried to explain that nothing happened, but he would not listen. She didn't react like this when he admitted to cheating. She was hurt, and still was, but because she loved him so, she did not go to this level of rage. *So much for romance and reconciliation.*

The next few weeks were filled with very little conversation, and no lovemaking. Rick took this opportunity to once again stay out late and come home with no explanation of where he had been. J noticed her body was changing and she had missed her period. She suspected she was pregnant. She did not want to tell Rick until she was sure, after the doctor confirmed she was pregnant. She had to wait for the right opportunity to tell Rick. Maybe this would be the one thing to save their marriage. One evening when they were speaking in general, she told him he was going to be a father. His reaction was mixed: "Are you sure? Wow, cool!" then to, "Is it mine?" The fight was really on now to try and help this man be a father to this baby. Over and over she explained that there was no one else, but he still doubted her. He said he would have to think about it, and left the house for the weekend.

J knew this was not going to work because they had too much bad history, and J could see the white picket fence coming down plank by plank. Rick came home that Sunday evening, very drunk and very angry. She had never seen him drunk. She called her cousin Donna to pick up Ava for the evening, because she had a feeling this evening could get messy. Whenever she and Rick went fishing, they took his shotgun along as protection from snakes. J questioned him about being out all weekend and being drunk around Ava. With red eyes, he started yelling about how much he wanted the baby, but could not stop thinking that it may not be his. Through slurred speech he told her how much he loved her, and would rather see her dead than with another man. Those words made J really afraid of what he may do. She tried to calm him down by telling him that when she came back from the farm, she had missed him, and that the love they made created this baby. He still insisted this was not his baby. J thought he had gone to the car to leave, but he came back with the shotgun!

As Rick threw the door open, J began to beg for her life and told him how wrong this was in the sight of God. She yelled at him that killing her and the baby would lead to him going to prison for the rest of his life. With tears in his eyes, he pointed the shotgun at J's forehead with his finger on the trigger. J could feel the cool steel on her forehead as she closed her eyes and prayed for her life, and the life of her baby. All she could imagine was the hot blast going through her brain, so she braced herself. The strain of the incident and crying must have caused J to hyperventilate and faint. When she came to, Rick was standing over her, holding the shotgun by the barrel and crying. He had picked her up and put her to bed. He apologized for almost killing her, and said it was best that he just left her alone. He said he loved her too much to kill her, but couldn't stay in the house with her. J told him she forgave him and begged him to stay, but he took the gun and some clothes, and left.

The months to follow were so lonely. J still continued to go to school and work—swollen belly, swollen feet and all. School was the one thing that kept her focused. Rick would come around from time to time when he tired of his girlfriend. They were still able to talk and be civil toward one another. J missed him so much and wanted them to be a family, but knew their relationship was too damaged, so she filed for divorce. Rick did not complain when J filed for divorce. He understood they would not be able to make it work. The divorce could not be granted until the baby was born, so they had time to still think things over. Rick had gotten an apartment, but said it was only temporary until they could work things out. J had heard of his girlfriend, and had seen them together at her father-in-law's store. All she could do was cry when she would see them together. *Where were all of these tears coming from?* They seemed to be endless.

J would call Rick and give him the doctor's report on the baby, and he would listen, but not respond. The morning she went into labor, J called Rick and asked him to come and take her to the hospital. He came by the house and sat with her for a while, but had to go to work. Claudia came and took her to the hospital and held her hands through numerous contractions. J called Rick repeatedly to see if he was coming. He finally answered and said he would be there after he got off work and changed clothes. J wanted him to be there for the birth of this child, to prove that it was his.

J was in the delivery room when Rick finally arrived just in time to see his son, Zack, come into the world. Zack was beautiful, strong, healthy, and looked just like Rick! For the first time in almost a year, Rick's face relaxed from worry. All of the nurses and the doctor exclaimed how much Zack looked like his father. Rick kissed J on the forehead and whispered in her ear, "I'm so sorry, please forgive me for not believing you." Rick took Zack in his arms, crying and kissing him like a real father. He could finally see that J had not deceived him. For a moment in that delivery room, they looked and felt like a real family. J prayed a silent prayer to God, thanking him for Zack, and offered her son to God. She promised to raise him to love God and to be a strong man of God.

After J and Zack were released, Claudia took them to the "blue bedroom" at her house to recover for two weeks. Claudia's bedroom was painted a calm blue with beautiful drapes and white furnishings. Everyone in the family who was sick or recovering went to the blue room to recover. Rick would come and visit, but would go home to his apartment and girlfriend. His anger and bitterness had thrown him into another relationship that he did not know how to handle. He wanted his family back, but felt too much pain and sorrow had come between him and J. Rick took J home from Claudia's and helped with Zack, but always went to his apartment at night. When J was stronger, she went to finalize the divorce, because there seemed to be nothing left to redeem in their marriage. Alone with two mouths to feed was not what she had planned. The white picket fence had been torn down, and the house was coming with it.

Zack was a beautiful, strong baby with a healthy appetite. He was smart, aggressive and athletic, and Ava loved her baby brother. When Zack was older, Rick had started driving commercial rigs and would promise to come and pick Zack up in the truck. Little Zack would get dressed and sit on the porch waiting for his dad to pick him up. It would be late at night and he would still be sitting there waiting, watching every car and truck that passed by. J would often have to pick up Zack's sleeping body off the porch and put him to bed. She would call Rick and let him have it for not keeping his word to his son. He would always have some frail excuse for not coming. Occasionally he would keep his word, but those times were few. Rick's family tried to make up for his lack of provision for Zack by babysitting when J had school, or keeping him on the weekends. Zack loved his grandparents. J often wished Bell could be alive to see Zack. How proud she would be of him.

J completed college when Zack was one year old. Donna, Ava, Zack and Claudia came to cheer her on. J missed her mother and wished she could have been there to see her go across the stage, since she had robbed her of that honor in high school. J had made sure to take the children to church, and that they participated in

Sunday school and youth activities. The children were bright, but J always felt she could do more. J would buy books and take the kids to the library to make sure they read well. She took them to any free educational events in town or at the college to expose them to different learning experiences. She wanted them to have a life better than hers. Zack's energy was a challenge, but a blessing, because he kept J on her toes and occupied. Ava and Zack were inseparable.

When Zack was seven years old, J received a call from Rick's father saying that Rick had been found dead from a heart attack in his truck. He had been dead several days before they found him. J had not seen him in about two years, but had talked to him occasionally when he called to speak to Zack. The last time J saw Rick, he had come by the house and spent the night because he said he and his wife *(the former girlfriend)* were having problems. J had an opportunity to be the "other woman" with her ex-husband. Their pillow talk consisted of him telling her he still loved her and regretted that their marriage had not worked out. Rick wished they could do it all over again. He told J how he was taking medication for heart problems he'd developed because of the stimulants he took to stay awake driving coast to coast. J told him that what was done was done between them, but he still had opportunities to build a good relationship with Zack. Rick promised to come by and pick Zack up the next time he was in town, but J did not tell Zack, because she did not want him to be disappointed if his dad did not show up. Little did J know that would be the last time she would hear from Rick. Little Zack cried when J told him his dad was dead and asked, "Does this mean he won't be coming to get me anymore?" J would often take Zack to visit his dad's grave and explain how his daddy loved him, and what death was about.

For some reason J felt like a widow, because in her heart she still felt Rick was her husband. She was lonely, and because of the divorce and dealing with Rick's death, J was left with feelings of failure and guilt. *Had God overlooked her happiness? When would it be her turn?* Sandy would try and encourage J by saying that she would someday meet the right person, and if she didn't, she would still be fine.

J's degree finally paid off when she got a job working as a social worker. She felt she was finally going to do what she felt she was created for, helping people. The past eight years of her life had been hell, and she was thankful for a mountaintop experience. Every mountaintop has a valley next door. J was excited about being in her career field and able to take care of her kids. Everyone at her new job was helpful and wanted to see her get off to a good start as she got her feet wet. One social worker in particular, Troy, took a special interest in J, but had other plans for their working relationship. J's supervisor, Sharon, knew Troy from being one of her schoolmates and warned her that he was a womanizer and not to get involved with him. J enjoyed the flattery Troy gave her on her clothes and appearance. He had no idea of the emptiness she had inside, or *did he sense it?*

Troy was educated, smooth and cunning. He invited J and the children out to dinners and movies, but Ava was always one for caution. For some reason, she did not like him. Troy impressed J with his academic achievements and his ability to interact with the clients. She had never dated a college educated man, feeling she was moving up in quality of men. He took her to restaurants she had only driven by, never thinking she would be able to go in and dine.

J told Sandy of Troy's intellectual qualities and the nice places they would dine in. Sandy's wisdom never failed. "You know there are some educated fools!" J felt Sandy was being overprotective. She quizzed Troy repeatedly about his reputation with women, asked if he was married, if he lived with another woman, and what were his intentions with dating her. She was determined to cover all of her bases this time. He said he was unattached, wanted her in his life, and was willing to accept her children. That was all J needed to hear—that someone wanted and needed her, and her alone. She did not want to share her man anymore. With questions satisfactorily answered, J agreed to try "love" again. Troy taught her how to love and be loved. They would talk of their future and how happy they would be, but J's experiences taught her that time would be the test. Troy formally introduced her and the children to his family, and she and his mother bonded right away. This was how relationships were supposed to go.

Alcohol had never been something J tolerated, even in her college party days, especially after she had seen how it made Rick act. Troy came to J's house one evening with a bottle of gin, and began to drink it straight! She wanted to know what this change was about. He told her this was how he relaxed in the evenings. Since she had met him, she had never known him to drink and told him that she did not want alcohol around her or her children. He promptly told her that this was what he did, and that she needed to get used to it if she wanted to be with him. J felt that familiar feeling in the pit of her soul that disappointment was coming. Troy's drinking became more and more frequent, and their relationship began to fall apart. J wanted to break it off, but Troy was determined that she was his possession. Their work relationship became strained because of his jealousy and possessiveness, and her supervisor Sharon continued to encourage J to break off the relationship with Troy before things got out of hand.

"If I can't have you, no one else will" is the most dangerous thing for any man to say to a woman. In J's case, it meant Troy was willing to do whatever it took to keep her, even kill her. *(After Rick and his shotgun incident, J was too familiar with those words.)* J finally told Troy it was over and never to come around her and the children anymore, but she still had to work with him. She started to apply for other jobs to get away from him. He would call her on the office work phone and threaten her about what he would do if she tried to leave him. J became frightened of what he might do, so she contacted a family friend who was in law enforcement to keep watch on her house at night, and to be on alert if she needed help at work.

J was an emotional wreck trying to concentrate on her job, raise her kids, and deal with the threats from Troy. One day at work, Troy called J with one of his threats and told her he was going to come to her house and settle the matter. J called her law enforcement escort and asked him to go with her as she gathered some of their things to take to Donna's house. J left the children with Donna, then she and her escort went to the house to get clothes. As her escort looked out, J gathered as much as she could in a bag, including a bottle of mayo and the salt shaker. *Fear can make you do strange things.*

As J and her escort were leaving the house, they heard footsteps all around the house. Fortunately they did not park in the driveway, but in front of the house. They ran to the car and sped off with the car doors open while lying down in the seat. Gunfire came from people standing on both sides of the house, in the driveway, and from the park across the street. They drove blindly down the street with the pedal to the floor, turning the corner at the end of the street on two wheels, almost flipping the car over! J screamed for 30 minutes before she could stop shaking. Troy really had tried to kill her!

The escort called the police to make a report and took J to his friend's house for the night for safety, because Troy knew where Donna lived. J called Donna and told her what Troy had done, and Donna assured her not to worry, she had a bigger gun than his. The next day J went to the courthouse to get a protective order against Troy because her law enforcement friend had found .45 caliber shell casings on the sides of the house, the driveway, and in the park across the street. J showed the judge the shell casings, and he issued a protective order that Troy could not come within 100 feet of her.

Troy was determined to finish the job and keep his word that no one else would have her. J had not gotten any sleep for days and was worn out from the threats. She did not feel safe in her own home, so she and the children slept in the same bed with their clothes on, in case they had to run in the middle of the night. J came to work early a few days after the incident, and as she walked into her office, Troy came in behind her. He had been hiding in a room across from her office. Troy's 6'5" frame loomed over her as he threatened to kill her for having the order filed on him. Donna had given J a pellet gun that looked like a real pistol, if you didn't know anything about guns. With trembling hands, J pointed the pellet gun at him, and for an instant he backed up, but threatened to return. J was trembling so bad she could hardly hold the phone as she called the sheriff to report the incident. The sheriff came to the job, handcuffed Troy, and took him to jail. J and her supervisor spent the day praying and praising God that J's life was spared.

Troy and J had to go to trial for the violation of the protective order, and at the hearing Troy attempted to file "threat to kill" charges on J because she had "pulled a gun" on him. The judge shut him down and yelled at Troy, "Shut up! You obviously know a real gun from a pellet gun. I am tired of pronouncing young women who are mothers of young children dead because of abusive men like you! You will NOT come in and insult this court!" The judge sentenced Troy to two weeks in jail and a $2,000 fine. J felt a sense of power as the deputies took a defeated Troy off in handcuffs. She also feared that when he got out, he may try to finish the job.

When Troy came back to work, he was restricted from coming into J's work area, and he never bothered her again. They would have to occasionally pass one another in the hall, but it was very cold and distant. J later found out from Sandy's husband that Troy had a history of abusing, beating, and bullying women, but none of them had ever filed charges against him. J would cross paths with him later in life, but Troy treated her with respect and did not confront her. He was a coward, and he knew she would fight back.

J took a sabbatical from men. She just wanted to heal and find peace and live a normal life with her children, because they had been through a lot and needed her full attention. She felt she was a magnet for dysfunctional men. She had different church members and friends trying to help her out of her well by trying to introduce her to friends of theirs, but she could only see men like Mel, Rick, and Troy, and their flaws. Her hairdresser would style her hair and try to bring a smile to her face, and for a moment she would feel pretty and special, only to crawl back into her shell. She felt God was punishing her, so she no longer believed in prayer or its power. She went through the motions at church, sang in the choir, but her faith was weak. No one could see the sadness deep in her heart.

One evening while getting her hair done, the hairdresser introduced her to her neighbor, Evan. The hairdresser cut his hair and had told him about J. He was tall, handsome, and had a beautiful smile. J considered him, but was very fearful of failing again, so she passed on the offer. J noticed that each time she came to get her hair done, Evan would drop by the shop and make small talk with her. After a few months of these chance meeting, J eventually agreed to give him her number. She informed him up front that she would not tolerate any abuse or mistreatment. She told him she was recently divorced, had two kids, and was not up for games. Evan appreciated her being upfront and told her he had a daughter by a previous relationship, but was otherwise just a hardworking single man. After a few months on the phone, and occasionally meeting at the beauty shop, J agreed to go out with him. They went out, and J hated to admit that she had a good time. She was still wounded and cautious.

Evan was a perfect gentleman, and was determined to convince J that he was not in her life to hurt her. His kindness made it easy for her to confide in him and trust him. They decided to take their relationship to another level, and it was all J had imagined. She knew that sex outside of marriage was wrong, but her loneliness had overtaken her better judgment. She would sit in church on Sundays with her physical needs met, but would leave church feeling guilty for her intimacy with Evan the night before.

J finally confided in Sandy about her relationship with Evan. Sandy was always non-judgmental, and told J she had to make her own decisions and be able to live with the consequences of those decisions. J brought Evan by Sandy's house to meet her and her husband.

Sandy was very cordial, and thoroughly looked him over. Sandy's husband was familiar with those who "ran the streets" and said he had seen him around, but hadn't heard anything bad about him. Sandy's oldest son, Randy, knew Evan from school and knew him to be a "ladies man." A red flag went up!

For some reason, J had a feeling she was headed for heartache with Evan. She wanted to have someone in her life who brought some positive energy, and at the moment, Evan was it. Randy told J that he thought Evan was living with his girlfriend. J's heart dropped at the thought of sharing her man again. She questioned Evan intensely about the girlfriend, and he denied it. J noticed that he would never invite her over to his place, but always came to hers. Whenever she would ask to meet his daughter or any of his family, he was very evasive. The red flag was still waving.

J met his cousin and sister at the beauty shop, but other than that, he did not make his family available. He wanted to spend time with her, but was not very interested in them going public places with her children as an outing. She again asked Evan about the accusation that he lived with his girlfriend, and he finally admitted that he did live with her and they had a daughter together. J felt her heart break again as she felt betrayed and used by Evan. She put him out of her bed and her life. She felt so embarrassed and used, and called Sandy to tell her about Evan's confession. In her kind way, Sandy told her that life was not over, and "this too shall pass." J was sure she was being punished by God for being disobedient. She did not feel the need to pray; it would do no good. God was going to punish her regardless.

A month after the breakup, J again missed her period, and she knew what that meant. She had always been regular as clockwork, only missing for pregnancy.

She did not have insurance and could not afford to go to the doctor, so she called Sandy with the news of her suspicion. Sandy told her about a free clinic for women she could go to, and offered to go with her. J felt comforted and also embarrassed for Sandy to be there with her. The test was positive, she was pregnant. J cried in the doctor's office and would cry daily for the next 8 months. She worried about how she would feed and clothe another mouth, and about what the church folk would think. They had never seen Evan and did not know she was even seeing anyone. This was going to be a mess.

J called Evan with the news about the pregnancy, and he was silent. Then he said the wrong thing:, "How can I be sure it is mine?" J let him have it! She was not going to go through that again. J knew that there was no one else it could be but him. Then Evan did another wrong thing—he made J a proposition that he would help her with the baby, if she would give up her other two children. He said he was not going to take care of anyone else's children but his. J unloaded on him again and told him that it was all or nothing. His next bad move was to ask if she had considered having an abortion. *What?* She did not believe in abortion, not even in this tough situation.

J told Sandy about Evan's offers, and for the first time J saw her angry. Sandy could not believe that he could be so sorry and lowdown! J knew God was punishing her, and even though Sandy told her God was a forgiving God, J felt guilty. J had to do the one thing that had haunted her—facing the church folk before she started showing. She went before the church and asked for forgiveness. She felt like she did when she was pregnant with Ava, standing before the church in shame and asking for forgiveness. *Would she ever learn?* Here she was, 10 years after the first unwed pregnancy, in the same situation. The church folks' reactions were mixed. Then came the biggest blowup imaginable—one of the women in the church accused Sandy's son, Randy, of being the father of J's baby! None of the church folk had ever met Evan, and J felt it was not their business who the baby' father was, so they started speculating. Sandy told J that she would be proud to have her as the mother of her grandchild, and J assured her that it was not the case.

Sandy and J would have a big laugh whenever some nosy person at church would kid Sandy about being a grandmother. Randy was not laughing, especially when he got into a huge argument at church about how people were treating J. She was like a sister to him, and he told them to mind their own damn business. That stopped the face-to-face assaults on J, but the behind-the-back gossip continued.

J was in bad shape financially and physically due to her job being phased out and no insurance. She was not able to find work, because no one would hire her being pregnant. She had to go to the free clinic for prenatal care, and received food stamps. The only income she had was the death benefits for Zack from Rick's death. A guy named Ty, one of Donna's classmates, worked at the cotton classing office and helped J get into the cotton classing school. The training was tough, but J learned fast and was able to pass the test. Ty felt J owed him something because he had helped her, so he asked her out. She refused because she had enough problems. Living in her Aunt Mae's *(Claudia's sister)* rent house with cheap rent was the only thing that saved her and her children from being homeless.

The utilities were often off each month, and good quality food was not always affordable. J would call Sandy almost every day, sometimes late at night, crying from guilt. For eight months J felt she was a sinner and

God did not love her because of her disobedience with men. Men had raped her, used her, abused her, and even tried to kill her. It must be something wrong with her! J read the entire book of Job over and over, searching for answers and comfort, because it was the only story that spoke to her pain. Her Bible was worn out with tear stains throughout the book of Job. *Was God testing her? If so, would she pass the test?* Sandy was patient and kind, always trying to help her to understand that God was a God of love and forgiveness. J knew she loved her unborn child, but was fearful of the future. She felt like a failure.

Sandy encouraged J to attend nursing school after the baby was born in order to have a more stable income. Sandy had been an LVN for over 35 years. J told her she did not think she was nursing material, but Sandy finally convinced her to try it. *(J would eventually attend LVN school first, and then take her prerequisites for the diploma RN school. Because she had a degree, she did not need as many classes. As an LVN, she tested out of the first year of RN school and only had to attend for one year.)* J was on a mission toward stability, and saving a year of school worked for her. Ty continued to ask her out, and she continued to say no.

When J went into labor, there was three feet of snow on the ground, and she was snowed in. The fire department had to make a path for the ambulance to pick her up, and the fire truck dropped Ava and Zack off at Aunt Mae's. J would have to go through labor all alone, because no one was able to get to the hospital. She had contacted Evan before going to the hospital, and he said there was nothing he could do. J was in labor for hours, with no one with her but the hospital staff that had gotten snowed in. The loneliness hurt more than the labor pains. Finally, one of men from church had a four-wheel drive truck and was able to bring Sandy to the hospital. J was so overwhelmed when she saw Sandy come into her room. What a dear friend she was! J let out screams, not just from the birth pains, but from the stress and strain of years of inner hurt and pain. She screamed until she did not have strength to push her beautiful 8 lb. 15 oz. baby boy, Caleb, into the world. The nurse and doctor had to help her, and Sandy was right there coaching her. By then, other friends from church had made their way to the hospital and were in the waiting room. When they heard it was another boy, everyone moaned. They wanted it to be a girl. J did not mind what it was, as long as it was healthy. She did her silent prayer of thanks to God for bringing her through the delivery and offered her son to God. J had just enough faith left to utter that prayer.

J went back to school after only two weeks recovery following Caleb's birth. She was not able to pass all of her classes, because the two weeks out put her behind. She was disappointed about the time lost, because she felt she needed to complete school as soon as possible due to having three hungry, growing children to feed. The nursing school recommended that she take the chemistry and microbiology classes at the junior college level that offered classes just for nursing students. Sandy helped J make the decision to go to LVN school, get on her feet, then go to RN school after she had worked as an LVN for a while. J felt it was going backwards, but now with three mouths to feed, she had to be practical. Evan came by to see Caleb, took one look at him and declared it was his son, because Caleb looked just like him! He left two cans of formula and did not come back. His cousin and sister would visit or call occasionally, but not him.

When Caleb was a few months old, J applied for LVN school and Aunt Mae reduced her rent to $100 a month to help her out. J worked as a nurse's aide while in LVN school to have some income. She worked mornings 7 a.m. to 3 p.m. at the hospital for school credit, and the evening 3 p.m. to 11 p.m. shift as a nurse's aide for work. The children spent most of the year between Claudia's and Donna's. J's off days were precious, and she and the children would try and cuddle, talk, and have as much free fun as they could find. She would tell them, "It's all going to pay off in the end." Sandy had to help J several times get her utilities turned on. J had inherited Bell's old Chevy Impala that had a good motor, but had poor tires. She would often find herself with a flat at least once a week. With three kids, $600 a month did not go very far. Those lean years would make J and her children forever a close-knit group.

Nursing became J's passion, and she thanked Sandy for encouraging her to pursue that career. RN school was a reality check, and J was finally now on a new path, working every extra shift she could. She continued to work seasonally at the cotton classing office for extra money. Ty continued to ask her out, but this time she said yes. She felt she had gotten on her feet and was ready to rebuild her picket fence. Ty had known her for four years and knew all about her. During those long hours at the classing office, they had time to talk about things that concerned them both. He had been a classmate of Donna's and they knew a lot of the same people. Donna liked him and thought he was worth considering. J had to clear him with Sandy's husband, who knew the streets. All she needed was another disaster crossing her path. Sandy's husband said Ty used to be in the streets but had turned his life around. Ty did not mind going to church with J and the children, and gave her all the space she needed. J decided if she got into this relationship, it would be for keeps. She did something she had not done with the other relationships—she prayed to God for guidance. She did not trust her own judgment.

The hospital nursing school program was a two-year program, but because J was an LVN, she was allowed to test out of the first year and would only have to do one year to become an RN. She felt she did not have an extra year to donate to school and away from her children; they had sacrificed enough. Ty proposed marriage and explained to her how he would add to her life instead of taking away. He explained how he would help support her during nursing school, and she would not have to work so many hours. J appreciated someone looking out for her interests for a change. She talked it over with Ava, who was 12, to make sure she was comfortable with having a stepfather. Ava wanted whatever made her mother happy. J set the date for six months, to give her a chance to see if this really was what she wanted. They set up counseling sessions with their pastor, and he felt they were ready.

A week before they were to be married in the pastor's office, Ty lost his job at the cotton office due to cutbacks. J wanted to wait, but he insisted they go ahead, because he would be able to find another job. The day of the ceremony, Ty was an hour late. Later, J would see these incidents as God saying NO! When he arrived, he did not have the ring he had promised. Again, J wanted to cancel the ceremony, but Ty insisted that they would go together and buy nice rings. Sandy and Ava were there to stand as witnesses, but after it was all over, Ava told J that she did not want her to marry Ty because she felt he would not make J happy. J began to have regrets.

The honeymoon was a disaster! Ty had no money, and J had to pay for everything. Ty took her to the pawn shop for rings and bought her a cheap $20 fake wedding set. He promised he would make it up to her, and that they would move out of the hood into a better place once he started working. J was already planning her departure from this marriage, because history had taught her that it would only be a matter of time before the madness would start. *What had she done wrong?* She prayed to God to make sure this was the right thing to do, with the right person, and it was still messed up!

Six months had passed and Ty still had not found a job, and J had all of the financial responsibility of three children, a husband, and going to RN school. The arguments over money soon began, and J grew to resent Ty more and more. One evening Ty came home from "job hunting" smelling of alcohol. She had never known him to drink, and his excuse was he had a sip of a friend's beer. J let him know that there would be no drinking, and if he did not get a job soon, no marriage. He flew into a rage and grabbed her and slapped her across the face. The blow sent her flying across the bed into the wall. She was stunned! She ran for the bedroom door, but his body blocked it and he hit her again. She screamed for Ava to go next door for help. She heard the children go out the door, so she fought as hard as she could to get out of the room. When she reached the front door, Ava was carrying Caleb, and Zack, who was 8 years old, let her know the police were on the way. Zack saw J's swollen face, wet with tears, and he flew into Ty with his little fist balled up, shouting, "You better not hurt my Mama again!" Ty raised his hand to hit Caleb, but J stepped in between them, and he hit her instead. A blow from a 250-pound man would have crushed a small boy's skull.

Ty left before the police arrived, and the officer suggested that J and the kids go to a safe place. J did not want to leave her house and asked the police to make Ty move. They said they could not legally put him out, and she would have to go to the judge for eviction orders. J was shaking all over as she packed a few items for her and the children to take to Aunt Mae's house, who always had a pistol someplace in the house and wasn't afraid to use it.

J couldn't afford to miss any days from school, so Aunt Mae worked on getting her face swelling down to look presentable for school. J went to the house the next day to get her nursing school uniforms and found that Ty had taken all of her uniforms, her nursing cap, supplies, and books, torn them all to pieces and threw them out in the front yard! *(J would later find out that Ty's rationale for destroying her nursing things was his warped idea that she would leave him when she became an RN, and she would make more money than he would.)* Destroying her school things was his way of trying to stop her from bettering herself. J sobbed as she picked up her things from the ground, and some of her neighbors walked by and shook their heads sadly at the display, but no one stopped to help.

J put her destroyed nursing items in a bag and took them to school. She was embarrassed to share her personal life with her teachers, but she had no choice but to tell them why she had to withdraw from school. One of her teachers began to cry when she saw the torn items in the bag. Her teachers refused to accept her withdrawal, but instead gave her uniforms, a new nursing cap, supplies, and books that had been donated by former students. J was so grateful for their care and understanding, and because of that she never missed a day of school. The teachers had the school security guard watch out for J's coming to and from class, and the hospital security guard walked her to her car after her shifts. None of the other students ever knew what she was going through.

J tried to determine where she and Ty had gone wrong. Perhaps she had not have been as supportive of him as she needed to be in his struggle to find work. She remembered how her marriage to Rick had fallen apart, and she just didn't want to fail twice at the same game. About two weeks after the fight, Ty called and begged to come over and apologize. He brought her flowers and a small box with the rings he had promised. The ring set was cheap, thin, and had a very, very small diamond setting. He said he had drank because of the stress of not being able to help out financially, and apologized over and over for hitting her. He begged her for another chance to get it right. He apologized to the children, and took the boys to the amusement park. Ava did not go, and did not accept his apology.

Ty and J decided to move out of Aunt Mae's rent house and start fresh. It was a hard move with a lot of memories for J, but she felt she was smothering in the bad memories. They found a nice, large three-bedroom, two-bath house on the other side of town, where the children would have a nice back yard to play in safely. Try as they would, it wasn't long before the senseless arguments started. They were in a new environment, but brought the same baggage. *New wine in old wineskins.*

J was trying to make it work, but Ty became more and more argumentative. One evening before the children came home from school, Ty came home drunk and insisted that J have sex with him. She hated the fact that he was drunk, and she wanted nothing to do with him. When she refused, he grabbed her and threw her around the living room. She thanked God the children were not there to see this. She went for the phone to call the police, but only got a few words in before he snatched the phone out of the wall and began hitting her with it. He demanded she have sex with him, and began to drag her by her arms into the bedroom. She fought, kicked, and screamed to him, "This is rape!

How can you rape your own wife?" This angered him even more and he tore her clothes off, forcing her to have sex with him. When he finished, he left the house. Crying, J just wanted to wash his scent off her and end this nightmare of a marriage. She was too embarrassed to call Sandy, and didn't want the children to see her like that.

After she took several baths and straightened up the house, she picked the children up from school. Ty came to the house later as if nothing had happened, but J would not him in. Instead she called the police and argued with him in the doorway until the officers got there. They took Ty off in handcuffs for some old tickets he had not paid. The female officer said they could only hold him for a few hours, and that J should use that time to get her and the children to a shelter. The officer gave her a number to call. J talked to the shelter representative and arranged a meeting place.

Here she was, on the run again. She took some of her valuable items to a co-worker's home and put them in her garage, then she and the children met the shelter representative at a local grocery store parking lot. The shelter was an old motel that had been converted to a battered women's shelter. J and the children were placed in a one-bedroom unit with one double bed. The shelter provided them with some used clothing, toiletries, and snacks.

The children kept asking J why they could not go home, and how long they would be there. J did not have any answers. All she could think of was Ty getting out of jail and being even angrier than before. The shelter required J to watch a film for orientation about the shelter that told of how 95% of boys who witness their mothers being beaten could themselves become batterers one day. This information haunted J, because the last thing she wanted was for her boys to become like Ty.

While in the shelter, they helped her file for divorce and a get a protective order in place. As J sat there in the shelter, wearing borrowed clothes and underwear, she vowed this was the last straw. From now on, she was fighting back.

J and the children stayed in the shelter for a week after it was determined that Ty was not in the house. He had been given orders to stay away. When they got home, J and the children gathered in the living room and prayed together. J could not understand why God had allowed this to happen to her, but had just enough faith in God that He would see her through. She had not been raised in violence and did not know how to fight men, but she was learning. Ty began calling, wanting her to take him back and saying how sorry he was. J told him she had filed for divorce, and he made a statement she had heard before, "If I can't have you, no one else will!" She took that statement very seriously. A protective order would not stop a bullet!

J was so unnerved that she would check the locks on the doors at least 10 times a night and looked in on the children constantly while they slept. She had the security guard at the hospital escort her to and from the car at the end of her shift. She lived in constant fear, and she couldn't help but think, "This is not living!" Sandy would ask her if she was okay when they would meet at church, and J would say all was well. J was losing weight, not sleeping, and looking haunted. Ty had control over her, and he wasn't even in the house. J finally came to the point of spiritual and emotional collapse and went into her closet, got down on the floor and curled in a ball. She cried and prayed to God to help her out of this mess. She knew she was too weak to do it alone, and she did not want to live the rest of her life in fear, or her children to be motherless. If God was truly her God, surely he would help her. For the first time in a long time, she heard God speak to her in a calming spirit that said, "You will be able to walk around without fear." J did not know the meaning of the message, but trusted that God would come through.

A few weeks later, J got a call from a nurse friend who worked for the city, and she invited J for lunch to catch up. J was informed by her friend that Ty had been reported by several women as spreading syphilis, and because J was his wife, she wanted her to know. J almost fainted! She said the health department had sent letters to the house, but Ty must have intercepted them. He had been in for treatment, but never told J she was at risk. This was the ultimate humiliation! Her friend helped her get into the clinic, tested her, and gave her the shots in case she had been infected. She made J's clinic visit seem as if they were old friends visiting, and allowed J go out though the employee exit, away from public display. J thanked her friend over and over for taking care of her. J's test came back negative, but the insult had been done.

Suddenly she realized that this was the "way" God would deliver her from this nightmare and the cloud of fear. J called Ty and told him what happened with the clinic. She screamed at him to tell the truth about taking the letters, or she would tell his employer, his family, and his friends what he had done. Ty finally broke down and admitted that he had intercepted the letters and was afraid to tell her the truth. He had been sleeping with several young girls on his job who had given him the disease. J was glad that she had stopped sleeping with him, but the rape had put her at risk. J called him a coward, and said that she finally saw him for the lowlife he was. She told him she no longer feared him, and said to him, "If I even have a bad dream that you have thought about hurting me or my kids, I will hunt your down, and you will be so sorry!" He told her he was going to check into rehab and get some help for his drinking. J said she did not care what he did, as long as it didn't include her. J had looked the devil in the face, he had taken his best shots, but she was still standing!

J woke up the next day renewed, refreshed and without fear. God had kept his word and revealed who Ty really was—a coward. She felt free for the first time in three years, because God had reduced the fire-breathing monster to a puff of smoke. Ty sent her a long letter about how he was in AA *(Alcoholics Anonymous)*, and one of the recovery steps he was working was asking for forgiveness from those you have wronged. J called him and acknowledged his letter and said she forgave him—not for his sake, but for hers. She promised herself and God that she would never let another man hurt her again. Ty told her about how he had developed a phobia that if he got near the house, he would develop anxiety attacks. All J could think was, "Look at God!" From that point on, J would see Ty in public settings, and it was as if he was not there. She was truly through with this chapter of her life. God had answered her prayers, and she was a believer. J promised God that she would go wherever He sent her and do whatever He asked. No task was too great or small.

Since that time of rededication, J has been challenged by God to move to the Dallas area to help with a church plant, where she developed a ministry for teens: the YES (Youth Expecting Success) Program, to provide at-risk teens with life skills classes that will help them be successful in life. She wants to help them avoid teen pregnancy and other pitfalls she had experienced. Because of her trials of being a survivor of domestic abuse, she also developed a ministry to support women who've had those same experiences (Tapestry Women's Ministry).

J has come to understand that God chose her for the trials she endured to be able to minister to others who were going through similar experiences. She became a licensed minister in 2005 and completed her Masters of Divinity Degree in 2014. She is on track to ordained ministry with the United Methodist Church. J has dedicated her life to preaching and teaching the gospel of Christ to help those who struggle with hearing God's voice in times of trouble. The long journey from victim to minister has been stained with laughter and tears, but J would not take anything for her journey. Her children have grown up to finish school and college, and she is a proud grandmother. She wakes up each day with a view from the back seat, because she allows God to drive, and it is a scenic route!

Reflection of J's Story

By Dr. Esther Mombo

"I have no husband ... the fact is you have had five husbands, and the man you now have is not your husband."John 4:16-14

Reading J's story was both sad and illuminating. When you think of women in the Bible, the Samaritan woman comes to mind, especially her response to Jesus: "I have no husband." The traditional reading of the narrative of the Samaritan woman is used to put emphasis on her as a sinful woman. This kind of reading distracts us from seeing the woman as knowledgeable, intelligent, open-minded, sincere, and theologically shrewd. She knew her ancestral tradition, history, lifestyle, religion, and the worship practices. She respected and valued them, and tried to clarify them with Jesus.

The marital status of this woman is not clear, and the text does not reveal this. We can only deduce from the local customs and imagine that she may have been remarried several times, if the husbands died. In a context where levirate marriage *(a custom where a man can marry the widow of his deceased brother)* was the custom, it is possible she was being remarried to keep up with the custom (e.g. Tamar in Genesis 38:8, and Ruth in Ruth 1:12-13, 3:13-14; 4:8-12). In the Deuteronomy law, a man was allowed to divorce his wife if he found her indecent in anything (Deuteronomy 24:1-3). The Samaritan woman may have divorced several times in a context where only the man could initiate divorce. Why she may have been divorced, we do not know, but in a patriarchal society, many reasons could suffice. Maybe she did not have children. Maybe she was one who expected to be treated as a full human being, and not a woman to be defined by society's standards.

In a patriarchal society, the Samaritan woman carried the pain alone, and meeting with Jesus gave her a new lease on life. Jesus did not make any moral judgments about her relations with five men. Jesus engaged her intellect, and her spiritual questions led her to become an evangelist for her people. Whatever society thought about her, she was empowered by meeting with Jesus. She was then transformed to tell everyone she encountered about Jesus, a man she said knew everything about her but still treated her with respect, answering all the questions she had.

Like the Samaritan woman, the story of J is about an intelligent woman, a woman with resilience, who tries to follow her physical and spiritual desires and is vulnerable to men in society. Despite the heartache, the story of J reveals a woman who is resilient and has a will to live on, and not to be defined by society. While her journey has been marred with heartache, it is not heartache that defines her, but her faith in God which leads her. Her empowerment makes her the witness of what God can do, and how a scorned woman can be a human being defined by God and not society. J and the Samaritan woman are women who were sinned against, but delivered by God to be instruments of empowering other women.

Reflection Authors

Minister Neisha Strambler-Butler, MBA

Minister Neisha Strambler-Butler is a faithful servant of God and serves at St. Paul United Methodist Church, Dallas, Texas, under the leadership of her husband, Pastor Richie Butler, Senior Pastor. In this role she oversees the Women's Ministry, special projects, and is an anointed speaker and teacher of the gospel. She teaches

Bible study and preaches at St. Paul and other local churches.

Minister Strambler-Butler is also an experienced human resource professional who is currently the director of global benefits at Texas Instruments, and holds a Bachelor's in Accounting and Organization Behavior & Business Policy from Southern Methodist University, Dallas, Texas, and a Master's in Business Administration from Northeastern University, Boston, Massachusetts. She is the proud mother of Emily Elizabeth Butler and Bradford Christian (Ford) Butler.

Pastor Brenda K. Carradine, R.N., MPH

Pastor Brenda Carradine is an evangelist, author of the book *"Lady Preacher,"* and is co-pastor of International Harvest Christian Fellowship Church, Saginaw, Texas, where her husband, Bishop Ernest Carradine, is senior pastor. Pastor Brenda has been a requested speaker for the Protestant Women of the Chapel's Annual Military Conference in Guam, Iceland,

Asia, Germany, Italy, and the United Kingdom. She travels with her husband nationally and internationally, conducting marriage, praise and worship, and empowerment seminars.

Pastor Carradine is the founder of the Palm of Deborah Ministries, Women of the Cloth, and Lady Preacher, Inc. Her book *"Lady Preacher"* is the second-place winner of the 2013 Five Star Publishers, Royal Dragonfly National Book Contest for Christian books and literature. Her book has also earned attention on the Tom Joyner Morning Show, KHVN, and UAN TV. Brenda holds a Bachelor's of Science in Nursing from Texas Christian University, Ft. Worth, Texas, and a Master of Public Administration from Troy University, Alabama.

Minister Leah B. Jordon, M. Div.

Minister Jordan is a native of Ft. Worth, Texas, and a graduate of the University of North Texas with a

Bachelor of Science degree in Rehabilitation Studies, and received her Masters of Divinity degree from Brite Divinity School at Texas Christian University, Ft. Worth, Texas, with a focus in Black Church Studies. Because of her dynamic preaching style, she was the recipient of the Walker Preaching Scholarship during her studies at Brite Divinity.

Minister Jordan is the founding pastor of Logos, a young adult group in Ft. Worth, Texas, where her ministerial focus is the spiritual development of young adults on college campuses, and young adults between the ages of 18 to 35. Minister Leah Jordan is a member of Shiloh Missionary Baptist Church, Ft. Worth, Texas, where her grandfather, the late Rev. Albert Chew, was the Senior Pastor. Minister Jordan is a dynamic pastor in her own right and carries on the preaching legacy of her grandfather.

Rev. Ella McCarroll, M. Div., Board Certified Chaplain

Rev. McCarroll has been ordained in Christian Ministry since 1993 and has served in the role of chaplain in hospital pastoral care since 1995. She has obtained a Bachelor of Science degree in Business Education from Texas College in Tyler, Texas, and a

Master of Science degree in Rehabilitation Counseling from the University of Arkansas, Conway, Arkansas. After her call to ministry, she obtained a Master of Arts degree with a Masters of Divinity focus from Southwestern Baptist Theological Seminary, Fort Worth.

Rev. McCarroll is a certified Bereavement Specialist, and leads grief seminars around the state assisting churches in starting bereavement ministries, as well as other ministries that support church and spiritual growth. Rev. McCarroll is a powerful preacher who has a unique call to minister to women's issues. Rev. McCarroll is a Board Certified Chaplain with the Association of Professional Chaplains, and was the first African-American female staff chaplain with the Baylor Healthcare System (now Baylor Scott & White Health). She currently serves at Baylor All Saints Hospital, Fort Worth, Texas. She is a member of Cornerstone Baptist Church, Arlington, Texas; Dwight McKissic, Sr. Pastor.

Minister Esther Mombo, Ph.D.

Dr. Esther Mombo is a professor at St. Paul's University Limuru, Nairobi, Kenya. For fifteen years she served in administration as academic dean, and as the Deputy Vice-Chancellor of Academics. Her areas of teaching include history, theology, and interfaith issues. She is an activist regarding issues of social justice that impact women in the church. Under Dr. Mombo's leadership, St. Paul's University has actively recruited women students by using creative strategies to bypass discriminatory rules and policies that would discourage women applicants. She has been known to say, "Biblical patriarchy, Western patriarchy, and African patriarchy have formed a very solid rock!"

Dr. Mombo has also created mentoring programs to oppose gender discrimination and violence against women. As a member of the Circle of Concerned Women Theologians, she has continued to teach about HIV/AIDS, poverty, and disability. She works closely with the Program for Christian and Muslim Relations in Africa and is a member of the WCC Commission on

376

Ecumenical Education and Formation (EEF). She is an experienced conference leader and effectively networks across communities and institutions nationwide. Dr. Mombo earned her Bachelors of Divinity from St. Paul's United Theological College, Nairobi, Kenya; Masters of Philosophy from Trinity College, Dublin; and Ph.D. from Edinburgh University, Scotland. She holds an honorary Doctorate from Virginia Theological Seminary, Alexandria, Virginia.

J.Harris, R.N., M. Div.

J. Harris, the author of the ***Healing Voices*** book, is a native Texan and has resided in the Dallas, Texas, area for the last 20-plus years. She is a graduate of Texas Tech University, Lubbock, Texas, with a Bachelor of Art degree in Social Welfare, and of the Methodist Hospital School of Nursing, Lubbock, Texas, with a Diploma in Nursing, and was licensed as a Registered Nurse. Harris accepted her call to ministry in 2005 and was licensed under the leadership of Rev. Richie Butler of Union Cathedral Dallas, Texas. She obtained her Master of Divinity degree from Brite Divinity School, Texas Christian University, Ft. Worth, Texas, in 2014. In 2013 she received training as a chaplain at Methodist Hospital System in Dallas. She is a member of St. Paul United Methodist Church, Dallas, Texas, where Rev. Richie Butler is Senior Pastor, and Harris serves on the Pastoral Care team and the Health and Wellness Ministry. She is the Community Health Nurse for CitySquare Community Health Services Clinic, Dallas, Texas.

J. Harris received training as a Parish Nurse *(now referred to as Faith Community Nursing)* in 1998, and sees her service and ministry to the community through the lens of her Parish Nursing practice. In 2000 she founded, and still serves as Program Coordinator of, the Youth Expecting Success (YES) Program for teens that provides SAT preparation and life skills classes. She founded Tapestry Ministries, Inc. in 2009 to support the YES Program and develop the Tapestry Women's Ministry, which ministers to women affected by domestic violence. She is the proud mother of four children and one grandson.

Chaplain Thelma Osai, M. Div.

Chaplain Osai is an ingenious leader, strategic magnate, and perceptive bridge-gapper. Chaplain Thelma facilitates others in becoming psychologically congruent while increasing their capacity to live out God's intent as a centered individual. She is committed to bring awareness, hope, transformation, affirmation, and healing for the purpose of going forth. Chaplain Thelma draws from her distinct knowledge and history with her rich resource of spiritual insights to offer a potent new viewpoint, lasting solutions to problems, and a set of tools that can be used to address stubborn problems in your everyday life and work.

With a shepherd's heart, she accompanies others by becoming a spiritual companion as she enables individuals to take control over their situations. With her credentials as a clinical chaplain, she provides pastoral care, crisis ministry, and end-of-life care. Chaplain Thelma obtained a distinct perceptive with her exposure to mental health first aid and bicultural competence. She is a magnetic speaker, experienced entrepreneur, system practitioner, communication and etiquette consultant, and an SAP consultant. She is associated with the Assemblies of God Church and married with one daughter.

Websites:

www.thelmaosei.com

www.soronkocompany.com

Rev. Tomeca Richardson, M. Div.

Rev. Richardson is a native of Ft. Worth, Texas, who was educated by Ft. Worth school district schools. She received her undergraduate degree from Paul Quinn College, Dallas, Texas, and her Masters of Divinity Degree from Brite Divinity School, Texas Christian University, Ft. Worth, Texas. She has worked and volunteered for many years in her community with neighborhood support programs. While serving as a volunteer creative writing instructor for one of the area women's correctional facilities, she was inspired to write and publish her autobiographical book, *"Hoochie to Holy: The Process of Sanctification."*

Rev. Richardson is a licensed and ordained minister in the United Methodist Church and currently serves as a full-time pastor with the Central Texas Conference of the United Methodist Church. She is dedicated to the work of sanctification and encouraging God's people to live with divine purpose.

Rev. Charlane Yvette Russell, M. Th.

Rev. Russell is a native of Lubbock, Texas, and resides in Dallas, Texas. She is a graduate of the University of North Texas, Denton, Texas, with a Bachelor of Arts degree in Sociology, and received a Masters of Theology degree and ordination from Grace Theological Seminary, Dallas, Texas. Over the last 10 years, Rev. Russell has worked in the mental health and substance abuse community as a counselor, social worker, and program coordinator. She has a powerful preaching and teaching style, and has done numerous motivational teaching engagements.

Rev. Russell lends her talent to numerous community service organizations in volunteerism and serves as vice president of Tapestry Ministries, Inc. , a non-profit organization that provides life skills classes to teens through the Youth Expecting Success (YES) Program. She has also been instrumental in the development of new ministers by leading minister training programs. She currently serves on the ministerial staff of the St. Paul United Methodist Church, Dallas, Texas.

Rev. Dr. Marjorie Hamilton Scott, M. Div., Ph.D.

Rev. Dr. Marjorie Hamilton Scott was ordained as an Itinerant Elder in the African Methodist Episcopal Church at the 2007 North Texas Annual Conference under Bishop Gregory G.M. Ingram. She currently serves as senior pastor for St. Luke AME Church in Garland, Texas. She is a board member of the North

Texas Conference Board of Examiners, and a member of Alpha Kappa Alpha Sorority, Inc.

Dr. Scott received her Bachelor of Arts Degree from Loyola University of Chicago, Illinois, and a Master of Divinity Degree from Garrett Evangelical Theology Seminary in Evanston, Illinois. She earned her Doctor of Ministry Degree from Houston Graduate School of Theology. Dr. Scott has served as Associate Pastor of Youth Ministries at Second Baptist Church in Evanston, Illinois, where she was ordained in 1995. She has served at Hartford Memorial Baptist Church in Detroit, Michigan, as Assistant to the Pastor and Director of Christian Education. She has also served as Associate Pastor at St. Luke Community United Methodist Church in Dallas, Texas, and as Executive Minister at St. Paul AME Church. She was a founding member and Assistant Pastor of Union Cathedral under the leadership of Rev. Richie Butler. She has also served as Hospice Chaplain for the Visiting Nurses Association of Texas.

Dr. Scott is fully committed to the teaching and preaching of a uncompromised gospel to the social consciousness of a people, encouraging and challenging them to act, grow, believe, and love. She is the mother of two daughters, Sidney and Shelby.

Rev. Dr. Alfie Wines, M. Div., Ph.D.

Rev. Dr. Alphonetta Beth (Alfie) Terry Wines is a pastor, biblical scholar and theologian residing in Saginaw, Texas, and is founder, president and CEO of **Living Water Drinking Deeply Ministries.** Known by many as "Dr. Alfie," she draws upon her unquenchable passions for biblical interpretation, biblical and religious literacy, worship, music, prayer, and leadership to enlighten, edify, and empower others. Utilizing her gifts as a teacher, preacher, writer, and musician, she is committed to encouraging compassionate living through a deeper understanding of the biblical text. She energizes and inspires others to exemplify a spirit of excellence, wholeness, love, and justice in every endeavor.

She is an ordained minister in the United Methodist Church and serves as full-time minister with the Central Texas Conference of the United Methodist Church.

What is Domestic Violence?

DOMESTIC VIOLENCE IS A PATTERN OF ABUSE from a partner/ex-partner or family member (including in-laws) that can take many forms:

- It can be physical abuse like hitting or kicking
- It can include emotional abuse like blackmail, mental torture, threats to disown you, or to kill you or your children
- It can also be controlling, meaning that you are not allowed out of the home on your own or to make contact with your family or friends, or to have access to money, or to obtain a job of your choice
- It can be sexual harassment, and stalking can also be a feature of both domestic and sexual abuse
- It can be rape – being married doesn't mean that your husband has the right to have sex with you against your will

It is important to realize that you are not to blame for the abuser's actions, and that you do not have to put up with the behavior.

If you are living with an abusive person, it is important to make some plans for a future escape because of violence and abuse. Keep the following items safely hidden at home or, preferably, with a trusted friend:

- Important documents such as birth certificates, driver's license, passports, immigration documents, court orders, and legal, property and financial papers, and extra credit and debit cards
- A bag packed with clothes for you and for your children, and a spare front door and car key, a fully charged mobile phone, cash, and other important items, such as extra prescription medicine. Do not worry if you cannot take these belongings with you if you do have to leave – you can always return with the police to collect them. If it is safe to do so, take your children with you. If not, contact the police, a family solicitor and a domestic women's organization or adviser to get help.

Think of three safe places you can go in an emergency:

- Police station
- A friend's house
- A women's refuge or domestic/sexual violence support agency

Source:https://www.gov.uk/government/uploads/system/uploads/attachment_data/file/97924/english-3-steps.pdf

The Warning Signs of Abuse
You may be in an emotionally abusive relationship if your partner:

- Controls what you do, who you see, and where you go
- Calls you names, puts you down, or humiliates you
- Makes you feel ashamed, isolated, wrong, stupid, scared, worthless, or crazy
- Acts jealous, accuses you unjustly of cheating, flirting, or having affairs

- Threatens you or makes you feel afraid
- Punishes you by withholding affection
- Constantly criticizes you and your children
- Blames you for arguments or problems in the relationship
- Makes non-verbal gestures intended to intimidate you
- Isolates you from friends or family
- Makes you feel guilty for spending time with someone else
- Threatens to take the children from you
- Monitors your phone calls
- Continually tracks your whereabouts by cell phone, pager, text messaging or GPS system
- Causes problems for you at work or at school
- Continually harasses you at work, either by telephone, fax, or e-mail
- Takes your money, withholds money, makes you ask for money, or makes you account for the money you spend, or spends large sums of money and refuses to tell you why or what the money was spent on
- Refuses to let you sleep at night
- Uses your immigration status or personal history against you
- Tells you that he/she cannot live without you and threatens suicide if you leave

You may be in a physically abusive relationship if your partner:

- Throws or breaks objects, punches walls, kicks doors in your home during arguments
- Destroys your personal property or sentimental items
- Pushes, slaps, bites, kicks or chokes you
- Uses or threatens to use a weapon against you or your children

- Drives recklessly with you and/or your children in the car during an argument
- Threatens to hurt or hurts pets
- Forces or pressures you to have sex against your will, prevents you from using birth control or from having safe sex, or makes you do things during sex that make you feel uncomfortable
- Traps you in your home or keeps you from leaving
- Tells you that you will never belong to anyone else, or that you will never be allowed to leave the relationship
- Prevents you from calling the police or seeking medical attention
- Withholds your medication

The Cycle of Domestic Violence

Violent relationships follow a common pattern or cycle. The entire cycle may happen in one day, or it may take weeks or months. It is different for every relationship, and not all relationships follow the cycle—many report a constant stage of violence with little relief.

This cycle has three parts:

1. Tension building phase—Tension builds over common domestic issues like money, children or jobs. Verbal abuse begins. The victim tries to control the situation by pleasing the abuser, giving in, or avoiding the abuse. None of these will stop the violence. Eventually, the tension reaches a boiling point and physical abuse begins.

2. Acute battering episode—When the tension peaks, the physical violence begins. It is usually triggered by the presence of an external event or by the abuser's emotional state, but not by the victim's behavior. This means that the start of a battering episode is unpredictable and beyond the victim's control.

3. **The honeymoon phase**—First, the abuser is ashamed of his/her behavior. He/she expresses remorse, tries to play down the abuse and might even blame it on the victim. He may then show loving, kind behavior followed by apologies, generosity and helpfulness. He will genuinely attempt to convince the victim that the abuse will not happen again. This loving behavior strengthens the bond between the partners and will probably convince the victim, once again, that leaving the relationship is not necessary.

Source:
http://www.domesticviolenceroundtable.org/domestic-violence-cycle.html   ;
http://www.domesticviolenceroundtable.org/domestic-violence-cycle.html

Statistics regarding domestic violence:

➢   Every 9 seconds in the United States, a woman is assaulted or beaten.

➢   At least one in every three women in the world has been beaten, coerced into sex, or otherwise abused during her lifetime. Most often the abuser is a member of her own family.

➢   Domestic violence is the leading cause of injury to women—more than car accidents, muggings, and rapes combined.

➢   Nearly 1 in 5 teenage girls who have been in a relationship say that a boyfriend has threatened violence or self-harm if presented with a breakup.

➢   One in every four women will experience domestic violence in her lifetime.

Domestic Violence Statistics:
www.domesticviolencestatistics.org 2014.

CHILDREN WHO WITNESS ABUSE

➤ Witnessing violence between one's parents or caretakers is the strongest risk factor of transmitting violent behavior from one generation to the next.

➤ Men who witnessed their parents' domestic violence were *twice as likely* to abuse their own wives or partners and their children.

➤ 30% to 60% of perpetrators of intimate partner violence also abuse children in the household.

HOMICIDE AND INJURY

➤ Almost one-third of female homicide victims are killed by an intimate partner.

➤ In 70-80% of intimate partner homicides, no matter which partner was killed, the man physically abused the woman before the murder.

➤ Less than one-fifth of victims reporting an injury from intimate partner violence sought medical treatment following the injury.

➤ Intimate partner violence results in more than 18.5 million mental health care interventions each year.

Source: National Coalition Against Domestic Violence:
http://www.ncadv.org/files/DomesticViolenceFactSheet(National).pdf, 2014.

National Domestic Violence Hotline Number:

1-800-799-SAFE (7233) | 1-800-787-3224 (TTY)

$\mathscr{H}$istory of $\mathscr{T}$apestry $\mathscr{M}$inistries, $\mathscr{I}$nc.

MINISTRIES, INC.

IN 2000 MS. JOHNRICE HARRIS NEWTON, Tapestry founder and president, conducted a sex education forum for teens in the inner city of Dallas, Texas, to address some behavior issues that she recognized as potentially problematic for the youth. The response from the parents and youth were overwhelming, and parents wanted to know if there would be other classes. Many of the youth came from broken homes, were homeless, abandoned, or living in unsafe environments.

Ms. Newton noticed that traditional debutante programs were too expensive for the poorer inner city parents, but the inner city youth were just as deserving of the same experience. She, her daughter Johnice Woods, Rev. Donald Parish, Jr., and friend Ms. Charlane Russell set out to develop a program that would have all of the elements of spiritual growth, as well as cultural enrichment. The program included spiritual growth, etiquette and grooming, money management, public speaking, health and wellness, and sex education.

In 2001, the group piloted the program with seven young ladies who were a part of the sex education class. Monetary and in-kind donations were solicited from businesses, churches, and other organizations in the community. A large local department store agreed to loan clothing (casual, business attire and formal wear) for the graduation event that included the youth performing talents, public speaking, fashion shows, and presenting the young ladies to society. Shopping for the clothing was another tool used to teach proper attire for different occasions. A local donor was so impressed with the changes in the young ladies that she purchased the casual outfits the young ladies modeled as a gift to them. The young ladies enjoyed the program, and the parents appreciated the changes the young ladies had made in self-esteem, behavior and decision-making. *(Three of the young ladies have completed college and have obtained advanced degrees. All were first generation college attendees.)* Currently the program still relies on private and philanthropic donations for funding, and all staff members are volunteers.

The decision was made to expand to include girls and boys, and now includes SAT *(Scholastic Aptitude or Assessment Test)* preparation, reading and math improvement, sex education (You Are Worth Waiting For), money management, career development, healthy lifestyle choices, etiquette and grooming, and drug/alcohol abuse prevention. Tapestry Ministries, Inc., a 501c3 non-profit organization, was established in 2009 to support the YES (Youth Expecting Success) Program and the Tapestry Women's Ministry and *Healing Voices* book project. Since the inception of the YES Program, over 30 youth are currently attending universities and colleges nationwide, and approximately 30-plus have graduated from college. Several have gone on to obtain advanced degrees. Many of the YES students are now teachers, nurses, architects, business owners, and community leaders.

Below are detailed descriptions of the programs provided by Tapestry:

The YES (Youth Expecting Success) Program provided the following services:

It Can...

1. For youth (young men and women) ages 13 to 18 years old attending public, private or charter schools. (There is no cost, cultural, economic or zip code restrictions to participate.)

2. Classes are held once a year from January to May in a neighborhood setting.

3. For youth interested in furthering their education by attending a college/university, junior college or trade school readiness is provided.

4. High School Youth: are taught the "how to" of taking the SAT exam using the Grammitix, Inc. curriculum taught by university prepared volunteer professionals. These series of classes enable students to gain test-taking skills to succeed when taking the actual SAT exam.

5. Junior High Youth: Standardized testing elements along with math and reading preparation is provided to

assist students with higher achievement in the classroom.

Youth are pre- and post-tested in both groups to assess knowledge improvement.

6. *YES Program Life Skills classes:*

A. Class presentations consist of: Spiritual Growth (faith based); Sex Education: "You are Worth Waiting For"; Etiquette and Grooming; Money Management; Career Exposure; Community Service; Healthy Lifestyle Choices; and Alcohol/Drug Abuse Prevention.

The Tapestry Women's Ministry

1. Provides support services to women who have been victims of various forms of abuse—domestic violence, incest, rape, violent crimes and sex trafficking— by providing emergency assistance to women who are seeking safety from violent and unsafe situations, and helping to find safe shelter and support services.

2. Support the publication and promotion of the *Healing Voices* book project.

3. Provide ongoing support groups, seminars and Bible studies in the community that will uplift and encourage women to live life purposefully.

Contact information:
214-476-7410
tapestrycares@gmail.com / www.tapestrycares.org

Lightning Source UK Ltd.
Milton Keynes UK
UKHW020611190419
341311UK00013B/1021/P

9 780997 265606